STRAIGHT WHITE MALE

PERFORMANCE STUDIES
Expressive Behavior in Culture
Sally Harrison-Pepper, General Editor

STRAIGHT WHITE MALE

Performance Art Monologues

Michael Peterson

UNIVERSITY PRESS OF MISSISSIPPI
Jackson

Copyright © 1997 by University Press of Mississippi
All rights reserved
Manufactured in the United States of America

The paper in this book meets the guidelines for permanence and durability of the Committee on Production Guidelines for Book Longevity of the Council on Library Resources.

Library of Congress Cataloging-in-Publication Data

Peterson, Michael, 1964–
    Straight white male : performance art monologues / Michael Peterson.
        p.   cm.—(Performance studies : expressive behavior in culture)
    Includes bibliographical references and index.
    ISBN 0-87805-977-6 (cloth : alk. paper).—ISBN 0-87805-978-4 (paper : alk. paper)
    1. American drama—Men authors—History and criticism.
    2. American drama—White authors—History and criticism.
    3. American drama—20th century—History and criticism.
    4. Monologues, American—History and criticism.   5. Performance art—United States.   6. Heterosexuality in literature.   7. White men in literature.   8. Monologue.   I. Title.   II. Series: Performance studies (Jackson, Miss.)
PS338.M46P48   1997
812'.045099286—dc21   96-30086
                                                                              CIP

British Library Cataloging-in-Publication data available

Contents

Preface	vii
1. The Artist Present in the Work	3
2. Monologue Culture	21
3. Loss as a Means of Mastery: Spalding Gray's Autobiographical Performance	48
4. Uncanny Resemblance: Eric Bogosian's Multiple-Character Performance	80
5. Performing Identity Privilege	119
6. The Universal, the Essential, the Particular, the Political	161
Notes	191
References	205
Index	215

Preface

Whatever else happens in performance, performers perform identity. And however else identity is constructed, performance plays a part in its production. One of the tasks of the study of performance is to investigate the function of identity in the making of meaning. One of the tasks facing those who would alter identity-linked structures of privilege and oppression is to study performances that maintain, mimic, or modify such social relations.

This book is a study of performances by white heterosexual men that might be considered part of the genre of "performance art monologues." The first chapter provisionally defines this genre, lays out some of the theoretical premises on which the study relies, and introduces the issues of identity and identity politics in performance. The second chapter offers a cultural contextualization of the genre, comparing it with stand-up comedy, traditions of Western poetry, the theatrical traditions of solo drama, and other forms of contemporary performance art.

Chapter 3 examines Spalding Gray, the first of two central examples. Arguably the most famous monologist in the United States, Gray began his performing career in regional theater, then moved to experimental theater, where he began experimenting with autobiographical monologue. He has now produced more than a dozen such monologues, two of which have been made into independent feature films. My analysis investigates the content of his best-known pieces and examines the manner in which his career-long autobiographical project converts every event that occurs within range of his performance into an element in the representation of that career.

Eric Bogosian is second only to Gray as a "cross-over" solo stage performer. Bogosian began performing in the New York experimental art scene, eventually moved on to theatrical venues, and then, like Gray, to feature films. Bogosian's work is not autobiographical; instead he uses his virtuoso acting talent to represent multiple characters in a series of short fictional monologues. In chapter 4 I examine several of his works for their depictions of characters from diverse social and economic backgrounds. I read his character anthologies as interpretations and representations of American social structure.

Chapter 5 explicitly analyzes monologists such as Wallace Shawn, Josh Kornbluth, Rob Becker, Andrew Dice Clay, and Denis Leary—alongside the work of Gray and Bogosian—in terms of the "identity politics" of straight white male performance. Shawn and Kornbluth are "serious" solo theatrical performers (at least in the instances cited); the other three are stand-up comedians. Yet each of these performances features both a "concept" and an implicit invitation to the audience to consider the "meaning" of the work as well as enjoy its humor. In this regard the generic distinctions between "art" monologues and comedy, which I seek to undermine in chapter 2, are further eroded.

The concluding chapter looks at Danny Hoch's performance *Some People* to identify specific strategies I see Hoch using to avoid many of the pitfalls other soloists encounter. Despite my qualified admiration for Hoch's work, I follow this section with a discussion of the cultural conditions that circumscribe contemporary solo performance. Foremost among these are the aesthetics of what I call "bourgeois avant-gardism," which in these monologues tends to operate hand in hand with identity essentialism to perpetuate traditionally conceived straight white manhood. Monologue performance, I contend, constructs a seeming community of straight white male subjects that is actually founded on the denial of the historical meaning of that identity. While I hope this identity is already destined for dissolution, monologue performance seems almost inevitably to conserve and reiterate it.

This form of performance is important because it is the most visible element of contemporary nondramatic theatrical performance, because it so frequently straddles the border between high art and popular culture, and because the individualism of solo work brings to the fore how identities—of authors, performers, spectators—work to organize both the literal and the extratextual meanings of performances. The identity terms "white," "male," and "heterosexual," while problematic if treated as essential, ahistorical, unchangeable formations, are important objects of study because so much power inheres in them so often. Monologue performances offer complex yet delimited terrain in which to contest and contend with these identities.

I have had the privilege of receiving the support and assistance of many remarkable people while working on this "monologue." Jill Dolan in particular has been a patient, encouraging, critical inspiration. That she cared about my work was enough to keep me at it.

I have never before had such a degree of on-going assistance from my peers as I have had from members of "the group." Stacy Wolf, Kari Kalve, Susan Koenig, Tracy McCabe, and Nicola Pitchford offered astute criticism, provided a scholarly community, and exemplified engaged critical thinking.

Sally Harrison-Pepper offered insight and encouragement at crucial stages. At various times many others provided feedback, support, information, and even lodging during my research: Sally Banes, Sandra Clark, Barbara Clayton, Mary Karen Dahl, Vivian Patraka, Donna Penoyer, Drew Richardson, Evie Warshawski, Morrie Warshawski, Craig Werner, Phillip Zarrilli.

Laurie Beth Clark has helped me immensely at every stage of this project, offering her provocative criticism, her support, and her library of performance-related sources and documents. I am immeasurably grateful.

Elizabeth Meyers Peterson was my first scholarly inspiration. Bill Peterson remains among my most treasured.

STRAIGHT WHITE MALE

Chapter One

THE ARTIST PRESENT IN THE WORK

THE MONOLOGIC APPARATUS

One dominant mode of the "Western dramatic tradition" (to the extent that this tradition can be said to actually exist as a single trajectory) is the monologic. When I received my undergraduate training as an actor, I was quite taken with the creation myth of European drama: Thespis steps away from the crowd/chorus/community and speaks to the assembled citizens, and a form is born. Even less legendary points of origin for theater, such as storytelling, are often viewed as originating in single-speaker modes.[1] In many later forms, the traditionally single voice of the writer merged with the body of a great performer to create the most privileged moments of aesthetic experience: the aria, the soliloquy, the great conquest or death speech, and hour upon hour of introspection. From purely monologic events to huge epic dramas, the single voice has become fundamental to theatrical performance.

The degree to which monologue has been naturalized as a condition of performance becomes clear in what is thought of as a relatively novel form: the performance art monologue. When I was still an actor preoccupied with auditions, the monologue seemed little more than a piece of play wrested from its context and used to decidedly selfish ends. Monologues always seemed cheap, somehow, when performed in venues like the actor's showcase. So I was a bit taken aback when I became aware of monologues being given pride of place as the center of a high art experience (probably when I first heard of Spalding Gray).

One attraction frequently mentioned by monologue spectators is the novelty of a single performer shouldering the burden of the audience's expectations. Beyond this novelty, however, the monologue form is "estranged" hardly at all. It is the (apparent) absence of the supportive apparatus that is remarked on in these comments, more than the absence of other speaking voices. The monologist is heroic in "doing without" the usual trappings, and spectators appreciate this. There is little new, and nothing disconcerting, for the well-trained theater-goer in watching a performance in which a single person is the focus. There is also nothing strange about a single person addressing us, speaking to us directly.[2] This, after all, is familiar from speeches, comedians, singers, and many contemporary religious structures.

It is not only cultural precedence that allows monologic performance to work so effectively upon an audience, for the form is not as unsupported by artifice as it might seem at first glance. In fact, it is possible to speak of a "monologic apparatus" nearly as complete as the general "theatrical apparatus" attended to by materialist feminist critics (among others).[3] This monologic apparatus includes material technical devices. Theater workers will be familiar with the effect even the subtlest stage lighting can produce, and the interest of the popular press in the clothing of some performers suggests that costume choices may signify beyond the functionality that is their primary connotation.[4]

Further, while an "empty" stage may signify a casual or unconscious use of stage space, in practice successful monologists tend to design that very emptiness; and even an undesigned stage space—at an "open mic" performance, for example—is likely to employ an elevated stage and seating arranged in the familiar theatrical orientation. Rows of theatrical seating, often slightly curved as if spectators were in orbit around the stage, shape the relationship of spectator and performer to an even greater extent when the center of that orbit is the single speaker. What little does occupy the stage in the way of props or set pieces—the stool and microphone stand of stand-up comedy, the single chair of Wallace Shawn's *The Fever,* or the table, notebook, and water glass of most of Spalding Gray's performances—constitutes and legitimates the presence of the solo performer in a manner more subtle than but perhaps as effective as more obvious design elements. Such physical elements of the monologic apparatus can emphasize the heroic aspect of the performance—they are the "doing with" that constitutes the apparent "doing without" theatrical support. A lone piece of furniture, a spot of light, and a voice amplified by electronics or acoustically aided by theatrical architecture dramatize the heroic act of speaking solo. This theatrical aesthetic might even be seen as more heavy-handed than the fictionalizing function of traditional design for dramatic theater.

But the monologic apparatus consists of more than the simple material elements, which require only the slightest effort of observation to notice. This apparatus is more productively conceived of as including the network of cultural precedent and expectation to which I have referred. Further, many hegemonic cultural traditions naturalize the singularity of artistic value through concepts such as genius and expressive individuality. Obviously such influences operate differently, if at all, for different spectators. Nevertheless, many spectators of monologues do view them from within some combination of such cultural factors. And certainly for a man raised as I was, in a polite white Southern middle-class milieu, a powerful if implicit cultural commandment enforces and is re-enforced by such performances: when someone (important) is speaking, one (less important) should naturally listen.

Because of the effectiveness of this literal and conceptual apparatus, it takes a degree of concentration (for me at least) to remember the strangeness, the arbitrary nature of a form that is so culturally centered, so basic to my experience of performance. This concentration is of value, however, for in gazing at the structure of one who speaks to many, I see the ideology of a hierarchical valuation of different voices stand out starkly. The monologue always contains, however sublimated or repressed, the question "Why are you listening?"

This peculiar circumstance—one person speaking, controlling the attention of a group—is arguably dominated in contemporary U.S. society (especially in the so-called "mainstream" and high art contexts) by speakers who are white and male. While the genre of performance art monologue (loosely defined) has been practiced as well, as complexly, and as (in)famously by women such as Karen Finley, Holly Hughes, Robbie McCauley, Rachel Rosenthal, Anna Deveare Smith, and many others, and by men of color from Guillermo Gomez-Peña to dancer-turned-occasional monologist Ishmail Houston-Jones, the position of single speaker, broadly construed, is still culturally occupied with greatest frequency by white men. Further, in the increasing body of artistic and critical work concerned with what "white man" means as a social sign, he-who-speaks is a prevalent trope. The monologic apparatus and various apparatuses of identity privilege thus work in concert, each tending to strengthen the other.

For these reasons, the genre of performance I am calling the "performance art monologue," as practiced by white men, is a highly concentrated, rarefied cultural production that depends on and participates in the construction of contemporary white male identity. This project examines the work of monologic performance artists (contemporary white males speaking alone while a great many people listen to them) to question how they occupy the territory of this "peculiar circumstance" in the midst of the rapidly shifting hierarchies, dizzying intertextualities, and crises in representation that, for many, herald "postmodernism." While I do not attempt to engage all the debates about the meaning of "postmodernism" and its explanatory power when applied to the contemporary, my concluding arguments should make clear that I consider a crisis of identity (which means a crisis of hierarchy and representation) one of the important conditions under which these monologues are spoken.

CRITICISM AND POLITICS

My project is a critical one in the sense suggested by Roland Barthes. Part of my objective is "setting the stereotype at a distance," reframing the representations I discuss. By stereotype I mean more than the common-sense meaning of "unjust generalization" (though I encounter a few of those). Barthes seems to define stereotype around a laxness or laziness in writing or representation, as constituted by a "necrosis of language, a prosthesis brought in to fill a hole in writing." Barthes says that "setting the stereotype at a distance is not a political task, for political language is itself made up of stereotypes, but a critical task, one that is, which aims to call language into crisis" (Barthes 1972: 387).

Borrowing for the moment Barthes's distinction between critical and political tasks (while recalling of course that Barthes is quite aware that there is always a politics to criticism), I admit that I also have "political" tasks in the sense in which he uses the word in this passage. That is, to a certain degree I deploy a stereotypical political language, in fact proclaim it, in pursuit of political desires. Certainly, the "straight white male" of my title is such a political stereotype—one that is at this moment in history absolutely vital. Still, Barthes argues that "to speak in stereotypes is to side with the power of language, an opportunism which must (today) be refused" (1972: 287).

Bearing in mind that Barthes maintains in his next paragraph that the wish to "transcend" stereotypes is "unrealistic," I struggle throughout this text to complicate this "straight white male," to make use of whatever leverage the terms may afford and at the same time to expand, undermine, or confound their meanings. I can begin this job, perhaps, with some attention to these three words and to my own relations to them.[5]

IDENTITY

My formative political and academic experiences were framed by feminist theory and the feminist movement both within and outside the academy. For straight white men in this position, working out one's relation to the category of gender often seems of primary importance. At the same time, the increasing attention to "race" on the part of white feminists has provided instructive examples—both positive and negative—of white scholarship that knows itself as such.

In a sense, then, the three adjectives of my title perhaps sketch in reverse the trajectory of my critical development. By this I mean to remind the reader and myself of a potential tendency to treat gender as primary, race as secondary. And in fact that is still the case to some degree in this study.

Of course, when used in heterosexist discourse, the phrase "white men" on some level "really" means white heterosexual men. Powerful cultural forces work to ensure that white heterosexual men can omit that specificity; they are assumed to occupy the sexual "default" setting. Whether as right-wing or liberal code words, contemporary appeals to the "white male" are based in a heterosexism that renders "straight" a monolithic term of privilege and seeks to deny the historical privilege of white maleness to those white men deemed to have a specific sexual orientation. But the increasing visibility of gay men in numerous vistas of straight male experience—from the marketplace to the political arena—has established yet another pressure point by which the strength of monolithic male, white, "het" identity can be undermined. The spreading notion that "straight" (whatever it means) is but one specific sexuality among many is one of a number of cultural phenomena that in fact threaten the privilege historically linked to that identity.

I therefore specify these performers with a third adjective as "straight" (or heterosexual), white, and male. I should briefly make two points about this gesture. First, while many of the performances under discussion include moments when the speaker "ins" himself as heterosexual, many performers do not so identify themselves.[6] They nevertheless "pass" as straight. For the performers on whom I focus, "straight" is a term of privilege every bit as central to their identities as white and male. It should be clear that I am not discussing the specific sexual practices of the men I critique, and do not claim any "factual" knowledge of their sexualities as lived outside of performance. Rather, for my purposes, the men I call heterosexual either "in" themselves or allow cultural heterosexism to frame their performances without resistance. Because I am concerned with discursive identity rather than clinical identification or actual sexual practice, I actually prefer "straight" to "heterosexual," though this move is not unproblematic, and is thinkable only in the context of the recent appropriation of "queer" as a term of pride.[7]

Secondly, and at the risk of belaboring what will to some seem obvious, there are compelling arguments against applying a straight-gay binary to performed identities. It can obviously be argued that such a binary fails in many ways to match up with lived experience. For example, even for "straight" male spectators watching "straight" male monologues, structures of pleasure operate that can hardly be called heterosexual.[8] Further, use of the binary threatens the political efficacy of undermining monolithic heterosexuality. And what of racial and gender binaries? Naming the white and male likewise reinforces disciplinary identity. Perhaps all these labels are best left unsaid.

Despite all this, I put aside my doubts about the label "heterosexual" because dropping the label remains unavoidably heterosexist. Ironically, this was recently reinforced for me in reading Robert Bly's preface to *Iron John: A Book about Men*.[9]

> Most of the language in this book speaks to heterosexual men but does not exclude homosexual men. It wasn't until the eighteenth century that people ever used the term homosexual; before that time gay men were understood simply as a part of the large community of men. The mythology as I see it does not make a big distinction between homosexual and heterosexual men. (Bly 1990: x)

Besides the suspicious similarity of construction between this statement and statements by an older generation of men suggesting that "man" had always included everyone before feminism quibbled about it, Bly's argument—so different in spirit from Foucault's reminder that "homosexuality" and therefore heterosexuality are relatively recent inventions—also makes clear his assumption that contemporary language does not constitute reality, while "ancient" language does. In other words, Bly dismisses a contemporary sense of difference (and its possible meanings for his readers) in favor of a biological essentialism he claims "does not exclude." If for no other reason than my deep disagreement with this sort of assumption, I have decided that it is necessary to name the "heterosexual" even at the risk of helping to perpetuate it.

To a greater or lesser extent, I am faced with a similar discomfort with regard to all terms for identity. My theoretical position on identity is an unreserved social constructionism, yet I am acutely aware that in actual political struggle—and in actual critical practice—such a refusal of stable identities is much more complicated than it seems. Ann Snitow has written compellingly of the "divide" within feminism between a desire to "build the identity 'woman'" and the "need to tear down the very category 'woman' and dismantle its all too-solid history" (Snitow 1990: 9). Snitow traces the various manifestations of this divide and feminism's "oscillation" between incarnations of the two positions. An important point of her essay is that both sides of this divide have produced important practical gains and theoretical progress.

In writing this study I felt a similar oscillation in myself every time I wrote the word "male" or "white" or "heterosexual." I am convinced that ultimately the solidity of such words—along with "bisexual," "black," and so forth—must be dissolved and reconfigured in order to produce fundamental social change. At the same time, like Snitow, I am well aware of how frequently such categories are of immediate political utility. Specifically, while my desire is for the dissolution of the identity juggernaut that is the white male heterosexual, this moment in the struggle over identity necessitates a frequent and insistent naming of that identity rather than a denial of its social reality.

That said, let me reiterate my interpretation of these monologues as part of a cultural conversation about what were previously the most stabilized of identities: whiteness, maleness, heterosexuality. That conversation is made up of and overlaps with many others. I would include seemingly quite divergent phenomena: the critique of political correctness, the backlash against civil rights and feminism, the reconstruction of masculinity. The right wing of our culture has of late taken to decrying the difficulty of being a white man in today's cultural climate. The new red scare constructed around an imaginary "politically correct" code of conduct is paralleled by cries of reverse discrimination; these twin paranoias act to shut down debate about cultural privilege and power. A different (though perhaps as reactionary) contemporary cultural gesture is the emergent "men's movement" and its assorted "new age" variants. New gurus (such as Bly) offer strategies for discovering or maintaining various aspects of the male; numerous therapeutic approaches suggest a striving for a "kinder, gentler," but still masculine man.

The theoretical difficulty of stabilizing any identity, while mobilized as a liberating potentiality for some, may at first have seemed a loss to those historical characters whose fixed certainty of personhood appeared a birthright under the terms of the Enlightenment or modernity. Bluntly, given the difficulty of knowing who anyone is, straight white men rightly feared the critique of identity and of identity privilege as a challenge to a luxury of being that was once taken for granted.

The fact that privilege is or was genuinely at risk does not mean that all the fears of straight white men have been justified. A *Newsweek* cover story in the early 1990s, "White Male Paranoia" (Gates 1993), is an interesting artifact of such fears. The piece carries a surprising sting, coming from a mainstream weekly. While the article gives vent to (and thus seems to validate) "white male paranoia," it does so with a consistently sarcastic tone and frequently undercuts (straight) white male stories of victimization with contradictory statistics.

The straight white male performance art I analyze arises from the context of the cultural climate *Newsweek* elaborates. This is not to say, however, that such performance is necessarily an active part of this climate. In chapters 5 and 6 I explore how such performance may unwittingly play into conservative male essentialism; the same structures may tend to subsume any straight white male performance under a general climate of straight white male paranoia. It is in this context that I examine a genre of performance in which white men stand alone, somewhat anxiously constituting themselves through language, uncertain as to which "others" are listening.[10]

These cultural developments also mean that any critique of what I call "identity privilege" must remain complex and flexible. While any particular straight white male individual might more or less passively inherit identity privilege from "Eurocentric heterosexist patriarchy," that privilege itself is more productively analyzed not as a quality of *being* white, male, or straight, but as the condition and result of the production or performance of those identities, both by individuals and by cultural institutions.

The emphasis on the performativity of identity has the advantage of encouraging the historicization of identity. The value of this is clear when we look at the performance of straight white class-privileged manhood in the contemporary scene. Several years ago, when I first began looking at them, such performances seemed related to desperate responses to the erosion of identity privilege, which seemed to be happening culturally despite the social conservatism of the Reagan-Bush years. More recently, the retrenchment of identity privilege as indicated by anti-immigrant, antigay, and anti–affirmative action developments suggest that some reactionary performances of straight white male identity have been more powerful than their frequently "wacko" extremism might have suggested.

While I do not disagree with the postmodernist traditions that see postmodernity as a "condition" of the state of knowledge (Lyotard) or as a product of change in the global organization of capital (Jameson), I do think that the "crisis of representation" as "experienced" or interpreted by those on whom this study focuses is most immediately tied to a crisis in representation of identity and identity privilege. And this crisis, while perhaps part and parcel of epistemological shifts or global economic reorganization, is about the gritty, uncomfortable terms of identity representation: race, gender, sexuality, and economic and cultural class.

GENRE

Like identity terms, generic divisions currently seem highly arbitrary and contingent. Genres are critical fictions that are inevitably founded on one or another privileged term, and the precise qualities that constitute them cannot be strictly delimited. To the "death of the author" might be added the death of the genre. That said, "genres" might still be of use as self-consciously constructed generalizations about certain "ways of speaking." The contradictions of this position become even more apparent when one desires a certain coherence among the works treated, and at the same time wants to further the tactic of emphasizing internal differences among those hegemonically "same" works.

To these questions might be added certain problems of discipline and venue. While much of the work I am concerned with tends to be framed and discussed as "performance art," formally the term is not clearly distinguishable from theater. For example, Eric Bogosian's *Talk Radio* exists as a playscript, derived from a club-style performance work; Wallace Shawn discusses his solo performance *The Fever* (and markets its text) as a dramatic work for one actor; Spalding Gray is almost ubiquitous in a certain stratum of the arts, ranging across the theater, film, and publishing worlds. My approach to this taxonomic problem is formalist, intuitive, and discursive.

Although I would argue that performance art cannot be defined in purely formal terms, I do find some formal commonality in a preponderance of those works called "performance art," especially in comparison with traditional dramatic theater. Performance art tends in some manner to privilege "reality" over "fictionality," or at least to toy with those terms. Metaphorically and often literally, performance art occurs in its actual space, while dramatic theater seeks to escape reality by overlaying the actual space with a fictive one. In many instances, performance art tends to involve a "special relationship" between the performing body and the text performed that is not, primarily, dramatic. This is to say that performance art differs from drama in that the performing body does not usually utter words or perform gestures scripted by a largely absent author-god. In performance art, it is much more likely that the author is present onstage in the body of the performer. In terms of spectatorship, this overlay of authorial ghost and performative body usually means that the performance is read as a single artistic utterance, rather than as an interpretive, contingent version of an original. In most performance art, it is the performing body of the author-figure that assumes the status of art object.

There are obvious exceptions to this categorization in the form of performance artists who do not appear in their own works and who use performers as one artistic element among many. Many of these works privilege "reality" over fictionality in some other way. For my current purposes I am operating on the proposition that what formally makes, say, Gray or Bogosian performance artists is the aura of authorship that surrounds the performer.

Theorizing speech as a broad category, Mikhail Bakhtin argues that "language is realized in the form of individual concrete utterances (oral and written) by participants in the various areas of human activity." Even though every utterance is in some sense unique and situated in an absolutely specific context, however, "each sphere in which language is used develops its own *relatively stable types* of these utterances. These we may call *speech genres*" (Bakhtin 1986: 60, emphasis in original).

Richard Bauman theorizes performance as a specific "way of speaking" (1977: 5). It is marked or coded so as to suggest an assumption of responsibility on the part of the performer, as well as sufficient competence in the performer and the audience. Bauman sketches the corollaries to these ideas, including the concept that performance is marked as such, is patterned in culture-specific ways, and is continuously "emergent," changing even though it is always involved to some degree with tradition.

It is my contention that performance art monologues, particularly as produced by white heterosexual men, are both a distinct "way of speaking" in Bauman's sense, and a relatively stable type of utterance, similar though diversely situated utterances within a speech genre, as Bakhtin describes. While viewers of these performances may not often spectate in this analytic manner, I would also argue for an intuitive recognition of these works as examples of a loose "genre." I suggest that many spectators, and certainly myself, consciously or unconsciously organize the performances I discuss in this project as a genre. While this may be based on an intuitive feeling rather than conscious formal analysis, that intuition may perhaps be explained by the specific characteristics discussed above.

Ultimately, however, these works are "performance art" because they are discursively constructed as such. Simply put, Gray and Bogosian are performance artists because critics and spectators so often use that term to describe them. Of course, other terms are invoked, drawn from theater, stand-up comedy, etc. In chapter 2 I argue that the difference between "performance art" and such related disciplines is discursive and not formal. The "performance art monologue" is, then, a genre within a form that is first and foremost a discursive rather than a formal entity. The specific instances of this genre produced by straight white men constitute a further subgrouping that speaks to and through discourses of art, theater, and even popular culture.

I argue for the consideration of these works as a genre even as I split them roughly between two subgenres. One is epitomized by Spalding Gray; a combination of soliloquy and aside, it is a first person speech delivered directly to the audience. The second is epitomized by Eric Bogosian and is well defined by the little-used word "monopolylogue": "a theatrical entertainment in which one performer plays several parts or characters."[11] This second type is sometimes directed at imaginary characters (that is, unacted characters conventionally imagined by performer and audience), and sometimes spoken to the audience as if they were a character or characters.

There are, of course, works that do not fit precisely into either of these subgenres. For example, many solo performers enact single "characters" who are not as clearly autobiographical as Gray's stage persona, but also not as wholly fictional as the individual characters in Bogosian's "monopolylogues." The experience of watching these forms differs, and I will explore this difference to some extent, since a formal analysis is central to my political analysis. Still, both forms emphasize the personality and performative power of a single author-performer. As much alike as they are different, they represent two checkpoints on a cultural boundary, a "discursive space" we must consider as a whole to grasp its power.

For my purposes, then, the performance art monologue is speech-based solo performance to which the audience can be assumed to assign some degree of "art" status. The scope of this project is bounded on one plane by this partly formal, partly contextual definition, and on another by the issues of identity discussed above. My topic is thus defined by the speaker (male, white, heterosexual), the speech (on a continuum between the two strands of talk-based performance epitomized by Gray and Bogosian), and those spoken to (an art or art-theater audience: not always the "art world," but never exactly "the masses").

I also return to stand-up comedy in chapter 5, discussing works that cannot really be called performance art under even the broadest definition. I include these examples to illustrate a similar functioning in what might be called "concept comedy." Andrew Dice Clay, Rob Becker, and

Dennis Leary are not performance artists, but their comedy shares strong affinities with artier solo work. These affinities are illustrated by the ease with which some comedians migrate from stand-up to theatrical monologue, Josh Kornbluth being one example.

Since all genres are critical constructions, they can be easily deconstructed. This genre in particular is tenuous, fragile. It is easy to imagine readers protesting that work A and work B are really more different than alike. For all its insufficiencies, however, a genre-based criticism has two important advantages. First, I think culture is rendered more or less intelligible to its members through such loose units of organization; we tend to "make sense" of culture by recognizing likeness and difference. Second, attention to genre—to the "in-common-ness" of works—can mean analyzing structures or choices in a general sense while remaining attentive to the particularities of individual works. In my case, I am interested in how these constructions/representations of straight white men can be examined as part of the theorization of identity politics and identity privilege.

I am also interested in reversing the question to ask how identity shapes performance. Bauman asserts the social marginality of performers (a topic long considered by theater historians) and links it not to moral ambivalence but to political anxiety.

> The consideration of the power inherent in performance to transform social structures opens the way to a range of additional considerations concerning the role of the performer in society. Perhaps there is a key here to the persistently documented tendency for performers to be both admired and feared—admired for their artistic skill and power and for the enhancement of experience they provide, feared because of the potential they represent for subverting and transforming the status quo. Here too may lie a reason for the equally persistent association between performers and marginality or deviance, for in the special emergent quality of performance the capacity for change may be highlighted and made manifest to the community. . . . If change is conceived of in opposition to the conventionality of the community at large, then it is only appropriate that the agents of that change be placed away from the center of that conventionality, on the margins of society. (Bauman 1977: 45)

In the arts scene in the contemporary United States, the impressive use of performance by already "marginalized" artists might be considered in light of this idea. In this study, especially in the conclusion, I might be thought of as asking, "What does it mean when a 'marginal' form like performance is used by those whose identities are so determined by their centrality?" In chapter 6, I argue that it is actually the operation of identity privilege to deny the "emergent quality of performance" (which I describe as the "here and now" of performance art) in some of the works I discuss. A mix of essentialism and universalism acts to keep privileged identity in a state of being rather than of becoming.

PRESENCE AND AUTHORSHIP

Performance art monologues by white heterosexual men intrigue me because they represent the intersection of a form that insists and depends on the forceful, charismatic power of the performer's presence with performers whose social identities are highly empowered in contemporary Western culture. I will refer repeatedly to the idea of "presence" in performance. While the word as I use it has productive links with more sophisticated philosophical ideas of presence, I more frequently invoke it as a theater-world cliché. As Joseph Chaikin defines it,

> This "presence" on the stage is a quality given to some and absent from others. All of the history of the theater refers to actors who possess this "presence." . . . It's a quality that makes you feel as though you're standing right next to the actor, no matter where you're sitting in the theater. (Chaikin 1991: 20)

As an essential quality that inheres in the bodies of the fortunate few, this presence is defined as an intangible quality allowing either the projection of the actor's person(ality) into the audience, or the drawing-in of the audience to the performer's field. Elinor Fuchs (1985) offers a more complicated definition that nonetheless builds on the one Chaikin invokes: "The notion of theatrical Presence has two fundamental components: the unique self-completion of the world of the spectacle, and the circle of heightened awareness flowing from actor to spectator and back that sustains the world" (1985: 163).

While I have no faith in the mythology of the actor's innate presence (I have no doubt it is a learned, if often unconscious, skill), I know very well the theatrical effect to which it refers. I borrow this term to refer to that performative power that "makes you feel" something in performance without any obvious explanation. It is not simply sympathy with a character, or identification, but a falling under the control (whether intentional or not) of the performer. My purpose is not to explain or account for the effects of presence, but to identify and critique some of its uses and abuses. In works signed as performance art, theatrical presence can work in concert with the "aura" of authenticity discussed by Walter Benjamin, and with the work of art's status as an "immanent object" (Sayre 1989: 1).[12]

"Presence" constitutes and is constituted by the illusion of directness. As Herbert Blau notes, "There is nothing more illusory in performance than the illusion of the unmediated. It is a very powerful illusion in the theatre, but it *is* theatre, and it is *theatre*, the truth of illusion, which haunts *all* performance, whether or not it occurs in the theatre" (1983: 143). These performers depend in different ways on the illusion of directness. For Bogosian, there is usually no pretense that "he" is speaking directly to the spectator. However, there is in the concentrated form of the dramatic monologue the suggestion of a very direct connection between the actor and his character. Further, twentieth-century Western theatrical practice has evolved a tradition of functional or minimal stagecraft that is founded in part on the belief that the actor unencumbered by elaborate scenery is somehow more directly connected to the audience. Gray structures his performance as a direct or unmediated address to the audience about him"self." But even his performance is obviously haunted by Blau's "truth of illusion." Gray, after all, performs his monologues hundreds of times, and this throws the idea of "genuine" emotion or expression into doubt.

These works both invoke and appear to dispense with illusionism and theatrical convention, which might be one strategy for securing their status as art. This kind of performance mixes and blurs the actual or iconic sign of performance art and the symbolic sign of fictive dramatic narrative. In doing so it appears to shift the theatrical gesture of direct address toward real speech. While there is a potentially unsettling aspect to this shift, it may also function as yet another guarantor of the authority of the speaker/performer. In a sense, this blurring offers a performer like Gray the best of both worlds: the "truth" of performance art and the power of theatrical illusion.

The construction of speech within tangible, real objects is traditionally the domain of high art (in the production of painting or sculpture, for example, which announce themselves as real objects even if they function as representations), while fictive representations (textual rather than "actual") are more often located within the realm of popular culture. In other words, the dominant experience of consuming, say, a Brancusi sculpture such as the abstracted streamlined metal "Bird in Flight" is of encountering a real object with a real history: it is located in this actual space, it can (almost) be touched, it was the center of a controversy over the definition of art when U.S. customs officials examined it, and so forth. This is despite the fact that Brancusi's "Bird in Flight" does function as representation on some level. On the other hand, the film *Star Wars* (1977) tends to be consumed as an intangible "text" and fantasy narrative—despite the fact that the film, or the print, or the projected light and sound, has an object status of its own. A Spalding Gray monologue seems to lie between these two poles. Performance art, as discussed in chapter 2, has traditionally exploited the performer's body as a tangible, sculptural object. The content of Gray's pieces, however, is anecdotal narrative. This is not to argue that the monologue represents the harmonious fusion of art objecthood and popular narrative. It is rather to witness the collapse of certain distinctions in this work.

Further questions are raised by the mediation of these pieces. If, following Walter Benjamin, one agrees that original paintings are no longer quite the same in the age of mechanical reproduction, how does the work of solo performance change in the wake of the film versions of Gray's *Swimming to Cambodia* or Bogosian's *Sex, Drugs, Rock and Roll*? At this point, it seems possible to say only "entirely" and "not very much" all at once: the film both destroys objecthood and reiterates the "truth of illusion."

The "presence" of the actor and the authenticity and immanence of the art object have been under attack for some time by critical theories and artistic practices that seek to undermine presence. Fuchs, in an article "rethinking theatre after Derrida," suggests that the "price" of the emergence of writing as an activity of performance "is the undermining of theatrical Presence" (Fuchs 1985: 163). Henry Sayre (1989) identifies as one threat to the aura of the art object the increasing acceptance in the last twenty years of photography as an art form. Because the art photograph always remains on some level a document of the moment(s) of its making, but also strives to be seen as an "immanent object," such photographs mark for Sayre the risk to an "aesthetics of presence" that the audience will recognize all art works as "relics" and view them in the same manner as "the arms and armor collection of the Metropolitan Museum of Art" (1989: 4).

> But I said that we are on the *edge* of admitting this transformation because the aesthetics of presence has a final line of defense—the audience. The audience has the privilege of ignoring the artwork's contingent status as a kind of documentary evidence; in fact, the audience knows first that it *is experiencing* art (it has come to the museum in order to do so) and the real presence of one masks—and paradoxically depends on—the absence of the other (the artist's). (Sayre 1989: 4)

In his treatment of the artist/author figure, Sayre almost constructs a Barthesian concept of the performer/artist/author figure. Barthes was able to announce theoretically the death of the author, but Sayre points out the author's persistence in the audience's involvement with the presence of the art object/actor. Barthes's description of what the "author" was before "his" death is applicable to the constructed "artist" that may be glimpsed behind the performance art monologue.

> The Author, when believed in, is always conceived of as the past of his own book: book and author stand automatically on a single line divided into a *before* and an *after*. The Author is thought to *nourish* the book, which is to say that he exists before it, thinks, suffers, lives for it, is in the same relation of antecedence to his work as a father to his child. (Barthes 1977: 145)

This is the presumed artist/author. It describes the Spalding Gray presumed to live the life anterior to the performance that narrates it; it describes the Eric Bogosian crafting a mosaic of social representation out of individually imagined characters. Despite the applicability to them of this traditional idea of the Author, these monologists are also described by the rest of this paragraph from Barthes:

> In complete contrast, the modern scriptor is born simultaneously with the text, is in no way equipped with a being preceding or exceeding the writing, is not the subject with the book as predicate; there is no other time than that of the enunciation and every text is eternally written *here and now*. (Barthes 1977: 145, emphasis in original)

For Bogosian and Gray are constituted in the moment of their enunciation, present "only" in that moment. Yet as repeated/repeatable performances, their works exist as "relics" or "documents" of their making. At the same time, after Sayre, we may say that the audience "has the privilege of ignoring" their "contingent status."

These and similar works of performance art are caught in a contradictory status, dependent on presence and immanence, yet unable, because of the author-function assigned to that presence, to jettison the antecedent author-god. There is one further complication to which I alluded earlier: because many of these works are more widely seen in documentation than in performance (and much of this study is based on performance documents such as film and videotape), the existence of such performance, at least of mainstream performance art, lies in documents of (not-)documents.

Issues of presence and presentness recur throughout my text. In my discussion of individual artists in chapters 3 (Gray), 4 (Bogosian), 5 (Becker, Clay, Kornbluth, Leary, Shawn), and 6 (Hoch) I explore the particular presence constructed in each body of work. First, however, I will consider critical and historical "documents" to sketch performance art monologues' presence among several other cultural traditions of artistic presence.

Chapter Two

Monologue Culture

My goal in this chapter is to lay out the contexts for the critical discussions to follow. This is not to suggest that the key to interpreting the performance texts under discussion lies hidden in some extraordinary historical context this chapter will unearth. However, even if my descriptions of the cultural contexts for performance art monologues are not especially dramatic, so to speak, there may be some value in rehearsing them as a way of suggesting a monologic strain or tendency within culture at large. The prevalent perception of cultural hierarchy in art, literature, and entertainment is an important context for performance art monologues. Performance art monologues attain a peculiar cultural class status through their associations with both high art and popular cultural forms.

I will structure this discussion of monologic forms as a comparison. Because "performance art" is still a contested term (to say nothing of the specific genre I propose), an articulation of the distinctions between performance art and other art forms may have a clarifying effect. One goal of the chapter is to construct a definition of performance art that accounts for both the critical value of the term and the potential value in its lack of precision. I have heard people say of Spalding Gray, for example, "What's the difference between him and stand-up comedians?" This chapter looks at solo dramatic works, dramatic monologue poems and performative poetry, stand-up comedy, and nonmonologic performance art to find such differences—but also to specify similarities. In fact, I go so far as to suggest that in some cases there is no meaningful inherent difference between performance art monologues and these other forms. Meaningful difference more often lies in the material circumstances of production and the cultural uses to which these forms are put. The chapter is intended to support my provisional definition of the "genre" of performance art monologues (and its two subgenres, autobiographical confession and multiple character impersonation), but also to reinforce that provisionality. This contextualization is also intended to indicate the traditional nature of this type of performance, so valued for its originality and avant-garde status.

Adena Rosmarin states provocatively that "we are able ... to read texts that are different as if they were similar because we are able and willing to make the edifying mistake of classification" (1985: 21-22). My aim is twofold: to delineate the differences between performance art monologues and other monologic cultural formations to "mistake" performance art monologues for a genre; and to trouble those distinctions. A critical appreciation of performance requires crossing the often elitist boundaries set up on the one hand to defend art from popular culture, and on the other to defend "theater" and even "dramatic literature" from performance art—even as one makes use of those boundaries to understand these terms as social realities.

SOLO DRAMA

The theatrical tradition of solo drama provides perhaps the clearest indication of the traditional nature of much contemporary monologic performance art. By the middle of the twentieth century, the solo show had developed a clear market niche in the theater industry, combining, as contemporary performance art monologues do, charismatic and virtuoso performers with subject matter not commonly presented in mainstream

Multiple-character performer Eric Bogosian (see Chapter 4)

theatrical forms. As entertainment commodities, solo drama and performance art have often been seen as novelty acts, refreshing diversions from mainstream performance.

In her study of "impersonated legend" performances—solo performances in which the performer assumes the role of a (usually) historical figure—Barbara Janoff distinguishes two strands of impersonated legend plays in a manner somewhat similar to my definition of two strands of monologic performance art. Janoff identifies her two strands as "platform performances," in which the performer reconstructs the legend character in a historical or pseudohistorical performance, and "autobiographies," which emphasize the character's first-person relation of a life story (1989: 5). The direct address and reflective tone of Gray's autobiographical monologues, for example, closely resembles Janoff's impersonated legend autobiographies, with the obvious difference that in the autobiographical monologue the performer is also the subject. In fact, Gray's tour of *Monster in a Box*, a 1991 monologue about the trials and tribulations of writing his first novel, *Impossible Vacation* (1992d), is in many ways similar to Hal Holbrook's reconstruction of Mark Twain's speaking career, or Emlyn Williams's impersonation of Charles Dickens—again, with the exception that the legendary author Gray impersonates is Gray himself.

The "platform performances" that constitute Janoff's other strand resemble some moments in multiple-character monologue performance art, as when Eric Bogosian impersonates a preacher, a lecturer, or even a street person ranting at passersby.[1] The resemblance is strongest in the "performer's direct address to the audience . . . so that (to a greater or lesser extent) *both* the performer and the audience have a role in the final dramatic product" (Janoff 1989: 48, emphasis in original). In other words, the listening audience becomes the hypothetical dramatic character(s) hearing the speaker's words.

Multiple-character monologues do not always invoke this structure, however. When his or her characters do not address an imagined audience for which the real audience stands in, the monologuist must draw on social and theatrical conventions to allow characters to speak. This is what many critics profess to dislike about works in Janoff's first category: the awkwardness of their dramatic construction. This is clearly revealed in Linda Winer's praise for Eileen Atkins's platform performance of Virginia Woolf's *A Room of One's Own* (as adapted by Patrick Garland in 1991):

> This is pure primary-source material—a one-person show for people who get annoyed with the form. Because Woolf wrote the words to be spoken aloud by herself, Atkins doesn't have to pretend to talk to imaginary characters or write letters to invisible friends or contrive methods to sneak in biographical details. She just talks. We merely lap it up. (Winer 1991: 277)

Work such as Spalding Gray's is entirely "platform performance," and a central part of his appeal is that his works are ostensibly made of "primary-source material" even purer than an adapted historical speech: his own hypothetically present speech. Most multiple-character performances are more reliant not only on the conventions of traditional theater, but on the additional conventions of the single-character play.

While Janoff's work provides useful formal analysis within a provocative political critique of "impersonated legend performances," a nonacademic has also written provocatively about solo drama. In *Acting Solo* (1989) Jordan R. Young, himself the author of a one-character play about Edna St. Vincent Millay, offers a popular history of "the art of one-man shows," as his subtitle puts it. Throughout, Young locates the specialness of the genre in the opportunities it presents for the actor, the depth of insight it can offer into its subjects, and the intimacy of its relation to its audiences. In a series of chapters focusing on solo performers and their works, from Hal Holbrook's perennial *Mark Twain Tonight!*, first performed in 1954, to Pat Carroll's 1979 *Gertrude Stein Gertrude Stein Gertrude Stein*, to Spalding Gray's *Swimming to Cambodia* (1984), Young uses a tone that is part celebrity biography, part theater history, and part how-to for the aspiring solo actor.

Young's representation of solo drama as personally meaningful to performers suggests one source of its appeal for audiences. His narratives of how actors came to do solo shows note that those shows represent breakthroughs in stalled careers, voyages of self-discovery, and even, in the case of Alec McCowen's *St. Mark's Gospel* (1977), an "act of faith" (Young 1989: 35). In effect, the novelty value of the solo form is enhanced by the sense that the performance itself, much more so than traditional drama, represents a remarkable achievement the audience is privileged to witness.

Young notes the formal distinctions between dramatically structured solo shows written by playwrights and autobiographical or self-authored works, but he also blurs that distinction, suggesting that the solo-ness common to the works is of primary importance in spectatorship. Young also implies but does not spell out a hierarchy of cultural value, noting that performers like Lily Tomlin and Eric Bogosian have "graduated from nightclubs to legitimate theatrical venues" and that Spalding Gray has "elevated the genre to an art" (1989: 25–26).

For my investigation of performance art monologues, Young's book actually blurs that sense of cultural hierarchy rather than establishing it. His prominent inclusion in an account of so many performers, many of them relatively unknown, does set Gray up as an artist among entertainers, but the very juxtaposition also undermines the constructed difference between entertainment theater and performance art. While I consider the perceived "special relationship" between performer and material an important element in shaping performance art spectatorship, the juxtaposition of Gray with, say, Holbrook indicates the degree to which "art" status is a function of the performer's background and the marketing of his or her work. Holbrook, for example, is almost never mentioned as the author/compiler of his work on Twain; instead he is celebrated for his remarkable acting ability. This is not because his work as "author" is not central to the piece, but because the established perception of Holbrook is as a theatrical actor. Had he an M.F.A. in visual arts, a background in Manhattan club performance, a career in experimental theater, or an avant-garde literary *oeuvre*, Holbrook's work as Twain might be considered from a very different perspective.

DRAMATIC MONOLOGUE POETRY

Especially in its romantic and modern manifestations, poetry exemplifies high culture as the expression of a brilliant individual's experience and way of seeing. It is thus a rich area to mine for paradigms of solo speaking.

One obvious place to search for parallels to performance art monologue is in the literary tradition of dramatic monologue poetry. Robert Browning's is probably the best known and most critically dissected work in this genre. Alan Sinfield in fact defines the genre as made up of poems "like" Browning's "Fra Lippo Lippi." The characteristics of dramatic monologue are "a first person speaker not the poet, a time and place, an [implied] auditor . . . revelation of character, colloquial language and some dramatic interaction between speaker and auditor." Like most critics of the genre, Sinfield emphasizes the theatrical structure of these works: "It may seem that dramatic monologue is a truncated play" (Sinfield 1977: 3).

Obviously, a "first person speaker not the poet" aligns dramatic monologue poetry more with the multiple character impersonation than with the autobiographical confession. On that "not" hinges much of the critical project of elaborating dramatic monologues, for most critics presuppose a reader's understanding of this written difference (and it would certainly produce a "misreading" to confuse, say, Danny Hoch with one of his characters). This perceived distance between writer and the "dramatic" character who speaks in the poem is what allows the reader to find the poem's meaning. The author's (or author/performer's) intention is the privileged site of meaning, and that intention includes the separation of the character/speaker from the poem and poet. Dramatic monologue, then, is essentially an *ironic* form. The reader reads the ironic text as a code in order to uncover the author's meaning, which is not wholly present and clarified within the poem.

The dramatic monologue poem combines the two main forms of irony as traditionally defined: "verbal" irony, "in which one meaning is stated and a different, usually antithetical, meaning is intended;" and "dramatic" irony, in which (to take the simplest definition) the spectators know more than the protagonist. Catherine Belsey points out that the irony of dramatic monologues constructs a position for the reader that seems to unite writer and reader: "The knowledge of the reader seems to surpass the knowledge of the speaker, but to be a knowledge shared with the author, so that author and reader independently produce a shared meaning which confirms the transcendence of each" (Belsey 1980: 78). Put another way, any "successful" reading of the poem must be identical to the authorial intention, however "independently" produced. To extend this to the contemporary performance of dramatic monologue performance art, the "successful" spectator must look *through* the words and actions of the character to the intention of the performer. The performance event involves both performer and audience in a collective observation of the character on display, and the cooperative spectator in a sense occupies the same position as the performer. For example, in Hoch's *Some People* (1994), spectators are hardly encouraged to identify with

Bill, the distasteful suburban yuppie concerned that "they" will damage his double-parked Jeep. Rather, even if they recognize something of themselves in the character, they are clearly asked by the performance to identify instead with Hoch's position as cultural critic.[2]

Traditional criticism of dramatic monologue poetry, however, has tended not to recognize the function of irony in prioritizing the author's interpretation. Rather, many dramatic monologue critics have used this stress on ironic distance to construe poems that are formally subjective (i.e., that communicate from within the characters' points of view) as operating *objectively* (as illuminating the world from a distance, from outside the characters' points of view). This strand of criticism sees irony as a tool for getting past a character's apparent meaning to a truer, almost disinterested interpretation. What is important in this understanding is what the monologues can teach readers about characters from the ordinary to the exotic.

The value placed on this kind of objective representation of subjectivity, and the assumed dependability of the reader's ironic understanding, can aid our consideration of the solo performance of multiple character impersonations (see chapter 4). At issue is whether the poet/performer's work can allow the reader/spectator to be sympathetic to the poem, and not simply to the character, as some critics suggest. Certainly many of Browning's monologues are quite sympathetic to the speaking character, but the critical appreciation of his work more often centers on his (and the reader's) ability to inhabit the speech of another person while simultaneously ironizing it. Multiple-character monologues might be said to offer a similar play of sympathy and irony.[3]

POETRY IN PERFORMANCE

The critical discussion of irony in dramatic monologue poetry usually presumes that the poems are read rather than spoken. The element of performance makes irony less stable in spoken poetry, especially since the contemporary poetic tradition of the poetry reading tends to privilege authenticity and immediacy over irony. Poetry readings thus suggest a key difference between written literature such as Browning's and performance art monologues. While dramatic monologue poetry has at times been a popular source for oral performance, the poems are typically considered as works on the page. To some degree, the mid-twentieth-century poetry reading institutionalizes the orality of poetry. For those in favor of the performance of poetry, the value of the reading is typically said to lie either in the "authenticity" of the interpretation offered or in the event of the reading itself. Poetry readings provide

> confirmation that poems are addressed to other people. Most poets, if there were no pay for readings, would read for nothing, not only because physical publication is appropriate to poetry's nature. In the poetry reading, the poet's physical presence delivers the poem in its volume, pitch, and resonance from mouth and tongue with body's muscles tapping the foot, body's hands keeping time in air—and this dance takes place no longer in the hermit's cave, to be reconstituted in the distant other caves of distant other hermits, but in community's open air.... The poetry reading suggests, mandates, or validates this notion of community only when it becomes, as in Gary Snyder's words, "an act of art." (Hall 1984: 77)

This emphasis on a seemingly organic relationship of word and movement, as well as the valorization of performance as a community event, is familiar to those with theatrical experience. Actors often speak of "finding" the right physical expression of a playwright's intention as embodied in the text.[4] The discourse of poetry readings is as likely to invoke intention as somehow immanent in the poet's own reading, transparently available when the interpreter and the interpreted are seen to be one and the same. As Hall notes, this seems to be a goal of the reading, rather than its necessary outcome. "By practice poets improve their ability to use voice and body to reinforce reference rather than to prevent it" (1981: 11). Hall contrasts this with the readings of inexperienced poets, which he implies do not "enforce or complement meaning" (1981: 11). The reading becomes caught in one of those delicious contradictions of authenticity. On the one hand, the author's body guarantees meaning (else why the emphasis on the presence of the actual poet?); on the other, poet/performers must aspire to a way of reading that does not interfere with the inherent authenticity of the event structure (see my discussion in chapter 4 of Goodman's distinction between autographic and allographic art).

The poetry reading is also seen as a gesture of courage on the part of the performer. The seemingly greater fixity of meaning is accompanied by an increase in that meaning's vulnerability.

> Consider what seems to be happening in performance: the poet presents the poem to a live audience. The poet differs from an actor per-

forming, in at least two important ways: the poet is not backed/ protected by the text, by an absent author, and the live audience can challenge the validity of the product in more intimate ways than walking out (which is the usual course of action employed by the disappointed theatergoer). For the poet/performer, the protection of middleman is removed. (Markham 1989: 121–22)

The simultaneous presence of author and "reading" (in both the performative and the interpretive sense) removes all alibis: the author is no longer buffered or excused by the interpretive activity of the performer (since they are the same), and the performer can neither sacrifice nor hide within the work of the author (because they are the same).

I will be arguing that the sensation of the "real" or "immediate" is a landmark common to most of what is usually termed "performance art." The poetry reading, at least in its idealized form, shares this immediacy. It transforms the poem from text into gesture, from an object into an event. In Snyder's words, the read poem becomes an "act of art." This is the most important point of comparison between poetry reading and performance art monologue: the spectator is encouraged to locate the author-function within the body of the speaker. This activity, which removes the writer/performer's alibi even as it amplifies the power of her or his presence, accentuates what Richard Bauman describes as the performer's "assumption of responsibility to an audience for a display of communicative competence" (1977: 11). The performance artist and the reading poet are doubly responsible, since they are both author and actor. Bauman's formulation of performative expectations of "communicative competence" might be (mis)read as including not simply that communicative competence that ensures a "quality" performance, but also a responsibility to engage competently with the social ramifications of that performance.[5]

The stakes of this responsibility are raised when the work performed is additionally presumed to have autobiographical reference. Because of the still prevalent romantic conception of art as expression of the artist's experience, this presumption of autobiography is likely to be present in any "lay" audience member's interpretation of a reading, unless the work is overtly coded as fictional (and perhaps even then). The performing poet in such a circumstance is responsible not only for the words and their "delivery," but for the very self that originates them. As I will argue in reference to Spalding Gray in chapter 3, autobiographical solo performance thrives on the anxiety of this responsibility.

In terms of poetry performance, the event structure of some confessional performance art (such as Gray's) is like a poetry reading in which the poems themselves are secondary in value to the event of their telling, and in which the event itself is known to be a candidate for inclusion in further confessional self-representation.[6] Like the poet, Gray in performance is without "the protection of the middle-man" or the alibi of the absent author. Unlike that of the typical reading poet, the spectacle of Gray's performance is not constituted by a (real or imaginary) object that exists prior to the performance (i.e., the poem); instead, the autobiographical monologue performance offers *itself* as the art object.

DRAMATIC MONOLOGUE POETRY "READINGS"

Returning for a moment to dramatic monologue poetry, we should note that it has at times been considered an oral as well as a literary medium. In *Browning and the Dramatic Monologue*, S. S. Curry (1908) makes his case for the appreciation and performance of Browning's and similar works. The first half of the book is devoted to arguing the importance of monologue as a literary form; the second half offers extensive instruction for "Dramatic Rendering of the Monologue."

Curry suggests that three principles should guide the interpreter of the monologue: "unity, centrality, and consistency" (1908: 236). He emphasizes the objective presentation of character in a manner similar to exclusively literary critics. "The monologue is as indirect as a play. It is the revelation of a soul, and to be used not to persuade, but to influence subtly. The truth is portrayed with living force, and the auditor left to draw his own conclusions and lessons" (Curry 1908: 244). In simultaneously emphasizing the literary significance and the performative accuracy of this genre of poetry, Curry combines elaborate poetic form with a basically realist performance aesthetic. His prescriptive instructions to the performer echo his descriptive accounts of the poet: portray the character as if real, without intruding too much. "Influence subtly." Curry finds social value in these twinned literary and performative exercises, suggesting that readers and auditors can learn about the world around them by the insights of the poet effectively transmitted through the effort of the performer. "It may be realized also that the evolution of the monologue is a part of the progressive spirit of our own time" (Curry 1908: 256).

Considering together dramatic monologue poems and contemporary poetry reading suggests a particular instance of performance: the dramatic monologue poet performing her or his own work. What if Robert Browning traveled through time to the present, to tour English departments and writing programs impersonating the characters in his work? This poetry reading—or the performance of these poems, if enacted in the manner Curry suggests—would combine the distanced structure of Browning's poetry (the reader apprehending Browning's "meaning" through the distinct entity of the character) with the authenticating "presence" of the poetry reading. While the audience at this hypothetical reading might not regard the fictional poems as "confessional" in the way described above, the presence of one "reputed to have written poems" in the body of the one performing them would emphasize the authenticity and the gestural "event-ness" of the speech.

What then is the difference between this hypothetical reading and contemporary multiple-character solo performance art? (This reading is really not so hypothetical, as there are contemporary poets who write "dramatic" poems in the voices of one or many characters.) In fact, there is no meaningful difference, other than that much of Browning's dramatic monologue poetry was written in verse, while the preponderance of performance art is not. My construction of a hypothetical poetry reading no different from performance art is not mere facetiousness; it reinforces my contention that performance art is discursively constituted rather than dependent on inherent formal rules. Multiple-character performances such as Bogosian's—or the even more nearly "poetic" ones of Hoch—are just such a meeting of poet and fictional poem, though obviously bounded by different verbal stylistics, performance venues, and audience expectations.

STAND-UP COMEDY

If poetry embodies (or once embodied) the high culture attributes to which performance art aspires, stand-up comedy might be said to typify corresponding attributes of popular culture. At the same time, stand-up, like theatrical performance and performance art, frequently grounds itself by invoking a purist aesthetic and a primitive origin.

A strict, limiting definition of stand-up comedy would describe an encounter between a single, standing performer behaving comically and/or saying funny things directly to an audience, unsupported by very much in the way of costume, prop, setting, or dramatic vehicle. Yet stand-up comedy's roots are . . . entwined with rites, rituals, and dramatic experiences that are richer, more complex than this simple definition can embrace. (Mintz 1985: 71)

Mintz's reluctance to pin down stand-up's definition is typical of both academic and popular discussions of the form, and marks its first commonality with performance art, which is often accorded a similarly privileged breadth. Its basic structural resemblance to monologic performance art is quite clear: a single performer talking before an audience, ostensibly speaking her or his own words. In its reception, stand-up often involves an extremely fine seam between performer and performance character, and almost all contemporary stand-up is built on ostensibly autobiographical material.

While Mintz notes that many writers on comedy begin by apologizing for even approaching the subject (1985: 71), stand-up has received serious attention for its social function. Stephanie Koziski's "The Stand-up Comedian as Anthropologist" (1984) is a clear example of a highly positive view of stand-up as a cultural force, in part because of her uncritical approval of the project of anthropology itself. Still, her combination of a progressive view of stand-up—she approves of stand-up for making "covert culture" visible (1984: 60) and focuses considerable attention on comedian Dick Gregory's social activism—with a more functionalist view (depicting the therapeutic activity of "airing feelings" the audience may tend to repress) is indicative of two ways the audience is said to respond to the perceived leadership of such cultural figures.

Mintz's view of "Stand-up Comedy as Social and Cultural Mediation" (1985) takes up the question of social function and seems to allow for both progressive demystification and a conservative gesture of reinforcement, in a "process of cultural affirmation and subversion." Mintz notes that the comedian is traditionally "defective in some way" and suggests that this allows "us" to laugh at "him" as a "negative exemplar." At the same time, "to the extent that we may identify with his expression or behavior, secretly recognize it as reflecting natural tendencies . . . he can become our comic spokesman" (1985: 74).

This role as spokesperson or even "as part of the public ritual of stand-up comedy" as "shaman" (Mintz 1985: 74) is relevant to our consideration of similar qualities frequently assigned to performance artists, and it certainly interests me in light of my feeling that these white male heterosexual performance artists are cultural leaders who function as icons of their identity groupings. With regard to leadership, Mintz further claims that comedians "accept this role more or less consciously, viewing their art as a protection of society" (Mintz 1985: 74 n. 6).

This conscious social involvement is certainly arguable if one considers ultracommercialized performers such as Bob Hope or Johnny Carson, but Borns in particular cites concerns expressed by numerous comedians about the damage done to the profession by performers who seem deliberately to refuse the role of social protector. This was the case with Andrew Dice Clay, the particularly outspoken comic whose racist, sexist, gay-bashing humor led to a partial boycott of his *Saturday Night Live* appearance by show regulars and musical guests. The degree to which stand-up is permitted to break social taboos is similar to that enjoyed by performance art, which has a reputation for outrageous material. Clay's defense of his material hinged on the "honesty" of his presentation of "Diceman," the offensive "character" he assumed while performing (Abrahams 1990). The same question of honest or objective distance between performer and character will be at issue in examining multiple-character performance art monologues.

Stand-up also raises issues of gender, sexuality, and power relevant to performance art. For many critics and comedians, these issues are quite material:

> In stand-up, the microphone as a means to gaining and holding power is viewed by comics in literal terms and, by male comics, in psychological terms revolving around virility and impotence. Paul [Reiser] describes a situation early in his career when his microphone was taken by someone in the audience: "It's like having your balls grabbed . . . you have no control." His feelings are corroborated by other male comedians, several of whom use the metaphor of "microphone as dick" to explain why there are many more men than women in stand-up comedy. (Borns 1987: 21)

While this last explanation for systematic discrimination seems particularly weak (and certainly open to an opposite Freudian interpretation), these observations are of interest for their graphic linkage of speech and phallic power. For now it may be sufficient to note, by way of connecting the scatological tendencies of stand-up to this image of the vocal phallus, that Derrida's extrapolations of Artaud suggest the degree to which speech "falls" away and should be considered excrement that is "lost" from the body and at the same time assumes a degree of power:

> Like excrement, like the turd, which is, as is also well known, a metaphor of the penis, the work should stand upright. But the work, as excrement, is but matter without life, without force or form. It always falls and collapses as soon as it is outside me. This is why the work—be it poetic or other—will never help me stand upright. (Derrida 1978: 183)

Stand-up, then, as a work of speech that "stands up," can be considered as a nexus of excremental art (that is, as Derrida says, all art except an art "without works") and doomed phallic signification.[7] "Shit," both as verbal trope in the works of comedians and performance art monologists and as a descriptive term applied to both genres by some dissatisfied spectators and critics, is in one sense a privileged term in both discourses, a connection between them at the levels of production and reception.

My pursuit of these metaphors casts a different light on Koziski's description of the "healthy release" offered by the comedian/anthropologist (1984: 72), and it suggests that a functionalist approach to either performance art monologue or stand-up perhaps ought to include a possible excremental function. Any critique of such seemingly outspoken work as Clay's or Bogosian's (and I am not equating them, but simply making Rosmarin's "edifying mistake" of recognizing some level of categorical similarity) must take seriously their justification on the ground of "release" or liberation of the repressed. This includes my own critique of works that construct themselves, at least in part, as speaking the unspoken.

For the moment, for purposes of definition, it remains to distinguish between stand-up and performance art monologue. This is not an easy task for formal analysis. Stand-up approximates the forms of performance art monologue so closely that critics and practitioners may find themselves hard put to make (up) a difference. For example, Spalding Gray has been called a "sit-down comic" (Young 1989: 178), and comedian Bob Goldthwait expresses a combination of an entertainer's cynicism and a dada or punk sensibility on the topic:

I was in a performance place in Boston not long ago, and I was like, "What's the big deal about a performance artist space? Next they're going to put a mechanical bull in here—what the fuck...." Last night there was a lull in my act, and I said, "Jesus, one more lull and I'm going to be a performance artist." I don't like the word "art" in general, it usually implies that you're hip, and I don't want to be hip. (Quoted in Borns 1987: 287)

There are certainly fewer laughs, on average, in monologue performance art, but this does not hold in all specific cases. Gray's *Monster in a Box* (1991), for example, was received with almost constant laughter when I attended. So even this analysis of reception or performer-spectator relationship cannot consistently distinguish performance art from stand-up, and certainly can't cope with either particularly funny monologue or particularly bad comedy.

Perhaps it would be better to abandon the distinction, and argue for a fundamental sameness of the genres. Lingering difference can perhaps be ascribed to an internal stratification:

> In stand-up, as opposed to other art forms, people are far less willing to stand back and let the "experts" tell them what is and isn't high art. Unlike a Jackson Pollock painting or a John Cage quartet, with comedy, almost everyone "gets it" to some degree, so everybody becomes an expert critic. It is hard to impose gradations of quality on an art form that, when innovative and brilliant, often elicits the same response from people as when it is derivative and vulgar. After all, a laugh is a laugh is a laugh is a laugh. The only solution would be to draw a distinction between "high laughs" and "low laughs" which, while instinctively done by comedians among themselves ... seems both elitist and unnecessary. (Borns 1987: 280-81)

The elitism Borns finds in the high/low distinction within comedy is arguably of a lesser order than the elitism preserving the boundary between stand-up and performance art. Perhaps an egalitarian criticism should be invested in collapsing the distinction altogether. Certainly there is a tension in popular press criticism of performance art monologue between a populist, everybody-gets-it strand and a fence-tending, "this is high art" attitude. Refusing a distinction between performance art and comedy might thus have a popularizing effect on the reception of performance, while simultaneously agitating for the artistic recognition some fear is inaccessible to comedians because of their unexalted content:

> Regardless of how enlightened civilians—and comics—become about the artistic attributes of stand-up comedy, Alan Harvey believes it will always have the residual stigma of being a second-rate art form because of its "unenlightened" subject matter. He says, "It's hard for me to explain to people that watching TV at night, going to see *Rambo* at three o'clock in the afternoon, and walking down the street are things that further my art—not just ways of passing time." This is a compelling question central to the "comedy as art" debate: in order to satirize trash, the satirist must, in a sense, wallow in it himself [sic] . . . does this then make the final product trash? It's anyone's guess. But perhaps, if the outcome is funny enough, the question is irrelevant. (Borns 1987: 291)

In the case of performance art monologues, this content analysis fails to separate the quotidian focus of stand-up from the mundane occurrences detailed in performance by Spalding Gray, David Cale, or Mark Anderson. All of their work relies to some degree on the same sense of amazement at, or critical distance from, occurrences of daily life.

To call such performance artists "stand-up comedians," however, would ultimately be inaccurate. Despite their humor, despite the laughter generated by many of their performances, and despite their everyday subjects, these artists arise from a different means of production, circulate in a different economy of cultural value, and are marketed to somewhat different audiences through an almost entirely distinct performative apparatus. In one sense, we "know" there is a difference between performance art and stand-up comedy because the marketplace tells us so.

If formal analysis, content analysis, and even audience response analysis cannot reliably distinguish performance art monologue from stand-up comedy, and if the only secure "difference" is this material question of the apparatus, what are the implications for the study of performance art monologues? Even if there were significant differences in content, form, and performer-audience relationship (and a different reading of these texts might produce these differences)—there is still no "essence" of performance art, nor of stand-up, and so there is no essential difference. All of which is only to say again that all generic distinction is socially (discursively) constructed.

One clear example of the formal indistinguishability of performance art and stand-up comedy is the later work of the comedian Lenny Bruce. Bruce's last performances, after his repeated legal battles over the alleged "obscenity" of his performances, consisted largely of Bruce reading his trial transcripts, with frequent wry explanatory asides (see Bruce 1973). These performances feature a single performer telling the audience directly about his amazing experiences, which are unquestionably framed as "real." In some ways this structure is formally purer than even Gray's autoperformance, since the veracity of Bruce's narrative is substantiated by the Law (even as Bruce undermines the authority of that text by demonstrating its contradictions). Lenny Bruce is not, however, the "father" of monologic performance art, if only because performance art as such can hardly be said to have existed at that time. That is, because at the time performance art as a term was much more restricted in use, and because Bruce has not been retroactively inducted into the canon of performance art (and it is certainly not my project to do so), he remains discursively bounded by comedy, as well as materially bounded by stand-up comedy venue, criticism, and history.

This emphasis on the interpretive, linguistic, arbitrary construction of critical truth does not imply that form, content, and audience are unimportant; on the contrary, it emphasizes their importance as sites of social signification. The meaning of stand-up and monologue performance as forms lies in the differing territory they occupy.

PERFORMANCE ART AND MONOLOGIC CULTURE

My objective here is not to present a capsule history of performance art, but rather to offer a few brief observations on the discourse around performance art and the formal qualities common to the works taken up by that discourse.[8]

I have argued in each section of this chapter that no absolutely secure formal distinction can be made between these forms and performance art. In the previous examples, I have shown how specific moments of poetry, drama, and comedy closely resemble performance art monologues. The structure of this argument might easily be turned around, as specific moments of "performance art" can be cited that closely resemble instances of dance, sculpture, social work, political action, etc. From a formal point of view, performance art is sometimes even defined as that which falls through the cracks of formal classification. For example, Silvio Gaggi claims that "traditional theater . . . incorporates live performance of character and action into a temporal structure. Traditional sculpture involves neither live performance nor temporal structure" (1986: 51). He then positions various instances of performance as closer to one or the other. Works of performance are in a sense constructed negatively, through their failure to meet the requirements for admission to another form.

In spite of—or perhaps because of—this tendency toward negative definition, "performance art" seems an infinitely flexible term. Goldberg (1988) discusses dada cabaret and futurist performance, which have also been treated by theater historians, as "performance art." Fluxus artists made performance—presented in "concerts" of bizarre acts, only some of which bore any relation to music—central to their aesthetic (see Frank and Friedman 1984). The Women's Building in Los Angeles became a center for public feminist media performance (see Roth 1983). Before returning to sculpture, Chris Burden sacrificed his body in acts of performative contemplation that were often read as scandalous provocation, as in his MFA performance, *Five-Day Locker Piece* (1979), in which he lived in his locker at UC Irvine for five days (Battcock and Nickas 1984: 224–26). Musician Laurie Anderson brought performance art new visibility with large concerts and the unlikely success of her single "O, Superman." Robert Wilson raised and spent millions to produce operatic spectacles such as *Einstein on the Beach*.

"Performance art" becomes both more and less meaningful by being so widely applicable. It loses meaning, certainly, as it loses specificity, but it also accrues meaning with each new instance of its application. I think finally that performance art is best considered as a marketing term, used to communicate to prospective audiences about the kind of cultural product on offer. In this way it certainly insulates, say, modern dance or ballet lovers from dance-based performance art, even as it attracts art audiences to dance work. At its best, "performance art" can serve as an identifying marker worn by people based in a variety of disciplines and fostering contact between them.

My choice to define performance art in terms of usage is not the only alternative to the would-be tidiness of strict formal definition. Noël Carroll, for example, approaches the problem "historically or genetically," suggesting that "the factors that produced an interest in performance and the ways these factors dovetail have caused contemporary performance to be a connected and living tradition, an arena of activity organized by historically shared concerns" (1986: 65). Because Carroll's account of performance attends to the dialogic relationship between art world performance and experimental theater, it avoids the relatively simplistic description of progress (or degeneration) to which purely formalist narratives of performance art are susceptible.

The story of performance is sometimes told as a journey from the gallery to the theater (to the cinema). In this reading, performance art originates as a challenge to the aesthetic conventions of the gallery, activated either by inserting the live body into the gallery or by using the body to create art outside the gallery. Burden's work offers examples of both movements. *Bed Piece* (1972), in which he lived in a bed in a gallery for several weeks, disrupted the gallery space with the insistent difference of a live rather than represented body. Various other living paintings and sculptural works by a number of artists can be said to fit in this category. On the other hand, Burden's *Trans-fixed* (1974), in which he lay crucified on top of a Volkswagen and had himself wheeled into the street, represents the creation of an image (albeit horrific) presented for aesthetic contemplation outside of traditional art spaces. Other examples of this kind of non- or antigallery performance can be found in the works of Linda Montano, from her public chicken impersonations of the early 1970s to her seven-year series of regular appearances at the New Museum of Contemporary Art in New York offering art counseling to museum visitors.

Such work certainly challenged not only gallery-goers' sense of propriety, but also traditional critics' understanding of art and aesthetic quality. As one critic infamously said of artistic minimalism, "Art degenerates as it approaches the condition of theater" (Fried 1968: 21). The stillness and simplicity of minimalist objects transformed them into gestures, affronting the sensibilities of those who looked to the object for the embodiment of craft and inspiration. In gallery-based performance art the gestures were even harder to ignore, for they were made not by objects but by the artists themselves.

By 1979 critics had begun to view monologue performance, at least implicitly, as a genre. John Howell noted that monologue was of particular use to visual artists amid art's current preoccupations:

> The assertion of an unmitigated self takes on a special emphasis in the face of contemporary art's sophisticated aesthetics of abstraction.

> Monologue performance allows for an intimate personalism, a private expression with its own material integrity valid beyond art's certification. (Howell 1979: 152–53)

Looking ahead to the next decade, Howell suggests an emergent use of personalist monologue in a collaborative context.

> And already a strange hybrid appears on the verge of the eighties, an even more blatant mix of personal, multi-media performance art and more complex theatre techniques. *Three Places in Rhode Island*, a trilogy of pieces by Spalding Gray and Elizabeth LeCompte, is the most marked of these syntheses. (Howell 1979: 158)

Howell's example of monologue synthesized with other production elements did not outlive the new decade, as Gray left the Wooster Group to become the best known of the 1980s monologists.

In the same year, *The Drama Review* published a special issue on "autoperformance." The journal, which at the time tended to focus on formalist analysis, sought to clarify performance art terminology and establish its own standard. Michael Kirby's introductory note suggested that autoperformance, "a term we have coined to refer to presentations conceived and performed by the same person," might be a more precise term for the works under discussion.

> To some extent, these performances overlap a rather vague theatre mode variously called "Artist's Performance," "Art Performance," or "Performance Art." These terms are vague, in part because they are sociological rather than functional or aesthetic. (Kirby 1979: 2)

While "autoperformance" is a relatively precise and thus very useful term—it describes, for example, all of the works considered in this at times "sociological" study—it did not replace "performance art" in either common or critical discourse. However, this special issue helped mark solo performance art as a multidisciplinary form, produced by artists—and suitable for consideration by critics—of diverse backgrounds and allegiances.

In this narrative of performance art, the 1980s witnessed a transition from the gallery to the theatrical space. New York's performance club scene, vibrant in the middle of the decade but quickly diminishing, can be considered a transitional moment.[9] In the mid- to late 1980s performers like Bogosian began to be noticed by venues such as the Public Theatre, and experimental theater groups such as The Wooster Group came to be thought of as doing "performance." The frame against which performance pushed, the white walls of gallery and museum, was not present in this new theatrical work. Without this sense of revolutionary challenge, some began to feel that performance artists were "selling out."

> It is precisely that repositioning of performance art from the art world into the theater world which is prompting concern about performance art going "commercial" these days. If the art world has trouble dealing with the commercial viability of an artist whose work is an ephemeral, time-based phenomenon, the theater world is used to the idea of art that exists only in time, in front of an audience. Indeed, the theater world seems prepared to welcome performance art with open arms. (Abell 1987: 31)

This narrative of performance art is problematic, in large part because art world performance art cannot be completely characterized as either chronologically or aesthetically prior to theatrical performance art. While theatrical performance art was undeniably influenced by goings-on in the art world, theatrical experimentation was also concerned with its own contexts and traditions. There was a point at which these two performance arts seemed on the verge of clear critical distinction: "If *art performance* was initially a reaction to certain prejudices and practices of the art galleries of the late fifties and early sixties, *performance art* was a reaction to prevailing tendencies in mainstream theater of the same period" (Carroll 1986: 71, emphasis added). This distinction between (art world) art performance and (theatrical) performance art has not been widely accepted, in part because of a lack of critical rigor in attending to the context of performance practices, but also because, as Carroll pointed out, "at present, as in the past, performance art and art performance appear convergent" (1986: 78).

For the purposes of this study, I am less interested in whether the theatrical success of a few artists means the "selling-out" of art-world performance than in what "performance art" means in a theatrical context. Briefly, the experimental theater that came to coexist with art performance (but which arguably began in the 1960s and traces its roots back much further) offered the same challenge to convention in a different conceptual frame. While performance in the gallery challenged the aesthetics of the dead but tangible object with a living body, the new "performance" in the theater challenged the representational duties of the actor's body by insisting on its status as a real, tangible object, and confronted dramatic narrative conventions through what Carroll characterizes as "the quest for the real event" (1986: 73).

Clear examples of such work can be found in the performances of the Performance Group and the Wooster Group. These works frequently involved such "real-time" activities as serving food, as the Performance Group did in its *Mother Courage* (1974–77; Schechner 1988: 201), or placing phone calls to actual locations outside the theater, as the Wooster Group did in *Route 1 & 9* (1981; Savran 1986: 23). The performances insist to some degree on the event status of the work. While traditional representational theater generally pretends to be nothing more than the narrative, these works deliberately exceeded the narrative, at times dispensing with it in favor of actual events. Theatrical "performance art" seems in one sense a logical continuation of one of the central Western theatrical projects in the twentieth century, often named for Brecht, but with roots stretching back to dada and futurism if not before: the radical acknowledgment of the simultaneous presence of performers and audience.[10]

What Eric Bogosian has said of talk radio, that "[n]othing invigorates the mass media the way reality does" (Bogosian 1988: xv), is true in a different way of theater-based performance. I maintain that "performance art" is best thought of as a marketing tool used to identify particular versions of established cultural products for specific audiences. However, I would still argue that the most common factor in what is called performance art is not some single formal quality or the involvement of a traditionally (visually) trained artist, but the intrusion of some "real" or actual circumstance apparently at odds with the set of conventions acting as the "host" of the performance. This can take many forms: dance conventions confronted with spoken autobiographical narrative, quotidian movement, or insistently real properties; gallery conventions thwarted by the insistent bodily functions of the artist on display; or the habits of theatrical fiction broken by Schechner's actuals or the Wooster Group's use of Spalding Gray's life as text. Certainly there is work called performance that does not follow this pattern—Robert Wilson's huge spectacles, perhaps (though the sheer length of some of them might be said to involve the "actual" circumstances of the audiences' bodies in the plot of the performance). But even a provisional formal account of performance art is useful when coupled with an understanding of the term as a figure of speech.

The straight white male monologue performers considered here fit this provisional formal account to varying degrees. As I will argue in chapter 3, Gray's work transforms every "real" event in his life into representation. Highly fictional constructions such as Bogosian's, however, do not at first glance appear to fit this formal scheme. Still, as I have tried to show in my discussion of the performance of dramatic monologue poetry, artists like Bogosian still trade on the simultaneous presence of author and work. No matter how fictional, the reception of such performance still involves the perception of authenticity and privileged meaning present in the poetry reading. This authorial/performative presence is just the sort of intrusion of the "real" into the representation I have described as typical, if not necessarily constitutive, of performance art.[11]

Within the broad field of performance art, some effort is required to "mistake" the array of contemporary solo performances for a genre, for solo performance is as varied in form and content as it is widespread and popular. Karen Finley is among the best known of contemporary performance artists because of the sensational publicity her work has received. This has commonly focused on her use of nudity and disconcerting stage action; one might read accounts of her work in the popular press and not find out that language is central to her performance. Tim Miller is dance-influenced, but his solo work, while it involves more movement than that of many monologists, is centered on storytelling. For example, *Sex/Love Stories* (1991) and *My Queer Body* (1992) aim to both anger and amuse the audience through Miller's recollections of gay male culture and his activist involvement with ACT UP. Ishmail Houston-Jones remains more fully inside the dance world, but some of his solos have placed narrative speech alongside strenuous movement.

Monologue as a device has an important role in much performance art that is not solo work. For example, the work of Pomo Afro Homos combines monologues, dance, and multiple-character scenes. Penny Arcade's *Bitch/Dyke/Faghag/Whore* (1992) is built around a series of monologues, seemingly autobiographical, performed by Arcade, but the piece also involves live and recorded video and performances by a number of exotic dancers in provocative costuming.

I might also provide a certain context for the two main figures of my study, Eric Bogosian and Spalding Gray, by referring to some solo performers who produce work strikingly similar to theirs in some ways, yet with significant differences. Guillermo Gomez-Peña, for example, might be compared to Bogosian in that both have produced solo work that involves rapidly portraying a variety of characters. Bogosian achieves meaning through traditional dramatic means, presenting in turn complete and essentially realist vignettes of each character; these are anthologized in his full-length performances to provide a seeming cross-section of society. Gomez-Peña, on the other hand, uses even more rapid oscillation, between characters ranging from historical to fantastic, to call his own identity as performer into question. In *Border Brujo* (1990), for example, Gomez-Peña shifts characters by changing accents, hats, and voice amplification, but he addresses the audience directly and continuously, and never firmly identifies his characters. Early in the videotaped version of this work, Gomez-Peña chants a seeming parody of Catholic liturgy, sliding from Latin to Spanish to English. While he has obviously adopted a persona, this moment in performance is not attributable to a "realistic" dramatic scene, as are all of the characters in Bogosian's well-known works. Gomez-Peña's more thoroughly avant-garde aesthetic continually disrupts itself, leaving a highly fragmented "text" for the spectator to investigate.

In discussing Spalding Gray, it may be worthwhile to keep in mind some other semi-autobiographical performances, such as Holly Hughes' *World Without End* (1989). Hughes is best known as a playwright, and might be discussed, like Bogosian, in terms of fictionality. Like Gray, Hughes relates stories that seem to be from her life, ranging from her Michigan childhood to current career crises. Unlike Gray, Hughes is willfully confrontational, emphasizing her difference from the spectators and flaunting her disregard for their opinions of her. Again, the posture is more avant-garde in its disruption of traditionally comfortable theatrical dynamics; at the same time, Hughes's piece and the bulk of Gray's work share an autobiographical, confessional premise.

All of these diverse performers constitute the genre of solo performance art, if only because they work alone in ways that are frequently labeled performance art. Further, a case could be made for the presence of the "actual" or of reality-based elements within each of their representations. I might provisionally define the genre considered here as any solo performance based primarily on words that is constructed through artistic/critical discourse as performance art, and/or contains aesthetically disruptive "reality" in the manner discussed above. This is further delimited by the identity-markers "white," "heterosexual," and "male."

THE GENIUS OF MONOLOGUE

Three forces are at play in the cultural arena under discussion here. First is a performance form that privileges personality, individual creative energy, and singular performative presence. Second is the array of identity privileges that accrue to whiteness, maleness, and heterosexuality. Third is the high value placed on monologic genius within modern Western conceptions of artistic quality.

Monologue is a cultural impulse within Western modernity visible in monologic genres within various art forms. These genres are often the clearest expressions of the phallic singularity of discourse privileged by the critical apparatus constructed around forms of artistic production. The mythic "great men"—great painters, poets, statesmen, philosophers—are the embodiment of this monologic impulse. It is not exclusively modern, of course, and is perhaps best traced back to the Renaissance, if not beyond. In any event, I aver that monologue-as-cultural-impulse is a particular movement of power within culture; performance art monologues are one of the traces of that movement.

Ken Frieden's *Genius and Monologue* (1985) is a sort of intellectual history, or even archaeology, of the connections between monologue as a literary form and "genius" as a discursive construction. A key moment in the construction of "genius" as a modern concept occurs in eighteenth-century England. "Beginning in the 1750s, a craze of theoretical writings urges that the inspired need not *have a genius*; instead an inspired author *has genius* or *is a genius*" (Frieden 1985: 66). Drawing on Derrida's "subversion of monologue" through the deconstruction of "presence," Frieden distinguishes "monologue" from "writing":

> While monologue affords a delusion of presence by suppression of absence, writing *is* the delusory making-present in absence. Derrida's "preference" for writing reflects his choice of explicit mediation as opposed to pretended immediacy. Monologue seeks to elude the inevitable play of presence and absence, of *différance*; masturbation enters into this play; writing sets up the conditions of possibility for presence and absence, "transcendental" conditions of mediated immediacy. (Frieden 1985: 95, emphasis in original)

A critique of monologic performance art may be constructed upon this distinction between writing and monologue. While performance art has historically emphasized the real as content and as event, it has also tended to foreground, even to fetishize, the mediation of reality. Whatever the inadequacies of experimental performance art of the 1960s and '70s, one of the successes of its formal experimentation was in not seeking to elude the "inevitable play of absence and presence," in refusing to pretend complete immediacy. In other words, the continuation of the Brechtian project I mentioned above meant in part the presence of "writing" in performance—sometimes literally (see Fuchs 1985). This writing—the visible marks of explicit mediation—is largely absent from the 1980s turn toward monologue. Seamlessness, seduction, charisma—presence—mark a turning away from "writing" to "monologue," a pretense of immediacy. There are suggestions, however, that a developing "critique of the culture of simulations" (Banes 1990: 22) might further question this presence:

> After World War II, American avant-garde theatre began to move away from realist-oriented mimesis, in search of an even more fundamental route to authenticity. But as we head into a new millennium, even the aspiration to authenticity begins to disclose itself as one more cultural construct. (Banes 1990: 23)[12]

In retrospect, the 1980s turn toward monologue might be seen as an introduction of "genius" (in the sense Frieden notes of "being" a genius) to the relatively anti-individualist medium of performance art, which in the '60s and '70s had a significant collectivist element. In a sense, "genius" performance art monologues mark the triumph of high modernist aesthetics over a form founded on postmodern disruption. The modernist art object—immanent, sufficient to itself—appeared within performance art as the monologue. It may be that "art" as conceived by high modernism fails as it approaches the condition of theater, but performance art returned to modernism when it incorporated the most essential modernist theatrical value: the self-sufficient presence of the actor. Closer examination of the two monologists in chapters 3 and 4 will suggest that monologues of genius are a conservative cultural development that tends to be exacerbated by the attendant identity politics of the white, male, and heterosexual.

Chapter Three

Loss as a Means of Mastery: Spalding Gray's Autobiographical Performance

> Performance Art's most radical and innovative work often involves a thrillingly difficult investigation of autobiography. By rejuvenating the possible ways of presenting and representing the self, Performance Art has changed the notion of theatrical presence and widened the methods by and through which the self can be narrated, parodied, held in contempt, and/or made to be the source of revelatory vision and thought. (Phelan 1988: 28)

> Representation is not defined directly by imitation: even if one gets rid of notions of the "real", of the "vraisemblable", of the "copy", there will still be representation for so long as a subject (author, reader, spectator or voyeur) casts his *gaze* towards a horizon on which he cuts out the base of a triangle, his eye (or his mind) forming the apex. (Barthes 1977: 69)

The tension between these two statements is my focus in this chapter. On the one hand, Phelan appropriately celebrates the role of autobiography in performance art, especially as a rejuvenating source of content. On the other hand, autobiographical performance can at times seem to imply an escape from representation (though Phelan herself discusses it in terms of "presenting and representing"). As Barthes describes it, representation is an effect, not an object or an action, and even that which seems to avoid "imitation" (i.e., some current autobiographical performance) must in fact produce the effect of representation. And representation, of course, begs the question of who controls representation, and who represents whom. Using the example of

Spalding Gray, in this chapter I look for some of the potential consequences of playing the real.

Spalding Gray is arguably the most widely known performance artist working in the United States today. His wry persona and carefully crafted autobiographical narratives have drawn a following outside the art and theater worlds on a scale previously achieved only by multimedia composer and performance artist Laurie Anderson. His position has been critically established by such authoritative voices as Mel Gussow's: Gray has "defined the performance art form of the autobiographical monologue" (Gussow 1986: 216). Particularly in newspapers and popular periodicals, his monologues are regarded by a majority of critics as providing just that revelatory vision described above by Peggy Phelan. For many consumers of popular culture, Spalding Gray *is* performance art, and *is* that new understanding of the self through performance. Further, the marketing of the Gray phenomenon often emphasizes the universality of that understanding, as when Vintage Books quotes the *Washington Post* on the cover of the monologue *Monster in a Box*: "Gray fishes up so much of the glory and chaos of our times. . . . Talking about himself—with candor, humor, imagination—he ends up talking about all of us."

Gray does not label himself a "performance artist," and often refers to his work as that of an actor playing himself. While this need not prevent us from labeling Gray's work "performance" as distinguished from dramatic theater, it is clear that Gray wishes to emphasize the performative values his work inherits from theatrical tradition. If it is true that "in traditional dramatic performance the actor's body acquires its mimetic and representational powers by becoming something other than itself, more and less than individual" (Elam 1980: 9), then Gray revises that process, not becoming "other than" himself, but rendering his "self" as "other" (Shank 1982: 170). Onstage, Gray is an actor: he interprets a text using an actor's tools. The difference, Gray seems to suggest, is that the text he works with is himself.

In this respect, Gray's monologues are among the most highly visible examples of the cultural impact of the phenomenon many have come to call simply "performance." Elizabeth Wright has enumerated some of the effects of that impact.

> The most significant features of performance are the subjection of the body to analysis, the use of space as an experimental object, and the

disturbance of certain boundaries, namely those between artist and spectator, spectator and art "object," art "object" and artist. (Wright 1989: 115)

In comparison to many leading figures in avant-garde performance, Gray subjects the body to analysis mostly through his relative immobility, and experiments with space largely through that minimalist use of movement; but he has made the disturbance of the boundary between art "object" and artist the center of his performance career. His rigorous presentation of his own life as an object of contemplation situates him within a performance art tradition of framing life as art.

Nonetheless, theatrically-minded critics experience considerable difficulty in advising the public about Gray's work. They tend to fall back on comparisons to performers in more established genres. He is frequently compared to Jewish comedians; one critic calls him "a sort of gentile Jackie Mason" (Watt 1990a: 129), another "a WASPish Woody Allen" (Kirkpatrick 1990: 129). A *Village Voice* critic, quoted prominently on the back of Gray's monologue anthology, *Sex and Death to the Age 14*, proclaims him "a sort of WASP Shelley Berman for the '80s." A fellow WASP has suggested that this is because "WASP's aren't supposed to reveal feelings and neuroses, but repress them out of existence, so another signifier is needed."[1] Just as Gray's generic identification is clarified by his resemblance to comedians, his performance of ethnicity seems explicable as a qualified WASPness. This ethnic identity is qualified precisely by Gray's comic performance of neurosis and extroversion—qualities apparently associated with Jews, or more precisely with Jewish comedians. Near-Jewishness as a supplementary signifier may have been a vital element in the descriptive criticism essential to the early marketing of Gray's work, but it is worth noting at this point that the contrast between Jewish and WASP or Gentile in these statements serves to "whiten" Gray's identity even as it specifies his personality. For while I include Jewish performers such as Josh Kornbluth and Danny Hoch as white monologists (see chapter 5), the construction of Gray as a Gentile performer who is talkative and funny in spite of not being a Jewish comedian indicates his ownership of an arguably greater (albeit specified) identity privilege.

Interviewed for a documentary about performance art, Gray himself describes the character he plays by means of comparison:

Spalding Gray

> I sit on stage and I play myself. . . . I sit at a table . . . and when I say I play myself, I play the recollection of the performance before, and I add to it. . . . And I develop a character that's Spalding Gray, who is kind of a combination, as I often say, of Mark Twain, Candide, Don Quixote, and Mad Max. (Gray, quoted in Dwyer and Vittaccio 1988)

While the text of this remark might seem egotistical, the delivery, as always with Gray, is heavy with irony. This stance makes it difficult to say precisely what Gray "really" thinks about anything. The preponderance of the evidence, however, suggests that he takes his performative mission very seriously.

> While in Santa Cruz, I began to sit in on a class taught by Amelie Rorty, called "The Philosophy of Emotions." . . . One day after class I was talking to Amelie about my diary and about how I felt that I'd come to the end of a way of working, that I didn't know where to turn next. Because my work had stopped I had a feeling that the world was also coming to an end. I told her I thought we had come to the end of the white middle-class world as we knew it. She took me at my word and said, "Well, Spalding, during the collapse of Rome, the last artists were the chroniclers." And all the bells went off inside me. (Gray 1986: xii)

While also a bit pompous, perhaps, this quotation, taken from Gray's preface to *Sex and Death*, is extremely attractive to a critic approaching Gray's work, since it conveniently packages Gray for positioning at a particular cultural moment, a specific turning point in history. Robert Siegle, in an admiring study of "downtown" Manhattan fiction by Kathy Acker, Constance DeJong, and others, includes this anecdote in a chapter on performance/fiction that features Gray and Eric Bogosian (Siegle 1989: 256). Siegle's agenda is to trace a certain apocalyptic or *fin-de-siècle* brand of avant-garde writing; Gray's statement fits neatly into a book titled *Suburban Ambush*. In 1992, Gray, who at times seems to have his entire life filed away on so many narrative mental note cards, included the story almost verbatim in the new incarnation of his monologue *A Personal History of the American Theatre*.

One of the central issues in criticism of Gray's work can be framed around his interest in this anecdote: does his admittedly virtuosic chronicling of a class (or culture, or *episteme*) in decline participate in a radical or reactionary cultural gesture? In the following discussion of Gray's career as a chronicler/performer, I will attempt both to evaluate the social meaning of his participation in the cultural collapse he describes, and to raise some further questions about how empowered speaking subjects (specifically, male heterosexual white speaking subjects) locate themselves on this society's rapidly shifting cultural topography when they avail themselves of avant-garde performance forms.

Spalding Gray's career as a theatrical actor includes performance in high school and college productions; a stint at the Alley Theater in Houston, Texas; and, starting in 1970, work with Richard Schechner's Performance Group, most notably in the role of Hoss in the Group's famous production of Sam Shepard's *The Tooth of Crime* (1973). In 1975 some members of the Performance Group began to produce original work with Elizabeth LeCompte, who had been Schechner's directorial assistant, as director. In 1980, as the Performance Group dissolved, LeCompte, Gray, and several others formed a company called The Wooster Group (Savran 1986: 2).[2]

The Wooster Group produced four pieces based on material from Spalding Gray's life—most famously on his mother's suicide. These works formed the trilogy *Three Places in Rhode Island*, made up of *Sakonnet Point* (1975), *Rumstick Road* (1977), and *Nayatt School* (1978), and an epilogue piece called *Point Judith* (1979). The Group's distinctive, highly experimental methods did not fashion this material into coherent narratives recounting Gray's family history; rather, the Group used his family history as starting points for explorations of memory and culture ranging in style from formalist to absurd. Elizabeth LeCompte says that the "Trilogy isn't his autobiography. He is a device to focus the material" (quoted in Savran 1986: 84). However, it was while working with the Group that Gray began to perform monologues as contained solo pieces.

Theodore Shank offers one account of the desires that moved Gray toward monologic performance:

> Gray says that by nature he is "extremely narcissistic and reflective." He has always been self-conscious and aware of his everyday actions. He wanted to use these qualities toward creating his own work. As long as he played characters, even if developed through observations of people, he could "only guess at knowing this other." He realized he did not want to study others as objects, he wanted to explore himself as other. He no longer wanted to pretend to be a character outside himself. He wanted to perform his own actions and be reflective at the

same time on stage before an audience. He says it became a kind of "public confession of this reflectiveness. It became 'Look at me. I am one who sees himself seeing himself.'" (Shank 1982: 170–71)

Gray has produced more than a dozen monologues in his solo career. He typically performs sitting behind a small table, facing the audience directly. He does not write his texts out as complete scripts, but works with a process of recording narratives, taking notes, and retelling (and re-recording) from those notes. He quite literally, as he says, performs the memory of the performance before. In New York City, his early solo appearances were most often in the Wooster Group's Performing Garage, before in-the-know lower Manhattan audiences.

Gray's topic is invariably himself: his observations, experiences, conversations, relationships. What prevents his monologues from wallowing in diaristic detail is a remarkable charisma and quirky presence. While he keeps verbal analysis or reflection to a minimum, he never holds back on attitude, always expressing feeling of some kind, even if only a dry amusement. By turns neurotic, superior, and naive, Gray still constantly preserves a shadow of authorial self in his performance. That is, there is always the sense of the judging, creative intellect at work behind the monologue. This second presence, however, is never made fully available to the audience. Gray's laconic tone, his wry smile, and his use of pauses to prepare the spectator for particularly unusual revelations or turns of phrase all contribute to the impression that somewhere inside he is conducting a real analysis of the situation, that he and the audience share an awareness of all the encrusted social, political, and metaphysical meanings of the anecdote. None of these meanings are made textual, but everything implies that they could be, were it not more interesting to Gray to move on to the next bit of story.

While some may find it unsatisfying that Gray seems to withhold some aspect of himself in performance, many have praised this aspect of his work as "objectivity." Further, this sense of another layer, of "one who sees himself seeing himself," is a vital part of Gray's remarkable performative charm and charisma. This doubled consciousness is also at the root of the pervasive sense of irony virtually every critic finds in Gray's persona.

Equally important to the power of Gray's presentation is the strong sense of presence, both material and temporal. That is, Gray is emphatically there, in the same space as the spectator, and in the same moment. Shank connects this to the structure of many of the pieces. Speaking of *Points of Interest (America)* (1980), Shank says,

> Finally, he relates what happened to him today, and concludes with "That was today. And here I am." Ending with the present moment is just one of the means Gray uses to bring focus to the present so that the performance is not merely a relating of past events. It is important that the spectator does not have the sense that Gray is "acting," but rather that he is speaking to them about real events. His style of delivery is flat, uncolored, and candid. He really looks at spectators, especially when they react to something he has said. He actually reflects while in front of them rather than speaking memorized lines and pretending to reflect. (Shank 1982: 178)

While I find Gray's delivery to be "colored" in various ways, and while Gray arguably reflects less and pretends more with each repetition of a monologue, I agree with Shank that much of what is intriguing about Gray lies in the sensation of witnessing a present event rather than a simple oral representation of the past. Even though Gray may be repeating an anecdote as he remembers it from the previous performance, the quality of active remembering separates this experience from that of a scripted reenactment. The spectator does not so much consume a representation as witness an event.

EARLY MONOLOGUES: *SEX AND DEATH TO THE AGE 14*

This sense of event is created in part by the explicitly confessional tone of Gray's work. This is especially evident in the monologue *Sex and Death to the Age 14* (1979), which in book form might almost be a transcription of early sessions of psychoanalysis.[3] True to the title, the monologue contains all the experiences Gray can recall about death and sex until he was 14. Gray rambles through the anecdotes in an amused manner, and rather than serving as the basis for an analysis of the formation of his psychology, or as an investigation of the material forces shaping his life, the funny, odd, and occasionally startling revelations are simply the foundation for the event of their telling. This continues in the following monologue, *Booze, Cars, and College Girls* (1979), though there the sense of transgression occurs not so much in his willingness to tell the audience about himself, but in his gleeful recounting of his sexual adventures, including the peculiarities of anatomy and desire of the women involved, whom he discusses by name.

To the degree that he actually manages to explore the role of childhood experience in shaping sexuality, Gray does put the form of the confessional monologue to a use it too often ignores. "Traditionally, the personal, psychological significance of the solo form remains unacknowledged in the performance, shielded, so to speak, by the display of virtuosity" (Carroll 1979: 51). What makes this aspect of Gray's work difficult to pin down is that the apparent "personal, psychological significance" of his verbal actions seems at the same time to be a product of a virtuosic imitation of the personal.

Further, Gray's confessional attitude is more a style of speaking than an offering of himself. There would seem to be no more vulnerable state than confession; yet, at least in certain Christian discourses, confession restores a certain spiritual invulnerability. In this model, Gray's noncommittal narration of his youthful adventures in *Booze, Cars and College Girls* (or his venial neocolonial sins in the Thailand of *Swimming to Cambodia*) restore the speaker to a position of power. In overcoming the "obstacles" to speaking—constituted formally, for the most part, as embarrassment, amusement, or circuitous stylistics—a stage master such as Gray can accumulate the sacrificial aura that accrues to confession and penance and return to a position of centrality.

Sex and Death to the Age 14 and *Booze, Cars and College Girls* are among six works in the anthology *Sex and Death to the Age 14* (1986), which also includes *Terrors of Pleasure: The House* (1986), a highly praised monologue that marked a professional advance for Gray when it opened at Lincoln Center's Mitzi Newhouse Theater. Critics found it charming and universal: Nelsen's comment that "Gray reveals in a most humorous manner the things about ourselves that we are ashamed of" (1986) is a typical reaction. In fact, Gray may reveal certain silly attitudes some people hold about property (the monologue centers in part on Gray's misadventures shopping for a house in the Catskills), but he does not exactly reveal anything *about* them. He clearly finds them amusing, but is content to leave it at that.

In 1987, the performance was adapted for an HBO cable television special with more than the usual anxiety endemic to such adaptations of live performances. HBO apparently doubted the viability of a talking solo performer who simply sat at a table, unmoving (a strong contrast to the HBO staple of stand-up comedians), so the producers opted to alternate performance footage with reenactments of the anecdotes that make up the monologue. The special illustrates the monologue with clips of Spalding with realtors, Spalding alone in his frightening house, Spalding on a trip to Hollywood.

The effect is uninteresting, and not because of poor execution. The television adaptation makes clear that part of the intriguing texture of Gray's performances is the elusive status of the referent or of truth. In performance the spectator is free to imagine a referent (producing a signified), but is simultaneously fully aware of a very present signifier: Gray as author. In the HBO version of *Terrors*, this imagined referent is replaced with a secondary "dramatic" signifier—the reenactment—that is blatantly neither truth nor referent. Rather than the frission resulting from watching Gray craft an ironic text that is presumed to have a "true" referent, the viewer of the HBO adaptation sees Gray ironizing about a visual text that is patently unreal.

SWIMMING TO CAMBODIA

A much more successful adaptation of a monologue resulted from Gray's best known solo piece, the two-part *Swimming to Cambodia*, which was developed at the Performing Garage (1985) and later filmed on location there by Jonathan Demme. *Swimming to Cambodia* is ostensibly about Gray's experiences playing a supporting role in Roland Jaffe's film *The Killing Fields*, which was shot in Thailand. In performing his wide-ranging narrative, Gray sits at his usual table, his only properties a glass of water, two maps of southeast Asia, and a pointer. While necessarily engaging in political questions raised by the film (and the process of its making), the monologue spends much time on Gray's career and personal relationships, particularly the details of his life with "Renée" (Shafransky, Gray's lover, later his wife, still later his ex-wife).

Despite the personalism of the piece, which is consistent with his other work, Gray does focus on the politics of *The Killing Fields*, global U.S. intervention, and his own ambivalent position. He continually points to uncomfortable cross-cultural (that is, neocolonial) moments of awkwardness, such as his own "ambivalence" about the "tradition" of hiring Thai prostitutes (1985b: 44). His own consumerist interest in the food, the beer, the drugs, the women, and the scenery is framed for the listening audience as amusing, to be laughed at, even while his sometimes graphic detail allows the vicarious secondhand consumption of his post-production search for his "perfect moment."

This piece, both as two live monologues and as converted for Demme's film, drew widespread praise from liberal critics for its personalization of difficult questions about politics and history. Just as they had praised Gray for capturing an apparently universal anxiety about home-buying in *Terrors of Pleasure*, critics now lauded his ability to render grand moral questions in a humorous work that nonetheless provoked viewers to consider themselves. Film critics were similarly responsive to the success Demme and Gray had in denaturalizing the cinematic truth status of *The Killing Fields*. As a critic for *Art in America* put it, "although Gray's monologue may have stripped these images of their original significance, and underlined their character as dramatizations, they have now also become markers of a more clearly understood historical moment" (Dika 1988: 39).

The film of the performance, while of course not a perfect documentation (such a record is impossible), allowed new scholarly "close readings" of specific aspects of Gray's work. In a study based on the videotape of the film, Jessica Prinz finds it surprising that Gray's gestures in *Swimming to Cambodia* "mirror and reinforce the spoken text," establishing a communicative redundancy that "ensures coherence and disambiguation." In contrast to an aggressive pre-postmodern avant-garde, Prinz asserts, Gray's performance mode is designed to "establish communication with his own audience as effectively as possible" (Prinz 1992: 158).

Prinz's article is one of the few works on gesture in avant-garde performance outside dance scholarship, and while some aspects of her analysis are quite valuable—for example, she convincingly details the way symmetrical gestures function in Gray's performances to emphasize his visual and narrative centrality—her reading of Gray's gestural "redundancy" as generously communicative is problematic. She and most other critical supporters of Gray's work recognize the radical uncertainty of the self in his monologues, but this misreading of Gray's gestures as helping us as spectators to connect with the meaning of "our" tragedy and "survival" as represented by Gray (Prinz 1992: 166) is symptomatic, indicative of the chronic elision of difference enacted by Gray and recycled by critics. That is, for Prinz Gray's gestures generously reinforce the communication that allows him to embody "our" position vis-à-vis history—in particular, the history of U.S. military activity in Southeast Asia and its genocidal repercussions.

The response to the multiple incarnations of *Swimming to Cambodia* was not completely positive, however. Some critics, who had perhaps found Gray's earlier works innocuous, were now disturbed at what seemed the reduction of genocide to personal anecdote. By far the most sophisticated critique was offered by Peggy Phelan, who found in the monologue and film a "failed ontology" and in Gray a "troubling inability" to see outside of his own circumstance. Phelan admits that Gray's work seems to participate in the activation of autobiography described in my epigraph for this chapter, but argues that

> he has not faced the truly radical innovative edge in his project. To face this edge in *Swimming* would require that Gray abandon his boyish unconsciousness and explore his own misogyny, racism, colonialism, and economic imperialism, which run like sludge throughout his text. Such an exploration would not abandon irony, but it would add to it a more challenging intelligence. I don't care one bit that Gray has all of these embarrassing attitudes toward other people and other cultures, most of us do; but what I find disappointing is his assumption that this can be glossed over without comment in favor of some boyish charm or political naivete. (Phelan 1988: 29)

The apparent political reflexivity in *Swimming* perhaps took some critics by surprise, since the content of the work is relatively uncommon, especially in feature films. Phelan's analysis looks beyond the seeming honesty of the work, however, and her reading suggests to me a central difficulty with Gray's entire performance project. Gray's mesmeric use of stage space, lighting, personal mythology, digressive structure, and gestures of conversational intimacy does not embody a natural, universal subject-in-history, as some critics seem to think; rather, it imposes a particular historical position as universal and natural. What Prinz reads literally as a helping hand that allows the spectator to confront history through a performance constructed as transparent and contiguous to the spectator should be seen as an ensemble of *de*-historicizing gestures constructing a shared point of view, an opportunity for "us" to confront and resolve our nagging historical guilt with a collective pat on the back.

What Phelan says of *Swimming to Cambodia* might easily be applied to Gray's other monologues, all of which privilege charm and naivete (or neurosis and bemusement, or wonder and appreciation) over analysis. The actual superficiality of Gray's work is merely exacerbated by the weight of the subject matter in *Swimming to Cambodia*; the same glancing irony is at work in the comic catalogue of *Sex and Death* or the seeming satire of bourgeois values in *Terrors of Pleasure*.

INTERVIEWING THE AUDIENCE

Some of Gray's works are not purely monological in structure, though they center on his personality and must ultimately be considered part of his solo performance career. Gray first developed *Interviewing the Audience* with the Wooster Group's Ron Vawter in 1980, but soon began performing the work himself. Typically, Gray mingles with the crowd as they arrive in the theater's lobby, asking quick questions and jotting names and responses onto note cards. When I saw *Interviewing* at Washington University in St. Louis (a stop on Gray's 1992 nationwide tour), Gray asked perhaps ten or fifteen people if they would like to be interviewed, and was refused by no more than one or two. He spoke with most candidates for less than a minute, then moved on. In this performance he interviewed three audience members, announced a short intermission, and interviewed two more. Gray called out the name of his next interviewee when he finished with the previous one, so each participant was seen emerging from the audience, visually, at least, contextualized as part of a specific community.

Gray's interviewing style, at least in the contemporary incarnation of this piece, is pleasant but probing. He begins (at least he did in the performance I attended) every interview by asking how the subject traveled to the theater that evening. A running joke about Japanese cars develops as person after person answers that they drove to the theater in a Toyota. Gray quickly moves on to more personal questioning: "Are you in therapy? How was your second marriage different from the first? Did you take on lovers? Do you smoke marijuana?"

The interviewees, to varying degrees, seem nervous and awkward, but Gray manages to project a similar feeling of discomfort, as if he is genuinely worried about what will come out. The interviewees seem trapped between anxiety about what they will reveal and a desire to be sufficiently entertaining. The first, a white woman in her sixties clearly comfortable in the role of a "character," seems for a while to be on the verge of taking over the performance. Quite funny and completely unabashed, she provides laugh after laugh for the audience as she tops Gray's bluntness with her answers. Eventually, however, Gray seems to outlast her, and she appears to be having second thoughts about having been so outspoken. "How are you perceiving me?" asks Gray. She replies "I wish I knew more about you and you knew less about me!" The audience laughs at this, but Gray is prepared: "My life is an open book," he protests.

At his prompting, the woman offers some anecdotes about serving subpoenas in her job as process server. Gray draws her out—the audience is rapt—but then rather suddenly changes tack: "Do you drink a lot at night?" he asks.

Near the end of this interview Gray establishes a pattern he follows with almost every interviewee that evening—the topic turns out to be him, as he begins to discuss his therapist and the audience member actually asks him a few questions. Still, the audience clearly approves of the first subject and gives her a strong burst of applause as an usher escorts her from the stage.

The rest of the evening follows the same general pattern, though each interviewee presents Gray with slightly different challenges. The next guest, a white man from London teaching directing at the university, is as comfortable on stage as Gray is, and is not startled into revealing much. Though he is charming and amusing, Gray keeps his interview shorter than the first. The next guest is a young white woman attending the university. Gray acts quite frightened of her frenetic energy, and seems a bit "out of it" when the woman makes a string of references to television shows Gray has never heard of. Gray controls the stage, however, and is able to maintain his position by slowing down his own tempo and letting her run on. Gradually, the audience seems to laugh less at Gray's situation and more at his attitude toward her.

Still, the young woman has her moments. "What drives you nuts?" Gray wants to know. "I hate being patronized," she replies, chuckling aside to the audience.

The first interviewee after intermission turns out to be a psychotherapist, a white man who describes himself as "a bit of a control freak." This man's reserve seems impenetrable, and Gray gets little in the way of titillation from his responses. The interview is destined to be short, but Gray takes full advantage of the opportunity to talk about therapy, asking detailed questions about the man's practice and what he could do for Gray. Gray also asks several questions about the man's aversion to children, stating that his personal dilemma at present is whether to have a child. More than any other interview, this one is about Gray. If anyone in the audience has begun to feel that the star of the evening is not performing enough, this round of discussion perhaps satisfies them, as it becomes clear that the monologuist's not-monologue is in many ways not so different from what they've seen of Gray on screen.

The next name Gray calls out is unanswered. "You left . . . you got cold feet . . . I don't blame you," Gray says, and then jokes that the man must not have a Toyota. His last subject is a white woman who announces her occupation as "flight attendant." Gray nonetheless calls her a "stewardess" and asks her age. When she answers that she is 37, he continues a theme from the previous interview and asks "So you've got to find someone quick to have babies with?" This comment, and his reference to her as a "stewardess," elicit a murmur from some spectators, but Gray's tone makes it hard to say whether his sexist remark is really participating in motherhood-as-moral-imperative, or is an ironic framing of that discourse.

After some further discussion of biological clocks and the desire for children, he asks her to describe what she will do after the show, prompting her for details: "will you dream? What will you dream?" And then, almost without warning, she begins apologetically to describe her experiences with chemotherapy; "I don't want to get maudlin," she says. Gray seems only a little surprised; the audience is stunned. Certainly the tone is suddenly very different, but the show goes on—after all, we all know that this is what we came for. This is either a very beautiful or a very disgusting moment, and my sense of "us" as an audience (or perhaps only of myself as a spectator) is that we can't decide which.

Interviewing the Audience provides a riveting evening of entertainment, if it can be called that. It is also a highly unorthodox event, in some ways more like a religious or educational structure than a theatrical one. The oddness is heightened by the sense of a production working against its theatrical environment: the houselights are up throughout, and Gray and guests are seated down center, against the background of an empty, unmasked stage. While Gray's charisma and the structure of the piece certainly suggest to the audience that it see the interviewees through Gray's perceptual lens, to react as he reacts, at the same time the actuality of the event is blatant, present, apparently unreconstructed.

In some ways, the piece is a sort of performance art *lehrstuck* (teaching play), in that the performers and audience are one, coexisting in a state of self-examination. Brecht's teaching plays were designed to be performed without any external audience, as exercises in political experience. Brecht might perhaps have dismissed Gray's piece as lacking in radical politics, but *Interviewing the Audience* nevertheless involves all present in a highly self-conscious and reflexive event structured as a thoroughly nondramatic performance. Further, since so much of Gray's fame is based on his reputation as a storyteller and as a dramatic (if avant-garde) actor, the nonnarrative structure of the work takes on an almost *antinarrative* cast. In form and content, *Interviewing the Audience* is bounded by experimental theater, town meeting traditions, and talk show conventions.

The piece affords one central pleasure I associate with early broadcasts of the television show *Late Night with David Letterman*. Letterman's guests are predominantly celebrities, but he occasionally interviews eccentric unknowns. The studio and television audiences watch these interviews in part to see Letterman make jokes at his guest's expense. (This was perhaps truer several years ago). Frequently, however, a guest will say or do something unexpected that embarrasses the host or throws him off balance. These moments are a central appeal of Letterman's interviews. The audience watches to see both his predictable exercise of sardonic wit upon a hapless celebrity and the oddities of the lesser-known. The pleasure is augmented when this established structure is momentarily unsettled by an accident or a guest's own quick-wittedness. Letterman thus offers a double identification, granting the viewer both a vicarious exercise of authority (albeit hiply unconventional) and, in the next moment, a surrogate rebellion. The implied viewer oscillates between identification with and subversion of authority.

This same structure of pleasure is made available to the spectator of *Interviewing the Audience*. Gray, after all, is the phenomenon; we've come to see him do his thing. The revelations he produces from his subjects are what we pay the ticket price for, and if embarrassment or anxiety are part of those revelations then they are ours to consume. On the other hand, if, say, one in every 50 spectators has been invited by Gray to join the pool of potential interviewees, then that anxiety must take on a certain communal quality. Next to Gray, the most empowered position in the theater is perhaps the friend or acquaintance of an interviewee. These spectators share the power of not being onstage while experiencing a close connection to the sacrificial spectator being interviewed. This position offers the strongest experience of the pattern of anxiety and relief that shapes the performance. To take pleasure in the performance, in this view, is to thrill in this back-and-forth play of power, to enjoy (at least vicariously) being helpless, then to enjoy a sudden rush of power, and then again to find oneself in the control of a master of presence.

When considered in this manner, *Interviewing the Audience* seems little different from many other cultural products; the available subject positions for many viewers of theatrical or cinematic narrative are said by some to involve such a play of identification and objectification. I would join in rejecting knee-jerk denunciations of pleasures that involve a play of power, especially given the recent emphasis on the spectator's power in the actual practice of spectating dramatic representation. It is precisely these antidramatic qualities, however, that make watching *Interviewing the Audience* so disconcerting. The guest/contestant/victim is summoned from within the audience, broken off from it; and the sudden movement of one body from the mass under the houselights to the more exposed space of the stage highlights the fact that there *is* a referent in what looks like representation. *Interviewing the Audience* stages an *agon* between theatrical and referential presence. It is more difficult to revel in oscillating identifications when the reality of one character and, by contrast, the celebrity and unreality of the other are so foregrounded. And in the meeting of signifier and referent, the signifier wins.

I had a strong personal reaction to *Interviewing*; I worried about the potential embarrassment or even heartbreak of his guests, and could not shake the feeling that they were being "used." *Theater Week* quotes Gray suggesting that a good interview can create "instant community in the theatre space" (Holbrook 1992: 33), but as a spectator I find myself concerned with the communities outside the theater. Holbrook notes that "one glitch in the interview process can be a guest's hesitancy to speak honestly. In small towns, interviewees often dodge personal questions, fearing that any public admissions will fan gossip" (1992: 33). How often do participants regret what they say? Isn't this thoroughly immoral? These questions mar my pleasure in Gray's skill and the interviewees' revelations. Still, everyone involved seems to enjoy it, and I can't find any comfortable way to simply denounce the performance.

In this respect, *Interviewing the Audience* seems oddly reminiscent of dwarf tossing, the controversial tavern entertainment/sport that received much attention in the late 1980s. In dwarf tossing, dwarves were paid to be thrown across the barroom by patrons competing for a prize. Syndicated columnist Mike Royko featured the sport and its controversy in at least five columns, and attacked commentators who opposed the practice and legislators who considered outlawing it. Royko responded to every criticism by noting that all the parties involved were consenting, that the dwarves were well-rewarded, and that many of the sport's most vocal supporters were participating dwarves. The columnist was dismissive of those who critiqued the values inherent in the practice and decried the censorship of what he considered a legitimate recreational activity.

While I am hardly interested in censoring *Interviewing the Audience* (or dwarf-tossing, for that matter), the feelings evoked in me by Royko's descriptions are the closest parallel I have found to my reaction to Gray's performance. Aside from moral discomfort,[4] however, the parallel is closest in the way that both activities so clearly reveal the structures of power that shape one's reactions. When it comes to performing an interview, the star monologist clearly outweighs his subjects theatrically, discursively, and experientially—which is part of the reason for the thrill discussed above that occurs when the roles are briefly reversed. But the "consent" of the participants (in Royko's framing of things) is a red herring; beyond any legal or even ethical question, the power differential between thrower and thrown becomes representation, is transformed into a metaphoric affirmation of the state of things. *Interviewing the Audience* is really a sort of paratheatrical game of king-of-the-mountain in which the outcome is never really in doubt. While it is a dialogue, perhaps, on the level of spoken language, *Interviewing the Audience*[5] is ultimately a monologue of theatrical power, a ritual thrashing of the audience's sacrificial representative, as if the work were in fact designed for nothing more than keeping the audience in its place.

A PERSONAL HISTORY OF THE AMERICAN THEATER

If the Friday evening performance of *Interviewing the Audience* created in me a deep distrust of Gray, his Saturday performance of *A Personal History of the American Theater* in the same house seemed in some ways a reversal of what I had so disliked the evening before.

Gray's career as a dramatic actor is the basis for the text of this second piece. In its original incarnation (portions of which were broadcast on the PBS show *Alive from Off Center* and excerpted in *TDR*), Gray recalls anecdotes of his theatrical experiences in random order, as the names of plays in which he has acted turn up in a shuffled deck of index cards. His recollections of supposedly Stanislavskian productions of *The Three Sisters*, Grotowski-inspired movement pieces, and wildly revisionist Shakespeare run the gamut of modern production styles. The anecdotes are funny on many levels, and seem constructed to appeal both to an "in-joke" crowd with some knowledge of contemporary theater personalities such as Richard Schechner, and to a more "mainstream" audience looking to laugh at the pretensions and absurdities of artists and performers more abstractly considered.

The random structuring of *A Personal History of the American Theater* in its first version produced a work that merged the "traditions" of performance art and theatrical performance. While Gray's use of his own life as material follows in the path of autobiographical explorations praised by critics like Phelan and C. Carr (1990), the thoroughly rehearsed (if not scripted) nature of the monologues participates more fully in a theatrical aesthetic. The shuffled index cards Gray used to structure the early performances of *A Personal History of the American Theater* introduce to the theatrical performance an indeterminacy that goes beyond improvisation to a tradition of "high" art performance aligned with the works of John Cage, Allen Kaprow, and others. The (theatrical) representation is troubled by the introduction of process, a second "actual" that transforms repeatable theatricality into the "one-time" event of performance art.

By 1992, however, Gray had dispensed with the shuffled note cards and was introducing *A Personal History of the American Theater* as a "talk" rather than a monologue. Disappointingly, however, he gave little explanation for the shift in terminology, except to suggest that he was somehow "performing" less, and genuinely "talking" to us more. While his performance was certainly coded as informal, the material presented was in fact persistently theatrical and clearly ordered.

In its new form, Gray presented the material from the old *Personal History* in chronological order, offering a capsule biography approximately forty minutes in length. He stood at a microphone, rather than sitting behind a table, and talked to the audience. His manner, however, was quite similar to that displayed in his earlier monologues. He told many of the same stories about his experiences as an actor. He repeated the anecdote cited earlier about the revelation in Santa Cruz of his destiny as a "chronicler" of "the end of the white middle-class world as we knew it," as well as another about the difficulty of Schechner's direction to him at the end of The Performance Group's *Tooth of Crime* that he should drop his character and simply look at the audience. The story as a whole took on much greater coherence, a much stronger narrative structure, until it began to seem rather inevitable that Gray should be standing on stage at this precise moment telling us the story of his life. Paradoxically, the chronological structure functioned to mystify history rather than to clarify it. Instead of generating a sense of the arbitrariness of Gray's position of (representational) power as the earlier structure (using the random note cards) had, the ordered events worked to naturalize his ascendancy. While the early version exhibited Gray's virtuoso ability to jump from narrative to narrative, the new structure contained at least the potential for the disruption of that power. The newer structure, as seamless and fluid as his other monologues, or traditional narrative fiction, combined that performative power with a form designed to maximize and reinforce it.

While I found the restructuring of the work's anecdotal components made for a much more conventional and conservative experience (one that was even more strongly monologic), the second half of the new *Personal History* did appear to invert the structure of the previous night's performance of *Interviewing the Audience*. At the conclusion of the narrative, having brought the audience up to date, Gray asked the audience to ask him questions. The result was remarkable. For a period at least equivalent to the narrative, audience members quizzed Gray on diverse topics, from his working process to his fame to issues raised in the performance the night before. Not surprisingly, perhaps, none of the questioners left their seats to use the microphones provided at the back of the house. Instead, 600 people sat in the lighted auditorium and fired questions at the single figure onstage. Gray was remarkably affable, showing only very slight flashes of irritation. While he answered some questions with sentences familiar from monologues past, he answered others with seemingly spontaneous frankness. For example, he became involved in a protracted discussion with a young man across the auditorium. Following up on a theme from the previous night, the man asked when Gray last took LSD. "November," Gray said, fast enough to draw a laugh. The spectator went on to recommend "having sex while tripping." Gray admitted to having never had this experience, but said he is very interested and asked several questions. Other questions were less personal, but the overwhelming impression was of the generosity of Gray's responses.

For a time during the performance, this sense of generosity alleviated my dislike of the display of power the weekend had so far seemed to be. Much more than in *Interviewing the Audience*, these spectators projected a feeling of agency in their involvement with the piece, if only for the relative power resulting from the location within, rather than singled out from, the anonymous mass of audience. While the sense of generosity Gray projected still seemed based in the almost sacrificial offering up of a charismatic personality, this portion of *Personal History* did seem to succeed in giving over to members of the audience the power to structure the piece, at least on a moment-to-moment level.

The mood of community, the feeling of spectatorial agency, and the sense of Gray's generosity all faded quickly, however, outside the theater. First, as an interactive performance nonetheless founded on a monologue, the new incarnation of *Personal History* seems to extend the peculiar and contradictory power of monologue identified by Deborah Geis.

> When a monologue seems to address the audience directly, as opposed to a dialogue in which one character engages with another character (or a monologue in which one character addresses the other), the paradoxical position of the audience in respect to the speaker intensifies. It is possible to argue that the speaker of such a monologue simultaneously includes the spectators in a more direct way than otherwise, and reasserts their very powerlessness. The audience seems to be addressed, yet its members are not in a position to respond, for to do so would involve, in [Erving] Goffman's terms, breaking the "dramatic frame." This impotence serves as a reminder that as spectators, they are helpless, frozen, powerless (and have chosen to accept that role); yet for the duration of the monologue addressed to them, they are given a privileged or pseudo-privileged status as the character's confidants. (Geis 1993: 17)

In this piece, Gray carries things a step further. Having begun by addressing a monologue to the audience, granting them pseudo-privileged status as confidants, he then invites them to break the already weakened "dramatic frame" and respond to him. Even this, however, is perhaps a pseudo-privilege, for the dramatic frame has been superseded by the epic frame of Gray's life. The spectators are granted a certain power within the structure of the piece, but they are in fact contained even more strongly by the art/life structure of Gray's work than by any dramatic presentation.[6]

This expanding frame leads to a variety of questions about the structure of power in the performance, particularly the simple materialist question of who benefits. Certainly the open question period was an unusual theatrical event, a solo of solos, with "audience participation" as a sort of bonus, but the feeling that this evening's performance somehow mirrored that of the night before brought back disturbing questions, and prompted me to think those unpleasant thoughts away from which Gray's pleasant persona had wooed me. In particular, the idea that the spectators were being "used" occurred again and again. What "use" was it I was witnessing? I found myself contrasting my reaction to Michael Quinn's relatively sympathetic comments, in an article on "Celebrity and the Semiotics of Acting," about "real actors" and the consequences of celebrity.

> The illusion of celebrity presence is most illusory of all to the star, trapped in a stable image of selfhood that bears limited correspondence to the desires and disappointments of the changing real. The standard talk-show format, which exists to allow celebrity and role to interact or merge in the mind of the prospective viewer of a polyphonic drama, exists for the celebrity as an extreme (late) form of the mirror stage: the star views and comments upon an image of the self not only objectified and retouched but commodified, all in the names of art and authenticity. (Quinn 1990: 160)

While Gray may to some degree be "trapped" in an image, he is not trapped, as are the celebrity actors Quinn describes, between dramatic character and the "real." Rather, it is Gray's explicit project to create an image of the self that seems to correspond to the real. For this reason, the activity of a questioning audience set up by the second part of *Personal History* cannot disrupt the illusion of celebrity presence. It can only feed it. Dramatic, fictional theater sometimes seems to take on nonfictional import in the context of the world outside (as is the case with much "allegorical" political theater). By contrast, the "real" questions of Gray's audience become fictional, or at least representational, as they move out of the theater. Gray's disruption of theatrical convention may free the audience from the role assigned by that convention, and "we" may (or may not) find the experience somehow pleasurable, but we spectators are quickly trapped in an orbital relation to the star.

MONSTER IN A BOX: THE BOOK, THE PERFORMANCE, THE BOOK, THE MOVIE

This gravitational effect is perhaps inadvertently acknowledged by the description on the back cover of the published version of Gray's thirteenth monologue, *Monster in a Box*. The copy writer frames Gray's recuperative power in a somewhat different metaphor; the new work "is further proof that Gray has not only captured the dangerous spirit of our age but swallowed it whole."

If Gray has in this effort consumed the spirit of "our age," he has done so as part of an elegantly productive gesture, for *Monster* is but one part of an ambitious multimedia event, a permeation of a certain stratum of U.S. culture with Gray's presence. The title of the new work refers to Gray's enormous novel, part of which was then published by Knopf under the title *Impossible Vacation* (1992d). The performance work—the text of which has also been published (1992c)—is about Gray's adventures as a novelist. In a manner even more digressive than the chronicling of events clustered around Gray's adventures as a supporting actor in *Swimming to Cambodia*, *Monster* ranges far afield from the book itself, returning to the novel's presence in Gray's life and the memories of his younger life contained in it. Also like *Swimming*, *Monster* was made into a film, directed by Nick Broomfield, with music again from Laurie Anderson. This is perhaps the archetypal example of performance art's move into more mainstream markets: one performance, two books, and a film.

The performance itself is standard Gray fare, dazzlingly simple, wry, all but unbelievable in spots. Gray sketches out the plot of the novel in the first few minutes, then says "that's all you need to know about the book tonight." The real monologue, he says, is "about all the interruptions that happened to me while I was trying to write the book" (1992c: 5). The stories that follow are all loosely connected to this theme. Most of them also involve situations peculiar to the new, famous, post-*Swimming* Gray. He describes a visit to Russia (where *Swimming* is part of a festival of American films), a trip with Renée to Nicaragua (they're disguised as radicals on a "fact-finding" tour, but they're really researching a film for Columbia Pictures), and a torturous period in Los Angeles (where he has lunch with movie executives desperate for "an idea").

For me, seeing *Monster* on tour in Milwaukee after seeing *Interviewing* and *Personal History* in St. Louis was surprisingly comfortable. Perhaps the event was still mostly about a superior wit making fun of the hapless mortals he encounters, but it was still rather funny, and these "victims" are practically fictional in comparison with the brave volunteers and questioners of the two more interactive pieces.

There was another factor working to make this a comfortable evening in the theater. Even in the heart of the Midwest, there was a feeling of participating in an established cultural treasure. Gray has achieved the status of an institution, and the audience was there to partake, to acquire some cultural capital. (Gray looks more like Hal Holbrook with each passing show.) Not that there's something "wrong" with the monologue; it is as good or better than the rest, strongly structured and benefiting from Shafransky's involvement (she was listed as director in the program). But there was a sense that the circumstances of production have changed. In *Monster* Gray is no longer recounting the life of an actor struggling through various avant-gardes (as in *Personal History*) or telling tales of an artist in midlife crisis grappling with cultural clashes surrounding a small role that might lead to a big break (as in *Swimming to Cambodia*). This is the same Gray who appears on the cover of the *New York Times Magazine*. At this event, Gray was a famous person, telling stories about being a famous person, and winning approval for being a famous person with a skeptical attitude toward that very fame. The monologue felt more like a media event than a theatrical performance. As a *New York Newsday* critic put it, *Monster in a Box* is "the world's most entertaining promotion for a novel" (Winer 1990: 131).

There was the particular quality of live performance, the flavor of immediacy to the work. But Gray himself didn't quite seem live (especially in contrast to his interactive pieces). The more famous he becomes, the less real he can seem, and the more his anecdotes resemble those of a good talk-show appearance. Further, because Gray plays himself, he cannot offer the audience the merging of celebrity and role that Quinn suggests a talk-show appearance usually does. Instead, the liveness that remains seems only just enough to verify that the person in the film, or the author of the book, actually exists. Philip Auslander (1992) has suggested that the function of the live event, such as a rock concert, is increasingly to verify or validate the seeming liveness of the televisual record of such events. Live events reassure the consumer of the quality of the recording. In watching Gray perform, does the audience simply verify that a "real" Gray exists to authorize their enjoyment of his mass distribution? Or, to look back to my comparison with poetry readings from the second chapter, does the performance constitute a "validation" of the subjectivity behind the poem/monologue?

It is a familiar story, that the success of an artist inevitably means that a special (and perhaps exclusionary) something is lost. But perhaps it is not a function of success at all, but simply of repetition. As Gray continues to produce his monologic performances, the repetition of the formula risks approaching inadvertent parody, and the form itself produces its own conventionality. Though *Monster* was widely praised by mainstream critics, some seemed to tire of the routine, including an otherwise admiring David Sterrit of the *Christian Science Monitor*:

> He has earned his success, and it's good to see a genuine maverick getting such wide recognition. But it would be even better, I can't help feeling, if he'd start questioning this brand of theater as radically and insistently as he once questioned mainstream and avant-garde styles of the past. (Sterrit 1990)

GRAY'S ANATOMY: A HISTORY OF PERSONAL NEOCOLONIALISM

In the interest of completeness I will discuss one more work in the monologue series, *Gray's Anatomy* (1993). While there are specific elements of interest in the work, it is very clearly a continuation of the standard Gray monologue. My chief feeling in watching it was that Gray was going out of his way to confirm my opinion of his other pieces, especially *Swimming to Cambodia*.

One of the unique qualities of the piece is the strong sympathy it elicits for Gray, and the actual suspense generated by the digressive narrative about an eye condition that almost, apparently, cost him his sight. My personal experience with multiple eye surgeries as a child contributed to my visceral identification with Gray, though I saw other spectators squirm when he described examinations and procedures. The suspense is a particularly interesting quality, for it illustrates the immediacy of Gray's work; the story is told in a mix of past and present tenses, but throughout there is the sense that the illness being described (a retinal condition with the conveniently comic name "macula pucker") might be right there on stage before us.

The basic elements of *Gray's Anatomy* are, first, the diagnosis of his condition and his visits to orthodox ophthalmologists, and then a series of alternative cures he pursues in exotic locales.

The early part of the monologue is the most interesting, for Gray's ambivalence about doctors is wrapped up in his mother's Christian Science beliefs that prayer, rather than medicine, is the answer to illness. When diagnosed and advised by his doctor to have surgery, Gray considers instead a Christian Science "practitioner" to pray him back to health. This occasions one of the childhood anecdotes that are the strength of the early performances. In recounting the teasing he received from other children about his faith—"Say if lightning hit this branch here and it fell down and hit your head and knocked your brains out and your brains were spilling out all over the ground. Would you go to a doctor then?" (1994: 15)—Gray creates a sense of internal difference or instability in his white middle-class New England upbringing. His own identity is focused, perhaps even "historicized" somewhat, while the intolerance of the neighborhood children is played for laughs.

Back in the "present" narrative, Gray rejects his practitioner's offer of prayer if Gray is "faithful" and sees no doctors. Depressed, he wanders Manhattan, finding himself in the Bowery, "which is now the perfect place for me to be. I feel right at home here, the way I'm dressed and the way I'm looking and feeling" (1994: 20). In a curious episode, Gray tells of being mistaken for a bum by a carload of Hasidic Jews who drive him to Williamsburg so he can clean their synagogue. "It turns out that every Sunday they go and pick up Bowery bums and bring them over to clean the place" (1994: 22). Gray plays along, earning $10 and a sense of energy from his new identity: "I think, there is something I can do if I lose my sight in my right eye. I can do something other than tell stories!" (1994: 22).

Gray's next attempt at healing involves a sweat lodge ritual in Minnesota, presided over by a tall blond woman who calls herself Azaria Thornbird. It was her gaze that seemed to Gray to mark the beginning of his eye trouble (1994: 3-4), and her spirituality he hopes will help him. Walking naked through the snow toward the sweat lodge with seventeen others, Gray is both disappointed by the inauthenticity of the participants and worried about the inappropriateness of his own involvement:

I'm just standing there, freezing, looking around, and I realize that there are really no American Indians there. Basically, these people are

Scandinavian. They all have blond hair and blue eyes.... Azaria tells us to cry out to the sky, as we enter, "All my ancestors!" ... My turn comes, and I yell, "All my ancestors!" and then I think, Wait a minute. ... All my ancestors—who were they? Pilgrims. What did they do shortly after they came to America? Kill the Indians. Where was I going? Into an Indian sweat lodge. GOOOOOOOD LUCK!!!!!!!!! (1994: 26–27)

Gray next works with an apparently white (his race is not specified) healer who has him rub his hands together and "palm" his eyes repeatedly. Then Gray turns briefly to someone billed as an "authentic Brazilian healer" before being referred to a "nutritional ophthalmologist" named Dr. Axe.

Dr. Axe is quite a character, and he and the rest of his presumptively white family (his assistant-brother and receptionist-mother) make up the long story at the center of *Gray's Anatomy*. After Gray's lifestyle is minutely interrogated, his blood and urine excessively examined, and his diet confined to raw vegetables, he returns to his mainstream eye doctor for an examination. In the waiting room, terrified of the surgery, he reminisces about receiving a "magical" drawing of a "little man" from a healer in Bali (1994: 56). In this state of mind, he leaps at the suggestion of another patient in the waiting room that a certain "Filipino psychic surgeon" might be of help. Without seeing his doctor, Gray leaves for the Philippines to "meet this healer named Pini Lopa, also known as the 'Elvis Presley of psychic surgeons'" (1994: 60).

As Gray recounts it, on his trip the East is like a nightmare. No one speaks English, and the healer's routine involves buckets of blood and theatrical violence as he plunges his hands magically into the bodies of his patients—Gray and forty Japanese. "Actually, twenty come for operations, and the other twenty have come to photograph" (1994: 61).

The more Gray describes his experience, the more it seems that the problem with his vision is racism rather than physical injury. Undecided about subjecting himself to the procedure, he watches a round of surgery. All the patients are lined up, nearly naked, as the surgeon magically penetrates the first woman. "Blood shoots up into the air, six feet into the air, hitting the other naked Japanese. They're all shouting, 'Woo! Oooh! Woooow!' like little children running under a bloody sprinkler in summertime" (1994: 63). Horrified by the spectacle, Gray gets drunk back at his hotel. He returns, though, after a long bout of anxiety about getting AIDS from contact with Japanese blood, determined to go through with it. "The only way I was going to get on that table was if I got right in with the Japanese—just got right in the middle of that kamikaze energy.... I have never seen people move with such determination and lack of doubt" (1994: 68).

Despite his own doubts, Gray does submit to the procedure: "I really feel like my eye is a vagina and his two fingers are erect bloody penises coming at me" (1994: 69). Afterwards, the anxious patient can find neither damage nor improvement. But the surgeon recommends fourteen further operations, at $50 each. Gray goes home and has the standard operation.

While not all of his encounters are with people of color (and the sweat lodge participants are suspect because they are not), Gray's journey toward clarity takes shape in the monologue as a white voyage of self-discovery through the mysterious culture of the other. His experiences with that otherness allow him not only to embrace Western medicine, but to finally marry his girlfriend, Renée. As for me, my sense of relief in my strong identification with his medical condition is overwhelmed by distaste for this narrative. As Phelan said of *Swimming*:

> I don't care one bit that Gray has all of these embarrassing attitudes toward other people and other cultures, most of us do; but what I find disappointing is his assumption that this can be glossed over without comment in favor of some boyish charm or political naivete. (Phelan 1988: 29)

In chapter 5 I will detail how in performance monologues whiteness and white self-knowledge frequently depend on interaction with the racial other. *Gray's Anatomy* is a prime example of this phenomenon. For the moment, however, two simple observations remain to be made about this piece.

The first is the zest for life celebrated in the closing section of the piece. With an ironic nod toward a central image in *Swimming to Cambodia*, Gray relates that he nearly drowned while swimming at a rented house on Long Island, days before the wedding on the beach. Rescued yet again, and having survived a case of cold feet ("looking more and more at women . . . why not her? You know? In order to diffuse that, I would cover my right eye and they'd all blur"—1994: 75), Gray finally marries. Though his sight is not yet fully restored, he celebrates the climax of both heterosexual convention and neocolonial exploration, for his "little Balinese man" received from the healer serves as witness. The concluding image is one of extensive consumption. "I ate and I drank and I smoked . . . *everything* that could make me blind" (1994: 80).

The second point is the action suggested by the William Wegman photo of Gray on the cover of both *Playbill* and the published text of *Gray's Anatomy*. Gray looks out from behind the title through a square magnifying glass that enlarges his right eye. In keeping with the narrative of the work, the photograph seems to invite us to examine Gray, but it is *he* who is holding the magnifier. Gray's eye is made larger than life, and it is his view of the world that the work produces, rather than any truly probing introspection. Gray himself notes the pun connecting organ and pronoun (1994: 11). In the final section of this chapter, I argue that despite his medical history, the racial, sexual, and spiritual comfort or satisfaction Gray seeks within his narratives is made possible by the power of that eye/I.

I will explicitly analyze Gray's performance of each of the three identity terms—white, male, and heterosexual—in chapter 5, which offers comparative discussions of a number of performers. In concluding this chapter devoted to Gray, however, I will focus on his construction of an all-consuming event with himself at the center. While this gesture is perhaps not the exclusive property of straight white male privilege, that privilege supports and is supported by not only a neocolonial content but a performance practice that is structurally colonizing.

SPALDING GRAY'S POLITICAL PERFORMANCE: THE PERSONAL IS THE HEGEMONIC

Gray's popularity with audiences has been echoed, for the most part, by critics. Nonetheless, a few, Phelan most articulately, have found his work apolitical or even reactionary in its functioning. Others have suggested that monologue performance, in its formal proximity to the stand-up comedy of popular culture, represents a highly commodified form of art performance.

The critical defense against the notion of "selling out" has taken two main forms. One clearly demonstrated by Shank is a liberal humanist politics of recognition that emphasizes the supposed universality of Gray's stories.

> The tone of the monologues is predominantly comic because of a distanced, ironic perspective. The audience may sense how Gray felt while undergoing the experiences, but now he is alive in front of them having survived to tell about them from an objective perspective. Furthermore, the archetypical American experiences—love, sex, booze, cars, embarrassing situations—are recognized by the audience as similar to their own. A kind of catharsis takes place, and an important connection is made between the performer and the spectators. (Shank 1982: 179)

The obvious problem with this attempt to assign social value to the monologues lies in the blatant elision of race, class, gender, and sexuality in Shank's appeal to "archetypical American experiences." But Shank is only the most explicit of the humanist critics; most positive reviews of Gray's work (written predominantly by white, male, and presumptively heterosexual critics) emphasize recognition as a central pleasure.[7]

Another defense of Gray is given by William Demastes, who takes umbrage particularly at unfavorable comparisons of Gray and the Wooster Group.

> Given his privileged upbringing, it would seem that Gray had two options in pursuing an avant-garde, political agenda. He could reject his personal history and join the ranks of those out of power in an effort to enact change from without, and thus come to the theatre as less than a historically genuine spokesperson—a "have" joining in with the "have-nots." Or he could accept his personal history of privilege and work from within, accepting, at least for rhetorical purposes, his position of authority—"to the manor born"—complete with the empowering tools of that system, language certainly included. This second option, at first glance hardly an option for an avant-garde performer, is the option Gray has chosen. Choosing that option, it seems, was the cause for his split with his former colleagues. (Demastes 1989: 86)

Whether Demastes's account of the Gray/Wooster split is to be accepted is beside the point; more important is the "white man's burden" tone of the argument. Demastes seems to suggest that Gray can do from "within" what the Wooster Group tried to do from its avant-garde "without", and furthermore that he can do it without an "alienating revolutionary contempt" (1989: 93).[8]

Demastes's defense of *Swimming* is based on the image of Gray as an extremely powerful but benevolent theatrical dictator, who can save the audience from the power of representation by enacting the same dominance with an ironic twist.

> The fact that Gray's work is *art* prevents it from exhibiting no authorial or presence power whatsoever. However, *Swimming to Cambodia* succeeds in minimizing that power in performance while, more importantly, it points out exactly how dangerously engulfing that power is. It critiques *The Killing Fields* and simultaneously undermines the perceived power of its own presence, whose spell has temporarily controlled the audience. Gray observes that we've all been consumed; in fact, he *demonstrates* it by "leading" with his own presence. Though [Philip] Auslander's wish [in "Toward a Concept of the Political in Postmodern Theatre," 1987] to see a movement toward no "power" at all seems fated never to occur, minimizing "power," undermining it, and demonstrating its danger seem to be the next best set of options, real options substituting for unreachable idealities. (Demastes 1989: 93–94, emphasis in original)

Demastes's attempt to reframe Gray's work as minimizing and critiquing power is ultimately unconvincing. I might partly agree that Gray plays on a grace that is built on a seeming awkwardness, a charisma built on the apparently mundane, and a presence paradoxically built on an "ordinary" body, unassuming gestures, and relatively nondramatic vocal displays. I disagree, however, on the outcome of that relationship to power. While I will certainly admit the possibility of subversive *audience* response to the monologues, I find that the surface of the performance texts executed by Gray reveals a will to power rather than a shedding of it. As a chronicler of a new fall of Rome, Gray accrues experience to himself and renders all the world textual and consumable, rather than warning of the dangers of that consumption. Even as he catalogues his loss, Gray engages in the construction of a totalizing, all-consuming event that is far removed from the simple observation that even daily life can become art.

Earlier I was tempted to describe Gray as suffusing theatrical performance with the Schechnerian "actual" now associated with performance art. As a performer, he might be said to fuse an actor's presence with a performance artist's, merging the flashy "wow" of the theater with the gripping "now" of the performance space. Perhaps, however, this goes too far, or fails to see just where the frame around Gray-as-event lies. Perhaps Gray isn't an actor playing himself, but an actor playing a performance artist. "Unlike most of the other performance artists engaged in rethinking autobiographical 'texts,' Gray's work consistently returns to one theme: his most consistently expressed emotion is one of loss" (Phelan 1988: 29).

Gray, as my title suggests, has developed a sort of capitalist Zen in which a distanced observation of the self's loss and the loss of the self allows the "Self" to accrue experience, admiration, and mastery of a disproportionate amount of theatrical territory. In one sense Gray exposes the decades-old fad of "self-actualization" as a methodology of self-aggrandizement; Gray himself is so self-actualized that it's hard to see, out in the auditorium, anything of the "actual." Having made his life larger-than-life, he occupies the whole of the perceptual field. Never mind that irony drapes thickly over everything in this theater, making it easy to be critical of Gray, to ask him hard questions, to wonder if he's "exploiting" someone. This is all contained by the Self under a manifest destiny of experience, and the critical, thinking spectator produced by the piece, the Brechtian spectator constructed by all that vertiginous distancing, the chuckling, tongue-clucking, or even hissing spectator is swallowed up by the spectacular gravity of the event. He has us right where he wants us. And if Gray disdains the label "performance artist" and prefers to be thought of as an actor playing himself, then spectators are in the same position, playing at spectatorship, and any ad libs we work in between the lines turn out to be already written out in the script contained in Gray's field of vision.

Chronicler of the fall of civilization? Perhaps. But in that case the perhaps postmodern strategy of textualizing everything as the referent evaporates functions to make Gray master of all he surveys. While the art/life revolution disturbs, again and again, the comfortable boundaries constraining theater and its audience, not all contemporary developments of that troubling question can be seen as liberating. The personal may be political, but that hardly means that "good" personality makes for good politics. Spalding Gray has not fashioned a progressive straight white male performance practice from the autobiographical inquiry so central to contemporary performance, and he has not altered the relations of the production of theatrical presence. Gray-as-event inters, rather than interviews, the audience; "we" are buried in representation, and as the quotation from Barthes with which I opened suggests, Gray's (conceptual) eye forms the apex of the pyramid that entombs us.

Chapter Four

UNCANNY RESEMBLANCE: ERIC BOGOSIAN'S MULTIPLE-CHARACTER PERFORMANCE

> There was a lot of moralizing in Bogosian's slice-of-life cliches, moralizing of the self-justifying sort (he writes his own scripts), but Bogosian never patronized these lost souls. His moral was appropriately double edged: aren't these people weird? said his material, and isn't there something of them in you and me? asked his all-out performance. (Howell 1985: 108)

> This class of characters can not only speak what the privileged class does not often hear, but, isolated in monologue, it can also make clear how "invisible," as one of them expresses it, they are to the suburban psyche. Moreover, casualties declaring themselves bring to the monologue a voice that undoes the kind of social relation (the passive nonintervention of entertainment) typical of the form. (Siegle 1989: 263)

This chapter investigates a second major strand of performance art monologue, one that involves the impersonation of multiple fictional characters. It focuses on the most visible practitioner of this subgenre, Eric Bogosian. Among his similarities to Gray are their shared identity privilege and their common deployment of performative presence—albeit differently framed. In other ways Bogosian's work is quite different from Gray's. Most importantly, his primary work is in multiple-character fictional performances, anthologies of characters who are often but by no means always comic. Another important difference is that Bogosian's performances imply—and, according to Bogosian, arise from—a politicized attitude toward the society he represents.

In spite of his different intentions, Bogosian's performances are often as politically problematic as Gray's. While I offer a loosely chronological overview of Bogosian's career, my primary goal is to give several overlapping accounts of the political functioning of his performances. Each of Bogosian's major works raises new issues for consideration and leads me to emphasize different questions. As in the previous chapter, I devote some attention to the content of the works, but ultimately focus my critique on their form. Again, while I do address explicit constructions of whiteness, maleness, and heterosexuality here, I also reserve many such examples for the comparative discussion of these issues in chapter 5.

There is really no "typical" Bogosian performance, since his work has evolved over a number of years. Even in the string of successful multiple-character performances of the 1980s and '90s, each work features different characters and juxtaposes their appearance in ways that structure the overall effect of the piece. Still, "an Eric Bogosian performance" does imply that multiple characters will be presented; that they will be connected thematically, perhaps, but not through any plot development; that Bogosian will probably not appear as himself—though this too has begun to change in his latest works. The typical Bogosian work is funny, its humor based on character more than situation. While Bogosian has played a broad range of characters over his career, the most common characters are, like Bogosian, straight white men. There is a great range among these characters, however, in terms of ethnicity and class, as well as in their opinions (from which much of the work's humor derives). Bogosian has experimented with other performance forms, appeared in films, and written for the stage; while these aspects of his career are important to a broad understanding of his work, most important to my study are the multiple-character solo performances.

As the two epigraphs to this chapter establish, Bogosian frequently provokes political readings of his performances. One frequent theme, expressed in all its ambiguity by Howell, is that Bogosian brings a repressed or othered social element challengingly close to his (presumably privileged) audience. Siegle's optimistic passage articulates a somewhat less common analysis; he sees Bogosian's confrontational *content*— "casualties declaring themselves"—as somehow overcoming the passiv-

Eric Bogosian

ity "typical of the *form*." In this chapter I attempt to give a full hearing to such positive political readings, while demonstrating that Bogosian's representation of social outcasts frequently functions conservatively and recuperatively, in large part because his content cannot escape the trap built of concentrated identity privilege and monologic form.

Like the previous chapter, then, this one analyzes the workings of power and privilege in the performance aesthetics of a single exemplary performance artist. The next chapter examines a broader assortment of straight white men at the "margins" of performance art in terms of their specific performances of race, gender, and sexual privilege. My conclusion examines several promising strategies in the work of Danny Hoch, then investigates the confinement represented by the larger aesthetic system within which the identity privilege of these performers circulates.

DOWNTOWN ARTIST

Beginning around 1975, Bogosian moved within New York's downtown art and performance scene, finding backstage work first at the Chelsea Westside Theatre and then at the performance space known as the Kitchen, where he eventually became dance curator (Bogosian 1987a: 3–5). By 1979, Bogosian was even a published authority on the farthest reaches of the downtown scene, with an essay in *The Drama Review* titled "Art World Underground." In it Bogosian sketches the performance activities of a thriving artistic milieu apparently unconcerned with established arts institutions or discourses: in Bogosian's words, a scene in which " 'underground' does not mean secretive, it means indifferent" (Bogosian 1979: 32). The implication is that the downtown avant-garde of the time actively ignored mainstream culture. His performance work of the late 1970s thus comes from an artist embedded institutionally and critically in an avant-garde subculture.

Bogosian produced solo work in various downtown venues, most notably as the abusive nightclub character Ricky Paul. Bogosian describes his character in the introduction to *Drinking in America*:

> In the guise of a comedian/entertainer, he had nothing positive to say about anybody or anything and reveled in the paranoia and decay of the modern world. And he did this as a "comedian" and as a singer exploding with patter and song at ninety miles an hour. As I wrote Ricky's monologues, I would aim for what would disturb and upset my audiences—and then laugh right into their worst fears and prejudices.

> If I was playing to a college crowd in Massachusetts, I'd talk about how lazy blacks are; for a feminist mother's group in Milwaukee, I'd crack jokes about how "you can't live with 'em and you can't live without 'em"; in Berlin I goose-stepped across the stage, *sieg heiled*, and then asked the audience if the theater I was in was built with American Marshall Plan money.... The desired effect was usually achieved. My performances were greeted by flying bottles, spit and people trying to climb onstage and grab the microphone.... (Bogosian 1987a: 15)

Of course any performer's description of his own work might be taken with a grain of salt, but for my purposes, the Ricky Paul persona is important chiefly in contrast to Bogosian's later multiple-character work. While Bogosian set out to offend with Ricky Paul, the later multiple-character pieces contain offensive material rather than being contained by it. That is, in the single-character performances Bogosian used Ricky Paul as a persona from within which to assault his audiences; the entire work is premised on offense. In later pieces, even the simplest multi-vocality created by more than one character suggests that the characters are to be studied, that another party (Bogosian) is presenting them for consideration by the audience. As one character, Bogosian wore a mask to get away with being insulting; multiple characters suggest a distanced observation, almost implying that the mask serves as a kind of sociological tool. The second option was more suited to Bogosian's goals as a performer and examiner of American characters. The multiple character solo also proved much more effective in terms of theatrical longevity and mainstream critical recognition.

Roselee Goldberg, in an essay celebrating the 1970s as the "Golden Years" of performance, articulates an aesthetic rationale for Bogosian's multiple-character works that focuses on his interest in actorly "presence."

> Eric Bogosian, a trained actor performing in the art context, looked to the tradition of solo performers—whether Lenny Bruce or Brother Theodore, Laurie Anderson or Julia Heyward—as confirmation of his concern for presence—the actor's live presence being the energy and the "humanity" of his work. Concerned first and foremost with content, Bogosian at the same time emphasizes acting itself, "framing" the medium as it were by tightly constructing each piece in terms of moves, lighting, and subtly mannered acting. The characters that people his one-person shows are a gallery of contemporary types, and their

appearance illustrates his virtuosity as well as his acknowledgment of classical actor training techniques. (Goldberg 1984: 87)

Despite the theatrical language she uses to describe his approach, Goldberg also situates Bogosian's virtuosic acting style within an art world context.

> Such "acting in relief" in images that are both two-dimensional—carefully choreographed against space and set—and three-dimensional in their breadth of "personality" is as much the result of Bogosian's own love of spectacle (his background was the rock concert, not Broadway) as the result of his proximity to the art scene. Particularly, Bogosian was influence by artists like Jack Goldstein, Robert Longo, Cindy Sherman, and Michael Zwack, some of whom had made performances alongside work in other media and all of whom have appropriated aspects of mass culture in their work. For these artists "growing up" meant being literate in movies and television, not books. The economy of means used to create an image in the media—cutting and cropping, editing and freeze-framing—encouraged an equivalent sensibility in their art and performances. (Goldberg 1984: 87–89)

Goldberg's account is of an actor's actor, an artist of theatrical presence, putting that presence in the service of a high (visual) arts aesthetic of mass media appropriation.

This televisual style can be seen in an early broadcast performance that shows Bogosian combining the multiple character impersonations for which he was to become famous with a "real-time" variable—a hallmark of art performance. In "7 Americans in 7 Minutes" (1982), aired as part of *The Live! Show* on Soho cable television, Bogosian creates a variety of instant characters, in one-minute vignettes. Stopwatch in hand, he moves breathlessly from one character to the next, and his face and body suggest a great effort of concentration and expression. This focus on the event, and on the demonstration of virtuosity, seems at least as important as the characters themselves. The speed of the impersonation and the presence of the stopwatch (which Bogosian resets each minute with an exaggerated gesture) contribute a Brechtian distantiation to a form that is more often primarily about the creation of an illusion.

This distancing is in line with Bogosian's stated goals of estranging the everyday:

> The meaning comes out of the juxtaposition of the segments. But also, the meaning comes out of something much more gigantic—the enor-

mous amount of information assaulting us every day. The audience already knows the story of every character I present.... The point is to create a sense of distance from totally familiar images. (quoted in Banes 1983b)

While the Brechtian devices of "7 Americans" are not found in Bogosian's "pure" monologues, even his most polished theatrical pieces fit Goldberg's description of the "framing" of character with acting in order to estrange the stories the audience somehow "already knows."

MEN INSIDE

Men Inside (which contains some material that overlaps with "7 Americans") represents a "break" in Bogosian's career. After opening at Franklin Furnace, a small avant-garde performance space, in February 1981, the show moved in July 1982 to the Public Theatre, a very serious but arguably more mainstream (and "public") venue. Bogosian presented it as the first half of an evening; his second show, called *Voices of America*, is a vocal tour de force structured as a scan across the radio dial, and clearly reflects the mass media sensibility Goldberg notes. Bogosian describes the "radio" piece as "pretty much standard 'comedy' fare" and claims that it was best performed "in places where people didn't speak English, or were drunk. Like clubs. The idea was to do it very fast and loud" (1987a: 134). Despite Bogosian's self-critical assessment, the radio piece reads well as parody, and Frank Rich, who gave Bogosian's career a significant boost with his review of the evening, calls *Voices of America* the "superior piece" in a "hit and miss" performance.

Nevertheless, in hindsight *Men Inside* is clearly the more important step in the development of Bogosian's career, since the "monopolylogue" form is what fulfilled the "bright enough" promise Rich saw in Bogosian (Rich 1982). In *Men Inside*, Bogosian constructed a representation of society by presenting a collection of male characters. Each character speaks from within one or more clearly identifiable ideologies. In this sense, Bogosian does present the "totally familiar" by offering fragments of recognizable discourses.

As collected, along with *Voices of America*, in the volume *Drinking in America* (1987a), *Men Inside* opens with a freakshow barker advertising his entertainment with a catalogue of offensive descriptions of the fat, disabled, and otherwise deviant people on display. These include the

"Offspring" of a "Negro and a Chinaman," billed as "a medical impossibility" (1987a: 111), and "not an imitation, not a duplication, but the real thing. A genuine, homosexual Siamese twin. Step right up" (1987a: 112).

After thus framing the piece as a collection of titillating oddities, Bogosian presents another catalogue of sorts in the next speech, in which a young boy pesters his father: "Hey Dad, when I grow up I'm gonna be just like you, huh Dad? I'm gonna be tall and strong and never make any mistakes and drink beer and shave and drive a car and get a check. I'm gonna be just like you, huh Dad?" (1987a: 113). The boy persists in his questioning, demanding reassurance that when he grows up he won't be poor, live in a box, be an alcoholic or a junkie, or a "homo" or a "nigger." " 'Cause you're not a nigger and Mom's not a nigger, huh? Huh? HUH? We're American, huh Dad?" (1987a: 114). Bogosian adds a sudden twist to this recitation of vicious ideologies when at the end the boy "begins stuttering and falls to the floor in a fit" (1987a: 114, stage direction). This has the effect, perhaps, of inviting the audience to sympathize almost against its will, or perhaps of suggesting that a weakness or disability has rendered this boy more apt to repeat this hateful discourse.

"Nice Shoes," the next vignette, stages *Men Inside*'s first direct confrontation across class, when Sonny, the leader of a group of (apparently white) working-class toughs confronts a well-dressed man walking through the neighborhood. Through a series of threats organized around homophobic descriptions of Mike, the victim, Sonny and his pals steal Mike's expensive shoes, leaving the invisible Mike (the audience?) crying on the sidewalk. This is followed by a self-proclaimed "superfly" who makes a pass, in black urban dialect, at a woman on the street. When she makes no response, he instantly switches to calling her a prostitute.

The next character masturbates over a porn magazine, coming, according to the stage directions, at the end of the brief monologue. Then a businessman blames his lover, Cheryl, for his impotence. He becomes increasingly angry at her, finally saying "I know what you need, you need a real insensitive, male-chauvinist-pig cowboy." The following character is a beer-drinking deer hunter, with a "high-pitched 'cowboy voice' " (1987a: 124), who celebrates fist-fights and harassing women on the street. A middle-aged Italian-American argues the value of marriage to his son, and offers as an example his own pleasure and pride at the family Christmas celebration: "I sit there at the table, Vinnie, and I look at my family and I think to myself: All this belongs to me" (1987a: 128).

In the final scene, "Looking Out for Number One," Bogosian becomes the leader of a success seminar, invoking the Bible, Andrew Carnegie, and Bob Hope to convince the audience that they should not feel guilty about success, that they cannot help the "have-nots," and that "love, my friends, love is loving yourself first. Thank you, Amen" (1987a: 131).

Men Inside can be read as a deeply political work. While it addresses race for the most part only implicitly, issues of sexuality and gender are central. The title itself, while somewhat universalist in its suggestion that Bogosian contains the essences of these men, does announce the performance as the display of specifically gendered characters. The title might even be read as suggesting that the characters are all "men" on the inside: that is, the title may point to the characters' internalization of masculinist ideology, as when the young boy displays a precocious vehemence in his racism and homophobia, or when the father equates contentment with owning a family. Vera Dika suggests that the title might even be read as referring "to his characters as they reside inside *you*" (1988: 18). The spectator is certainly implicated by the sideshow barker, who not only frames the piece as a collection of freaks and serves as a first example of abusive, voyeuristic, commercialized desire, but also offers the show itself to the audience as if it were a pornographic secret.

Sexuality and power—and the abuse of both—run though *Men Inside* as connected themes. Men are condescendingly solicitous of women; then, when their wishes are not met, they suddenly become abusive with equal consistency. Homophobia alternates with a drooling fixation on homosexuality. The voyeuristic pleasures of the freakshow culminate in homosexuality. Noncooperative women are assumed to be prostitutes and lesbians, yet the masturbating man also casts his fantasy women as lesbians. Some characters seemingly compensate for a lack of power on one plane with an abuse of sexually defined power, as when the working-class toughs structure Mike's robbery around his verbal homosexualization, or when the harried businessman takes out on his wife the pressures of competition.

When I read it with my assumptions about Bogosian's "intent" in mind, *Men Inside* seems a scathing catalogue of abusive male behavior, relating it to other forms of social injustice and holding it up to the spectator's critical judgment. In this unpleasant world, Bogosian's characters respond to stress, frustration, or loneliness by repeating familiar tropes of lust, bigotry, violence, and greed.

My reading of the piece as articulating a critical politics is abetted, however, by my use of the published script rather than a live performance as my primary text; it may be easier for me to transfer my sense of Bogosian's goals (really, of course, constructed by the critical discourse around him) onto the written document of the performance. In other words, because I read it without the complication of the performer's charismatic presence—because I read it as a drama—I can perform the interpretive work of distancing *myself* from the characters, analyzing their situations, judging them as I imagine the author does. This is quite in contrast with my experience as a spectator of later live performances. While I unquestionably felt invited to watch with a sense of moral or political judgment, the sheer force of the impersonations, the micro-spectacle of mimetic virtuosity, worked to seduce me toward a simple fascination with the other.

This is a difficulty with all of Bogosian's monologues. The presentation of isolated moments of behavior requires an interpretive act of criticism. There is little sense in the performance of an attitude toward the characters or their behavior. The risk is that the presence of the performer will mesmerize spectators, rather than allowing the necessary distance. In the words of one review of an early, unpublished performance by Bogosian, in which he apparently supplemented monologue with disturbing visual projections:

> [P]erformance is never mere reportage. Its intensity supplies it willy-nilly with a point of view. In this case, Bogosian's own charisma and control make the monologues take shape not as a string of facts but as privileged, thus sympathetic interior views. The material demands an editorializing component that can't be left up to the viewer. (Banes 1983a: 70)[1]

IRONY AND INTENTION

I have suggested that what this form offers in place of an "editorializing component" is an ironic structure that implies a distance or distinction between the author/performer and the character. In this regard, Bogosian's strand of monologue performance has much in common with the tradition of dramatic monologue poetry discussed in chapter 2. Alan Sinfield lists as its characteristics "a first person speaker not the poet, a time and place, an [implied] auditor . . . revelation of character, colloquial language and some dramatic interaction between speaker and auditor. It may seem that dramatic monologue is a truncated play" (1977: 3). The relationship to (at least the texts of) Bogosian's performances is clear: many of Sinfield's characteristics apply in almost every instance. Sinfield, Carleton, and others debate the positioning of the author's voice in a form in which the only access the reader has is to the character's voice. Does the erasure of the artist's commentary behind the voice of the character confuse the moral questions raised by the poem/performance and subject the reader to the will of the author, as I suggested in chapter 2; or might "the ironic element . . . bring us into a sympathetic relation to the poem which is not the same thing as subordinating our view to that offered by the monologue speaker" (Carleton 1977: v)? Sinfield appears to agree with Carleton, at least to some extent:

> What we experience in dramatic monologue—and it is a quality which is not easily gained in other modes—is a divided consciousness. We are impressed, with the full strength of first-person presentation, by the speaker and feel drawn into his point of view, but at the same time are aware that he is a dramatic creation and that there are other possible, even preferable perspectives. This condition is a precise consequence of the status of dramatic monologue as feint: we are obliged to posit simultaneously the speaking "I" and the poet's "I." (Sinfield 1977: 32)

The degree of awareness of the poet's I is vital; if it is minimal, the performance risks being taken literally. Frank Rich seems almost to suggest that this is what happens in Bogosian's work: "by inhabiting his characters instead of condescending to them, Mr. Bogosian doesn't allow anyone a safe distance" (Rich 1990: 385). Of course, spectators *do* remain conscious of Bogosian's existence prior to the characters; especially now, his star quality ensures that. In fact, work like Bogosian's is premised on the concept of a separation between actor and character. For many performers, this separation is the alibi that frees them to behave in socially unacceptable ways.

When C. Carr juxtaposes descriptions of Andrew Dice Clay and Bogosian (1990: 205) in the same paragraph, she perhaps implies a critique of Bogosian, or else suggests a distinction between the two. Clay is an "obscene, hate-mongering" comedian who gives voice to attitudes that should be kept quiet; yet men who hold such negative attitudes become "case studies" for "cross-over" performance artist Bogosian (Carr 1990: 205). Carr is engaged in a brief overview of 1980s performance, and so cannot expand on this distinction. However, this sort of comparison is critically commonplace. Does Clay's location in the popular culture realm of shock comedy mean that his characterization of the "Dice-man" can only reproduce and advocate the offensive views he expresses? And that Bogosian, apparently because he began with high-art credentials in place and only then crossed over into popular culture, "studies" these attitudes? Clay's material is arguably more offensive than even the most abrasive of Bogosian's characters (though what about his single character performances as Ricky Paul?), and Bogosian's own politics are publicly opposed to "hate-mongering" while Clay's are not quite clearly so. However, if Bogosian's performance is politically preferable to Clay's, it is not because of his performance art pedigree. In fact, Clay has used the same alibi of difference between his real self and his character ("the Dice-man") to defend his sexist and homophobic material (Abrahams 1990: 58). While I would agree that Bogosian's performance is much preferable to Clay's, any distinction between their performative modes is perhaps one of quality rather than kind.[2] Access to authorial intent is necessary to interpret, for example, their spoken sexism as other than sexism. Ultimately, both have recourse to the same ironic alibi. Both lay claim to the same presumption of ironic distance critics attribute to Browning.

The problem of securing ironic distance becomes more complex when the emphasis is on performance rather than text alone. In chapter 2 I suggested that the dynamic of performance art monologues like Bogosian's is a mix of the textual structure of dramatic monologue poetry and the event structure of the contemporary poetry reading. Even if the audience is called back to the presence of the author behind the character by the celebrity of the performer, the emphasis is not on the "writing" or the construction of the performance, but on the authenticity of its execution, illustrated by gestures performed by the hand that "wrote" it.

The use of irony as an alibi becomes more and more complicated, as I have suggested, as the relative cultural power of author and imaginary character become more disparate. In this respect, the homeless characters that became almost a Bogosian signature by the late 1980s might be compared to Browning's speaker in "Caliban upon Setebos." Bogosian often allows his street people to speak the most coherent social criticism couched in apparent raving about their urban environment. Similarly, Browning's Caliban (elaborated on the "monster" from Shakespeare's *Tempest*) discourses on the relationship of God and the world, drawing examples from the beasts around him. In both cases, as I read them, the author simultaneously challenges and reinforces the implied spectator's sense of superiority. The apparently intended challenge arises from the breaking of expectations about the character; Caliban and the homeless man demonstrate an insight not usually credited to the disenfranchised. On the other hand, it can be argued that seeing "method" in "madness" (whether that madness is constituted by insanity, physical difference, or poverty) is a not uncommon stereotype, in the broad sense used by Barthes. By allowing their audience to make the interpretive gesture of recognizing method in madness, Browning and Bogosian arguably contribute to the superior reader's condescension to the character.

CULTURE AND CLASS: *FUNHOUSE* AND *DRINKING IN AMERICA*

The published text of the next piece allows for a similar reading of politicized "intent" and potential problems in reception. *Funhouse* (1983) is similar to *Men Inside* in that it is a collection of disturbing speeches by men, loosely connected by a number of themes. Just as *Men Inside* is framed by the carnival barker's invitation to voyeurism, *Funhouse* begins with a monologue by a rubber fetishist seductively describing the pleasures of being alone in the dark, completely surrounded by a "black cocoon" (Bogosian 1987a: 75). The speaker is happily isolated in the dark: "I don't have to think, I don't have to feel . . . and the best part is . . . I don't have to see . . ." (1987a: 76). This speech offers another metaphor for theatrical pleasure (in conjunction, or perhaps in contrast, with the third vignette, a man on the street advertising pornographic performance to passers-by),[3] sets up a subtle theme of the denial of reality that runs through many of the subsequent monologues, and challenges spectators to look outside of their cocoons at the "real world" the piece is about to show them.

The monologues that follow depict both privileged and destitute characters, all of whom seem to be after something. In particular, food and starvation are important images in *Funhouse*. An insurance salesman interrupts a bourgeois family dinner to scare his client into a larger policy. A street person rants about pollution passing through the food chain. A cancer-ridden glutton worries about anorexia in a piece called "Calamari." The image of children starving somewhere in the world returns in several pieces, while a Richard Simmons-like character challenges the audience to exercise and diet. Bogosian charts physical and psychological needs and greeds that are seemingly insatiable. He ends the piece with a condemned murderer telling the audience, "I'm inside you" (1987a: 107).

More than most of his monologues, *Funhouse* uses the juxtaposition of characters and topics to critical effect. Especially in its thematizing of material necessity, the piece succeeds in representing a society in which resources are distributed unequally and a culture that seems likely to keep things that way. While it shares many of the complicated representational flaws of the rest of Bogosian's work, on the level of content *Funhouse* is among the more successful critiques.

Frank Rich of the *New York Times* certainly seemed to find in *Funhouse* a fulfillment of Bogosian's promise. In turn, Rich fulfilled Bogosian's ambition. As Bogosian told *Connoisseur*: "It was just that I wanted a critic to come ... just to tell me what they really think. I trust the *Times* that much. And Frank Rich shows up and proceeds to alter my life" (quoted in Carter 1987: 169). Rich, on the other hand, felt Bogosian was too good to be true: "As a satirist, Mr. Bogosian aims to kill, not wound, and he's far too lethal to receive mass exposure. The Public Theater deserves our gratitude for giving this renegade artist a showcase" (1983). To the degree that Rich was wrong about his potential for "mass exposure," Bogosian's trust in the *Times* would appear misplaced. Bogosian continued to refine his monologue formula, and Rich continued to champion him in the press. While Bogosian's mass exposure is slight by some pop cultural standards, his satire neither "killed" its subjects nor relegated him to obscurity.

Drinking in America (1985, collected in Bogosian 1987a) expands Bogosian's repertoire of characters slightly to include more members of the privileged classes, especially those involved in the production of culture. A talent agent in Los Angeles is awakened by a phone call, pauses to snort cocaine, and launches into a cynical speech about what actors can be had for different amounts of money: "He's no good, he's a drug addict ... FORGET ABOUT HIM! We'll go to his funeral ..." (1987a: 29). In "No Problems," a complacent middle-aged man casually describes his health, his family and sex life, and his financial security. He only briefly displays a troubled side: "You know, you turn on the news and uh ...

it's disturbing . . . I make myself watch it because I know I should. For their sake" (1987a: 59). The fortunate appear to be either hyper-alert and jaded, or placid and self-consciously content.

Street characters remain important in *Drinking*; there is a fantasizing black wino called "American Dreamer," a heroin addict, and a beggar lying on the ground singing "We Are the World." The longest and most complex monologue comes from Ritchie, a working-class white braggart who relives an enthusiastic crime spree that ends with him delivering a passed-out woman to her parents' house. He claims to be a "gentleman" who doesn't "mess with unconscious broads," and tells of wedging her behind the screen door, ringing the doorbell, and running away (1987a: 55).

Other characters with only slightly more privilege also mistreat or take advantage of those with even less power than themselves, such as the Greek restaurant owner abusing his employee in "Melting Pot." A convention-going ceramic tile salesman alternately advises and confesses to Michelle, a prostitute, first telling her that "there's no future in this escort business," then explaining that "I'm just a lonely guy . . . just a lonely little cowboy." By the end, despite referring to himself as her "Daddy" and calling her "one hell of a stimulating conversationalist," he still requests, with a wink, a "nice slow quick one" (1987a: 36–38).

Drinking in America centers around substance use and abuse. Inebriation serves as a through line for the pieces, holding them tenuously together. There is a brief disc jockey segment advertising nihilistic bands called "The Molesters" and "Cerebral Hemorrhage." Later, there is a scene in which someone called Eric records a commercial for Kronenbrau, the beer that sponsors the concert broadcast by the DJ. The effect of this motif is to suggest a simultaneity of all the scenes, as if the show were a snapshot of an intoxicated society. A final bit of cohesion is added when the street drunk at the end, like the wino from the second monologue, imagines he is waiting for his limousine.

The "snapshot" effect produced by *Funhouse* and most clearly by *Drinking* is, in my reading, central to Bogosian's performative project. These anthology works suggest a slice of life, or an objectified cross-section of society, held up to the audience for critical scrutiny. While unifying thematic elements, such as hunger or intoxication, can highlight this effect, most multiple-character monologues suggest a similar structure. As I have suggested, the awareness that an author-presence precedes the characters should lead the spectator to a somewhat critical approach to those characters, at least in the form of the "divided consciousness" Sinfield describes.

This performative stance of holding up a slice of life for the audience to contemplate is of course hardly the exclusive property of performers who possess straight white male privilege. Anna Deveare Smith, an African-American woman, has thoroughly and famously worked this vein (as Whoopi Goldberg did in a quite different way in her early character-based stand-up performances). Still, like Gray's all-consuming performance, the role of panoptic social observer is one that can build on and be built of identity privilege, perhaps inevitably at the expense of critical distantiation. That is, aside from any crucial formal differences in their performance styles, a straight white male performer and, for example, a black woman will signify differently as the "lens" through which the snapshot is taken. Simply by dint of history, a performer with a presumptive identity politics will imply a critical stance that is absent from the performance of identity privilege unless it is explicitly asserted. As my comparison with Clay is meant to suggest, this critical attitude is still more difficult to secure when the author-presence is submerged under the character(s). *Talk Radio*, in some ways an anomaly in Bogosian's career, features one alternative strategy for partially securing an ironic or critical attitude: the introduction of an authorial stand-in.

TALK RADIO

Bogosian's next big career advancement was a long-term project. He began work on what would become *Talk Radio* in 1982, and it finally opened as a play in 1987 at the New York Shakespeare Festival. Oliver Stone's film adaption, starring Bogosian, was released in 1989. While its later incarnations are far from solo performance, *Talk Radio* is of interest because of its use of monologue as an element, its metaphoric relation to performance art, and its impact on Bogosian's career.

Barry Champlain, the protagonist/host of *Talk Radio*, is an outspoken and at times obnoxious character whose job is, like Bogosian's, that of a heroic soloist. He spends the bulk of the play talking with listeners who've called in; Barry is alternately obnoxious, cajoling, broadly comic, angry. As Bogosian describes him:

> Champlain assumes the stance of indignant and enraged crusader, a man who sees through all the lies and hypocrisy and "tells it like it is."

Of course, Barry always has one eye on the Arbitron meter; he has to be careful to keep his show entertaining. (1988: xvii)

This might be a description of a 1980s performance artist, and certainly describes the position Bogosian found himself in as an emerging star. Like a true monologist, this radio dialogist must hold the stage/airwaves on the force of his presence alone. By the end of the play, the disillusioned Barry holds forth in an insulting monologue, haranguing his listeners and finally telling them to stop calling (1988: 90). But like a performance art audience, the radio listeners know to read such negativity as part of the act. They are impervious to antiradio; in fact, it is a high point in the show.

Talk Radio is an inversion of the structure of Bogosian's monologues. In his solo work, Bogosian speaks as assorted idiosyncratic characters; in *Talk Radio*, they talk to him and he replies. Of course, Champlain is not exactly Bogosian, and the film suggests that the spectator should also consider the DJ with a critical eye. However, Champlain to a great degree becomes an alter ego for the author. Conceptually, then, *Talk Radio* illustrates a utopian performance for Bogosian, since the spectator best equipped to read the ironic intent behind the characters is the first one to hear them, the channel through which they are heard by the audience. If a central problem with the monologues is that they seem to require that the spectator divine the artist's intent, the innovation of *Talk Radio* is to project that presence onto the stage as the protagonist of the drama. Perhaps the visibility the play and film brought Bogosian ensures that this character follows Bogosian as an intertext, a point of reference for future spectators of his performance art monologues. Even if this is the case, however, other problems arise in the charismatic representation of social stratification on a single body. These problems are exacerbated rather than ameliorated by Bogosian's increasing fame.

APOTHEOSIS: *SEX, DRUGS, ROCK & ROLL*

Sex, Drugs, Rock & Roll (1990) is a complicated mix of characters constructed of very precise writing and nuanced portrayals, a highly charismatic representation of a stratified society. The pieces are generally longer and more intricate than Bogosian's earlier work, and the characters are continually one-upping themselves. Just when it seems Bogosian has reached a logical break, revealed all the layers, or reached a comic high, the monologues swerve off in new directions, only to return to the original thematic point.

There is a fast-talking subway beggar who is funny primarily because he knows his role so well, and anticipates all the negative reactions his captive audience might have: "I am not a drug addict," he says repeatedly. He is followed by a monstrously egotistical British rock star, appearing on a talk show to mouth obviously hypocritical antidrug platitudes and promote his group's next show: a benefit concert, twenty percent of the proceeds from which will buy consumer electronic goods for Amazonian Indians. A callous businessman, with wife, mistress, employees and clients all on hold, barks orders at his secretary. "Bottleman," a nervous homeless person, calculates the price of basic necessities by the number of recyclables needed to purchase them. Yet another (the same one?) ethnic (Italian?) street tough describes a violent stag party he threw for a friend.

Two characters from *Funhouse* reappear here. The ravenous middle-aged man from "Calamari" returns in "Live," which begins with almost the same line: "Ugghhh . . . every time I have the fried calamari with the hot sauce, I feel like I'm gonna blow up!" (1990: 75). The rest of the monologue is an improvement on its prequel, however. Instead of emphasizing the funny but predictable humor about his appetite that is central to the piece from *Funhouse*, *Sex, Drugs, Rock & Roll* depicts him as a philosopher who catalogues his extravagant purchases—of cars, cigars, vacations—to explicate his doctrine of living life to the fullest. His attitude is still humorous, but he is serious and consistent, and Bogosian performs him with a gruff purposefulness that almost evokes respect for the character.

The homeless man from the *Funhouse* vignette titled "Shit, Fuck, Piss" returns in *Sex, Drugs, Rock & Roll* in an expansion of the earlier piece titled "Dirt." While in the first piece the humor (and warning about pollution) came in a quick, short burst of raving, in "Dirt" the chain of pollution goes on and on, from dog to ocean to oil spill, the character displaying a virtuoso work of homeless performance.

An equally broad political vision is elaborated in "Artist," by a dope-smoking dropout who resists "the system" by refusing to produce art: "the system only has one message, man—fear . . . Everybody's scared man—they're afraid they don't do what they're supposed to do, bang, they're homeless" (1990: 96). Homelessness, in fact, runs through *Sex,*

Drugs, Rock & Roll in the same way food occurs in *Funhouse*, or booze in *Drinking in America*. Even more central than in the earlier works, people who live in the street are the most sympathetic and even articulate characters, on the one hand, and the specters the privileged are desperate to avoid on the other.

Funhouse established Bogosian as a marketable theatrical performance artist; *Talk Radio* transformed him from performance artist to playwright to Hollywood star. *Sex, Drugs, Rock & Roll*—off-Broadway, in hardcover, on cassette and in the cinema—prepared the way for Bogosian's ascension into the pantheon of U.S. culture. Frank Rich in particular canonized him .

> [W]ith this brilliant show, his funniest and scariest yet, Mr. Bogosian has crossed the line that separates an exciting artist from a culture hero. What Lenny Bruce was to the 1950's, Bob Dylan to the 1960's, Woody Allen to the 1970's—that's what Eric Bogosian is to this frightening moment of drift in our history. (Rich 1990 385).

In Rich's review, Bogosian becomes both a saint and a great book. While deeply moral, this serious (yet funny) artist is above petty and unaesthetic politics:

> Mr. Bogosian isn't a documentarian, an X-rated Studs Terkel running a tape recorder. And he isn't a public scold of either the left or right, setting political agendas. His sketches don't end with neat moral codas but trail off, like distant radio stations vanishing into the night on a dark highway. (Rich 1990: 386)

This poetic image is far removed from the satirist who "aims to kill" that Rich had described in his positive review of *Funhouse*. Perhaps this is a symptom of success. Certainly by 1991 Bogosian is so important that only his last name (in large red letters) appears with the title on the book and audio cassette.

The secret of the critical success of *Sex, Drugs, Rock & Roll* perhaps lies in the sheer persistence of its creator, for Bogosian really creates the same old show all over again, only better. The balance and connectedness of the pieces, the virtuosity of the writing and acting certainly represent advances on earlier work, but the formula is tried and true: street people who behave outrageously, speaking truth in their madness, plus outrageously selfish wealthy people moving in a bubble of privilege isolated from the streets, plus the thick-headed, violent, beer-drinking working class, plus egotistical, drugged, otherwise out-of-touch cynics.

This assessment might be overly harsh if applied to a single Bogosian text, but the consistency of his multiple-character performances has hardened a single representation of society into almost a new genre composed of (relatively) original stereotypes. For example, while his homeless men are wonderfully varied in diction, dialect, posture, and mood, their basic outlines and dramatic function are as conventionalized as a commedia character's. And like any good conventionalized comic figure, they can be counted on for laughs.

UNCANNY LAUGHTER

The easy, consistent laughter produced by such conventions becomes uncomfortable for me as I become less sure of the proper shape of our (the performer's and my) ironic relation to the comic character. For example, the laughter of the audience is very present on the audio release of *Sex, Drugs, Rock & Roll*. Reading the text, I keep chuckling, and then listening to the tape I keep laughing out loud when the audience laughs. Why are we laughing? Often it's because Bogosian is pretending to be someone with more power than us, and showing us how stupid they are at the same time. This is fairly comfortable. Sometimes we laugh so that Bogosian can change emphasis slightly and make us see ourselves laughing (as in the subway beggar's speech). This laugh is uncomfortable, but then comfortable again, since that is so clearly the right reaction. What Bogosian can't do is make us see ourselves seeing ourselves, how smugly we savor this being caught laughing at something inappropriate.

Sitting in the audience watching the film version, I remember the strong laughter from the audio tape. The audience in the cinema, about the artiest crowd you can assemble in my part of the Midwest, is laughing, but a little more subdued than the audience on the tape. I want to know why we're laughing. We laugh at what the Bottleman says: (1) because he's a bum, (2) because he's being played by a guy who's not a bum, who's pretty well off now; (3) because he's saying crazy things that have a clever grain of truth in them; (4) because Bogosian, who's gotten to be pretty well off by pretending to be a bum, was smart enough to have a bum say these crazy things with a grain of truth in them; and (5) because the person next to me is laughing for reasons 1–4, and laughter is contagious. What's so uncomfortable to me here is that, with the possible exception of laugh number 5, there is no space for enjoyment that isn't first and foremost about exploiting and reinforcing my privilege.

But stage bums are good for more than a laugh. Rich's hagiographic review concludes by suggesting the potential for social change Bogosian's show represents.

> Leaving the show, one is struck not so much by the uncanny resemblance between the real-life beggars outside the theater and the fictional ones of Mr. Bogosian's impersonations as by the way *Sex, Drugs, Rock & Roll* as a whole forces the audience to examine its own roles in the larger drama that, however unwillingly, it shares daily with the dispossessed. (Rich 1990: 386)

Sex, Drugs, Rock & Roll might, in fact, provoke such self-examination in its audiences. I'm afraid, however, that Rich's statement points to a serious flaw—if not in *Sex, Drugs, Rock & Roll* or Bogosian's earlier pieces, then in that very audience. If "real-life" beggars are so available outside the theater, what is the need for an "uncanny resemblance?" Is all this laughter really part of a privileged audience examining its relations with the dispossessed? The silence of the author-presence, the blankly ironic frame that persists as the structuring element of his works, traps Bogosian in a conservative circle of laughter for as long as the audience is so relatively unchallenged in its preference for uncanny beggars over real ones. "Uncanny" often carries the sense of "eerie" or "mysterious." In the cumulative "mass exposure" of Bogosian's characters, aesthetic mystery coincides with political mystification, and his resemblance is no longer "more than expected" (another meaning of uncanny). Rather, the representations all too easily become exactly what is expected. Our familiar, easy, largely unchallenged laughter is the surest sign yet that the apparently apolitical attitude Rich praises is a deadly one for performance art. This laughter is another indication that some "editorializing component" is needed. The objective stance of the work resembles that of theatrical realism, and that is what the laughter makes *Sex, Drugs, Rock & Roll* resemble: a realist play—without set, without plot, without dialogue.

PERFORMANCE ARTIST/SHAMAN

While I compare Bogosian's work to realist drama in order to invoke the well-established political critique of realist mystification, there are four reasons to persist in calling Bogosian's monologues "performance art." The first is that Bogosian comes from an "authentic" performance art background and has appeared at performance art clubs, "gallery" venues such as Artist's Space and Los Angeles' Sushi gallery, and still appears in performance spaces such as P.S. 122.[4]

A second compelling reason is that the term "performance art," as a critical commonplace and as a marketing strategy, is continually applied to his work. For critics outside of art world publications, this designation is usually accompanied by enough ironizing to suggest the critic's sophisticated doubts about the term:

> For critical convenience, Bogosian, a thirty-four-year-old writer, actor, and monologuist, is usually classified as a "performance artist"—a New Age term invented a decade ago by New York's downtown grandees and applied to performers who aren't exactly actors, writers of scripts who aren't exactly playwrights, musicians who aren't exactly composers, and people who draw and paint but aren't exactly artists. (Carter 1987: 168)

Thirdly, Bogosian's performance (acting?) style, including its filmic mediation and critical reception, falls within a particular performative tradition within performance art. Bogosian's virtuosic character-switching can be viewed as a nonthreatening manifestation of a strain of "magic" that runs through performance art.

In its combinations of illusion, reality, and the body of the performer, performance art may be considered categorically similar to magic performance. Body artists such as Stellarc and Chris Burden are the Houdinis of performance (as well as its crucified messiahs); visually dazzling performance works echo stagy, illusionistic magic shows such as David Copperfield's; intense character performance often seems to invoke hypnotism and shamanism as intertexts. This last type of magical performance is exemplified by some of Karen Finley's work; critics commonly note her trance-like performance state and the sense that her body is possessed by the voices of her performance. It is at times suggested that this is not purely conscious behavior. In fact, Mark Levy compares Finley directly to shamanic practices, noting that "the ability to take on a different persona or personas while in an altered state of consciousness is typical of the shamanic 'shape shifting' " (Levy 1988: 60).[5]

While no one suggests that Bogosian is literally possessed by his characters, or that he performs in a trance state, critics often remark on the disappearance of the performer into the characters. Frank Rich calls him "a chameleon actor" (1990: 385), and John Howell says of *Drinking in America* that Bogosian "was so deeply and consistently inside his personas that it was almost magical to watch him disappear into them, with no theatrical hocus pocus" (Howell 1985: 108).[6] This disappearance of the actor (and of apparent artifice) is often a step toward a celebration of the "reality" of the characters: "While other eighties solo performers, like *Swimming to Cambodia*'s Spalding Gray, place themselves in the foreground, Bogosian disappears into his characters' minds—which look spookily familiar once your eyes adjust to the darkness" (Rosenberg 1990: 50).

The sense of familiar "real life" intruding on representation is the fourth reason for considering Bogosian's work performance art. As I suggested in chapter 2, the presence of apparent reality—autobiographical material, here-and-now event, or "real-time" structure—is the clearest identifying mark of the bulk of what is called performance art. While Bogosian's early "7 Americans in 7 Minutes" introduced the formal quality of a real-time structure, his later work draws on the sense of "magic" discussed above to evoke a documentary quality in the depiction of fictional characters. "His intent, his manifest talent, has pushed the form to frontiers more rooted in the real. He has infused in his disturbing collection of characters a knowing verity that makes what they say and do all the more chilling" (Carter 1987: 168). This sense of "knowing verity" in Bogosian's creations, especially his working-class ethnics and street characters, has led some critics virtually to mistake representation for the real. Bogosian is continually credited with exposing hidden aspects of society, revealing the very thoughts of people ranging from drug addicts to corporate big shots. Paradoxically, the "reality" of his presentations is valued precisely *because* they are fictional creations—once again, the aesthetics of performance art and realist theater brush against one another. One critic claimed that *Sex, Drugs, Rock & Roll* "cuts so close to the bone that the borderline between theater and the world outside seems almost nonexistent at times. Yet this is entertainment" (Watt 1990b: 384). While Gray is credited for transforming his real life into art, Bogosian is lauded for transforming his art into seemingly real lives.[7] Frank Rich offers Bogosian perhaps the highest honor the *Times* can bestow: "The highly original writing in *Sex, Drugs, Rock & Roll* is realer than journalism" (1990: 386). Even a liberal reader of Rich's paper might find that this favorable comparison to journalism inadvertently damns with faint praise.

THE PROXIMATE OTHER

If there is a subtle shamanic quality to Bogosian's work, the shaman is also ethnographer, for the focus of his performances, and certainly of many of his positive reviews, is on the investigation/representation of cultural "others." To a degree, of course, this is true of all character acting; what is desired is a coherent and convincing (realer than journalism) representation of something not well or entirely known by the audience. In general, this is true of ethnography as well. The pleasures I associate with the most conservative, traditional ethnographic writing lie in seeing one's own cultural position as the unexamined center, naturalized and validated by its capacity to catalogue curious differences. Arguably this is abetted in my viewing experience by the identity privilege I share with the ethnographer/performer. The unexamined center is not *simply* straight, white, and male, of course, but it is that; further, the habit of consuming difference is a prominent characteristic of identity privilege within contemporary "multicultural" economies.

The difference between Bogosian and most of his characters, however, does not seem so great as that between a stereotypical ethnographer and his native informant. With the exception of the Brit from *Sex, Drugs, Rock & Roll*, Bogosian does not play characters from non-U.S. cultures; he only occasionally plays other races (less and less in his later works); and I have never seen him play women or explicitly gay men. In attempting to "type" his characters, what first comes to mind is a certain range of ethnicities that occur most often. Actually, the "typical" Bogosian character is perhaps a white homeless man of unidentifiable ethnic background. Such characters (from one point of view) arguably differ from Bogosian only along lines of class and social status.

It is perhaps most accurate to say not that Bogosian expropriates characters from points far distant from himself or his audience, but that his very appeal lies in his representation of *proximate* others. I borrow my use of "proximate" from Jonathan Dollimore.

> Within metaphysical constructions of the Other what is typically occluded is the significance of the *proximate*—i.e., that which is (1) adja-

cent and *thereby* related temporally or spatially, or (2) that which is approaching (again either temporally or spatially) . . . (3) the opposite of *remote* or *ultimate* . . . the proximate is often constructed as the other, and in a process which facilitates displacement. But the proximate is also what enables a tracking-back of the "other" into the "same." I call this transgressive reinscription, which . . . may be regarded as the return of the repressed and/or the suppressed and/or the displaced via the proximate. (Dollimore 1991: 33)

Earlier, I called homeless men "specters" from which Bogosian's most privileged characters flee (this is the literal plot of "Rash Final," an "orphaned" monologue Bogosian includes as an Appendix to *Sex, Drugs, Rock & Roll*—1991a: 113–17). Metaphorically, the homeless must be othered by such men (whether in the piece or in the audience) because of their proximity. Rich's review makes clear the adjacence of real homeless to the theater audience in New York; the drugged artist of *Sex, Drugs, Rock & Roll* voices the fear that homelessness might be approaching ("bang, you're homeless"). Constructing the homeless as other becomes a necessity, in that it "facilitates" both a literal and a metaphorical "displacement" of them from their troubling proximity. Bogosian's wealthy characters must displace the homeless in this manner. His audience is also at liberty to "other" his homeless characters, for they are arguably less captive than the implied audience of the subway beggar, and being stuck on a train with a homeless person, however amusing, is an experience unlikely to change the thinking of most New Yorkers.

The problem that confronts the "Same" when othering that which is proximate is that otherness also increases the sense of threat it means to reduce. In this example, the homeless become the locus of numerous other social fears, such as crime, drugs, and mental illness and disease, only in part because of their "actual" involvement with such problems. This paradoxical increase in the disturbing power of the other increases the threat to the privileged of Dollimore's "transgressive reinscription."[8] Othering, that is to say, can backfire.

Bogosian's representation of proximate others effects, or allows the spectator to effect, a "tracking-back of the 'other' into the 'same'." Even as his performance emphasizes the differentness of the character (which, after all, is necessary for the display of virtuoso impersonation that is his trademark), Bogosian also solicits an identification with his characters, as well as (frequently) a more analytic recognition of commonality. At the level of content, this is one result of attributing a special wisdom to the apparently "crazy." And to the extent that this "backfires," this transgressive reinscription follows the pattern of the model I have imported from Dollimore's study, as the proximate returns to destabilize the norms from which it was at first apparently excluded. This allows for a reading of these pieces as challenging to a complacent audience. As the reviewer I quoted at the start of this chapter put it, "aren't these people weird? said his material, and isn't there something of them in you and me? asked his all-out performance" (Howell 1985: 108).

Of course, the body on which this all-out performance happens is Bogosian's body, not the bodies of the homeless or mentally ill. To the extent that the spectator is expected to identify with the performer rather than the characters (as is the case with such virtuosic/heroic work as Bogosian's), the portrayal of such characters is literally the reinscription of the other on the same. In identifying with the rewritten body, the spectator metaphorically becomes homeless. Considered in this light, such representation is truly subversive, and the ostensibly stable identity of privilege is shown as weak, contradicted, at best contingent.

Yet because of Bogosian's remarkable, almost shamanistic ability to write the other across his body, the homeless (and the drug addicts, mentally ill, and perhaps the entire working class) become theatrically dispensable. Just as consumer-driven ethnography obviates actual cultures, favoring ethnographic representation, so this variety of performance may serve to remove any need to consider the presumed referents and their conditions of existence. "We" don't, in fact, even need Rich's "real-life beggars outside the theatre." Like Baudrillard's Tasaday, knowing of their presence in the jungle is enough.

COMMODITIZATION

This two-way movement of othering and reinscription perhaps helps explain the successful commoditization of Bogosian products by the mechanisms of mass high culture distribution, and the success of an artist Rich predicted was "too lethal to receive mass exposure." Another critic's description of Bogosian's work suggests that the disappearance of actual bodies is a factor: "[T]he material's mainstream enough for TV and the Public Theater; you don't have to be afraid to sit in the front row. It's in your face but not in your lap" (McDonagh 1991: 70). Bogosian offers performance art about the homeless in which spectators need not worry that the artist will physically confront them. Because Bogosian works within the proscenium, neither need they worry—as they must on the street or the subway—that the homeless will physically confront them. Read in this way, Bogosian's work bears a relationship to the homeless equivalent to spending an expensive camping vacation "roughing it."

Within this dynamic of sameness and othering, Bogosian's very success may feed itself, since the more popular and wealthy he becomes, the more similarity (at least on the level of fantasy) there is between him and his audience. The *Connoisseur* profile seems to understand this, emphasizing his ability to be both bourgeois and avant-garde (a connection important to my argument in chapter 6): "He is really a kind of *faux* bohemian whose success has bought him the existence he has sought since his days in Woburn—a safe, comfortable, middle-class existence" (Carter 1987: 169). Bogosian puts it another way:

> I'm on the fringes of an incredible industry—the United States entertainment industry. I'm like a tiny island you can't even see, a little island of sand with one palm tree on it, but to be in any relationship at all with the entertainment industry means that the crumbs which fall off the table can leave me in a very comfortable situation. (Bogosian 1990: 135)

I think this statement captures why Bogosian is such an appealing almost-star. He remains on the "fringes" of entertainment, a position that might describe the feelings of one set of implied spectators for the film versions of his work—"art house" filmgoers (who might accurately—if simplistically—be characterized as straight white males) with a certain taste. Seeing *Sex, Drugs, Rock & Roll*, for example, is an experience a cut above "baser" stand-up; it's about seeing performance art that still has charisma, comedy, and characters; and it's about seeing a movie (site of guilty pleasure) with the alibi of serious theater. In general, consuming performance art as cinema means experiencing an object whose value lies in its ostensible connection to the real through the pleasurably distorting, empowering illusion generated by the prosthetic eye of the camera.

THE REAL AND THE REPRODUCIBLE

Bogosian's marketability, the durability of his "presence" across documentation, and other questions raised by the documentation of performance art are illuminated by Nelson Goodman's elaboration of "autographic" versus "allographic" art. Goodman arrives at the distinction by way of an extended consideration of what might constitute a meaningful difference between an original work of art and a forgery.

> Let us speak of a work of art as *autographic* if and only if the distinction between original and forgery of it is significant; or better, if and only if even the most exact duplication of it does not thereby count as genuine. If a work of art is autographic, we may also call that art autographic. Thus painting is autographic, music nonautographic, or *allographic*. (Goodman 1968: 113)

In autographic art, then, every work is an individual and distinct piece, while allographic works may exist in multiple iterations or instances. In terms of performance, an allographic work would be that which may be "authentically" restaged: a play or other "script." A hypothetical autographic performance in this system would be genuine only in its original occurrence; any subsequent occurrences would not be versions of an original, but essentially different and unique works of art.

Performance art has usually claimed autographic status, a fact made clear by the common distinction between a live performance and its "documentation." This is clearest in one-time events, such as most Happenings. The question of repeat performances is more complicated. If each performance is a distinct, autographic art object, then what is the status of that which is repeated? Many Fluxus artists simply adopted musical terminology, so that a work's "score" could be repeatedly performed in Fluxus "concerts," and could even be repeated by other artists.

Simply borrowing terms from music is not really effective, however, in explaining what happens when verbal, increasingly literary performance works are restaged again and again. There may be, for instance, a script or transcript of a Spalding Gray monologue, but that does not mean Gray's work as a whole is allographic and each performance of a piece simply an "instance" of the original (in Goodman's terms). This is so because what makes a Gray work inarguably "authentic" is the simultaneous presence of the living person and his autobiographical reminiscence. Perhaps this kind of performance should be seen as allographic only insofar as it is the original author-performer who produces successive reiterations or interpretations. The performer in this case becomes a sort of autographic engine, producing anew each time the trace of authenticity necessary for the work of art.[9]

Performance art's will to be autographic is complicated by the necessary marketing strategy of rendering it allographic. Autobiographical performance is complicated by the questions of authenticity and of truth versus fiction; if it's the life (say, of Spalding Gray) that constitutes performance, then each "instance" of performance (each appearance by the star) is the work. However, since the record or copy of that instance is marketable, and since that record or copy might be made from any of a number of appearances under the same title, this marketing suggests that the origin or ground of that authentic copy is reiterable (allographic). The very marketing of performance art documentation thus deconstructs the autographic authenticity of the "original" performance, and so in turn undermines the supposed value of the record or copy.

The body and thus identity are implicated in the tension between autographic and allographic performance. For instance, one factor in the relative difficulty performers of color have experienced in marketing their work (creating allographs) might be the racist and essentialist tendency of mainstream culture to value people of color for authentic *specificity*, while valuing whites (especially men) for their *universal* authenticity. That is, the content produced from within the white male subject is seen as universally applicable (allographic), while the content produced from within more marginalized identities is seen as restricted in its application, its meaning bound to its performance by "specific" bodies (that is, autographic). To return to Goodman's forgery test, "universal" experience is meaningful even if imperfectly copied (by those marginalized identities who aspire to privileged subjectivity), while "specific" (raced, gendered, etc.) experience cannot be meaningfully reproduced, but only autographically performed. Spalding Gray's achievement in this schema is his creation of relatively autographic performance from an allographic/colonial position.

While it may seem at first that this distinction has much to do with work like Gray's and little to do with work like Bogosian's, the secular shamanism (that is, the virtuoso acting) of Bogosian's work does offer itself as autographic: each performance is intensely unique and "in the moment"—and hence unrepeatable.[10] How then to explain the peculiar pleasures of consuming Bogosian's work on film? In part, this can be attributed (as I suggested) to the additional aestheticizing function of cinema, pleasurable in and of itself. But I think there must be another element, that there is a lingering trace (there need be no distinction between a real and an imaginary trace) of the "authenticity," the "real" presence of the live performance. Of course, since the performance displaces its possible referents, this trace is the trace of fiction. Nevertheless, the failed adaptation of *Funhouse* for television I will discuss next demonstrates the degree to which that trace of the real is the prerequisite for successful documentation of such work.

The adaptation of *Funhouse* for television also offers a particularly clear opening into issues of representation and identity important in all Bogosian's work. "The underside of the American Dream" is how the voice-over described Bogosian's 1987 appearance on PBS's *Alive from Off Center*. In that performance of *Funhouse*, Bogosian delivers monologues as a predatory insurance salesman, a frighteningly nonchalant consultant in torture techniques, a drunken veteran in a gutter singing "God Bless America" and futilely asking passers-by for help standing up, a yuppie arriving home after work, and a convict facing a death sentence speaking to his jury. Bogosian displays his considerable acting ability, using a wide range of physicality, dialect, and tone to distinguish his characterizations, which are connected through the recurrence of the street location and the fact that the convict appears on the yuppie's television (at least as broadcast by *Alive From Off Center*). The piece reads as a cross-section of U.S. society—though certainly not an all-encompassing one.

Like the HBO broadcast of Gray's *Terrors of Pleasure*, the PBS version of *Funhouse* is an instructive collision of "art" with mass distribution. PBS, of course, represents "high television," and *Alive from Off Center* came to be its outlet for avant-garde work. While HBO seemed determined to convert Gray's piece into something resembling the pilot for an offbeat comedy series, PBS emphasized the seriousness of Bogosian's work, in large part through the use of frequent tight shots and slow, thoughtful changes of angle.

It was clearly necessary to cut the performance text of *Funhouse*, both to fit *Alive From Off Center*'s program length and to meet censorship requirements. To this end, obviously, the speech titled "Shit, Fuck, Piss" was cut. One of Bogosian's more memorable street characters, this "Bowery Lear" describes the city as engulfed by a spreading pile of shit, punctuating his narrative with "shit fuck piss" and concluding with the admonition to "FLUSH THE TOILET! FLUSH THE TOILET!" (1987a: 82).

Despite the content limits imposed by television, *Funhouse* was in many ways ideal for *Alive From Off Center*. Before the program's opening credit sequence, a short version of "Sitcom" (which comes late in the published text) introduces the show. "Sid" tries to sell "Arnie" a ridiculous idea for a situation comedy set on the different levels of an apartment building. "We'll call the show *Upstairs, Downstairs* . . . Huh? Who's PBS? To hell with PBS!" (in the published text, he says "Fuck PBS"—1987a: 91).

Aside from this bit of self-reference, the PBS *Funhouse* minimizes the media critique of the piece and maximizes its ethnographic aspects. References to media and representation are missing: the porno advertisement, the TV preacher, the exercise guru of "Make Yourself New!," and an advertisement for the "College of Cashier Education" are all cut. While the context of a mediatized society is diminished, the eccentric characters—especially the poor and criminal ones—remain. The "Shit, Fuck, Piss" monologue was cut, but the drunken veteran on the sidewalk of "Honey, I'm Home" remains, as does the raving, apparently homeless character called "The Pacer." In this adaptation the death-row convict that concludes the piece becomes the strongest indicator of a cultural dimension to the characters' problems, speaking over the yuppie's television set. Even the apparently overt politics of the torture instructor monologue seem diminished and predictable in this shrunken context.

Bogosian's ability to represent the disenfranchised and sick is highlighted, but his ability to analyze the context of such situations is reduced. Whatever the specific process of adapting the script of *Funhouse* may have been, it seems to suggest that the mass high culture market finds his commodity status in his artful representation of the other rather than in his attempt to assert its contiguity with the rest of society and its relationship to cultural factors.

PBS and HBO displayed a common anxiety about the visual interest offered by a single unadorned performer on a "neutral" set. While Gray's relatively big-budget HBO special "opened out" his piece with location shots complimenting Gray's narrative, the PBS series simply embedded Bogosian's body in detailed sets and realistic costumes, though the sense of "television studio" remains present. In the chapter on Gray I argued that the adaptation robbed the piece of its interest by replacing the referent imagined by the audience with one imagined by the camera. The effect of the television adaptation of *Funhouse* is similar. The virtuoso pleasure offered by Bogosian lies in his ability to suggest character and environment through pure histrionics, through the deployment of a remarkable repertoire of vocal and physical characterizations. The addition of sets and costumes weakens this experience in two ways. First, the increased use of theatrical apparatus to assist the performer in fact deemphasizes the performer's role as virtuosic creator. Second, the PBS sets, especially because they appear "theatrical" on screen, call attention to the conventions of character impersonation, pointing to the actorliness of Bogosian's work. The shamanistic quality of the single performance artist who summons difference into his body evaporates, replaced by the technical competence of an actor on a set.[11]

This adaptation is more than a document. It is the autographic object treated as if it were allographic, the interpretation of performance as if it were drama. The PBS *Funhouse* is an instance of one illusion debunking another; the juxtaposition of the illusionistic body with obvious signifiers of theatricality (estranged somewhat further by the television camera's too-observant gaze) demonstrates that the body isn't really so magical after all, that it too is haunted by Blau's "theatre, the truth of illusion." In makeup and costume, in front of a painted flat, Bogosian no longer seems so natural pretending to be homeless. In fact, this specimen would seem much more at home on an almost bare stage, in a setting affecting the same neutrality as a microscope slide.

MEET THE AUTHOR

In most of his work Bogosian has moved from character to character without any real mark of his "own" identity, and assumed each character with little visible comment. The effect is to suggest that if Bogosian is behind these people somewhere, from the excruciatingly offensive comedian Ricky Paul to the torture expert in *Funhouse*, he stands in an almost objective relationship to the characters. This is not to say that Bogosian agrees with or justifies these men, simply that the performer seems almost to function as one of Baudrillard's blank screens. This aesthetic is not precisely the same as the realist theater's emphasis on hiding the process of production, for the screen itself, Bogosian's body, is arguably present to the audience both as character and as the "technology" of presentation. The effect is thus nonrealist without being Brechtian.

One might account for some of the unsettling quality of Bogosian's facile character changes through the floating, decentered subject of postmodernism. Any notion of a stable identity is troubled by the multiple personalities displayed. As Norine Dworkin wrote, Bogosian "slides smoothly from character to character like eggs off Teflon. So smoothly, that the only issue sticking in our heads after an evening with Bogosian is the memory of a virtuoso performer" (1989: 68). What Dworkin objects to in Bogosian's performance is perhaps not inherent in solo monologue performance, but located in its customary "Teflon" quality of presentation. The ease and virtuosity of much multiple-character monologic work also removes from its reception the sense of the artist's labor, and masks what I call, after Bauman, the performer's "assumption of responsibility" to the audience.

Dika reads the presentation of Bogosian's character works differently. While she uses language like Jameson's to describe Bogosian's parody, she argues that the absence of a clear and specific ironic stance sets up a complicated formal destruction of comfortable spectatorial habits:

> Bogosian's presentation of his material is impartial, his parody blank. Never cuing viewers as to his attitude to the role he is playing, he may lead them to find themselves tentatively sympathizing with the motivations of a rapist, or yearning for the banality of suburbia.... In Bogosian's truncated fragments ... the performer/author comes intermittently into focus, breaking up the fiction, and startling the viewer into an awareness of whatever identification has developed between him or her and the character. (Dika 1988: 18)

I agree with Dika that the more abrupt character switches in multiple-character monologues may tend to disrupt identification between spectator and character. However, as I hope my comparison with dramatic monologue poetry demonstrates, the spectator is expected to read through the characters presented to recognize authorial intention. The necessity of searching for the author behind a blank generalized sense of irony, coupled with the remarkable performative presence common to the genre, would seem to beckon the spectator into identification not with the character, but with the performer. Such a performer, in order to offer multiple characters with the expected virtuosic realism, must assume a position of universal understanding and deploy a physical presence of universal capability. The author/performer thus arrives at a place of epistemological and ontological privilege, and invites the spectator to join him there. This hypothesizes Bogosian as capable of knowing and being anyone, and presumes a spectator capable of identifying with anyone. But again, the pleasure on offer is not of "becoming" a crazy homeless person or smug suburbanite, but of becoming, through identification, like the artist, at once unique and universal. The audience of the "classic" Bogosian performance might be said to see itself in Bogosian, but this is less because he creates characters like them (though he does) than because spectators are invited to identify with the artist's act of seeing. Those few moments, more frequent in his later work, when the author does come "intermittently into focus" may disrupt the quasi-realist aesthetics of Bogosian's mimesis, but they may also abet this identification not with the character, but with the author/actor.

AUTOBIOGRAPHICAL MOMENTS

In the "classical" Bogosian, the artist is present as the omniscient creative will behind the work, but not usually "represented" on stage. Occasional ironic references may appear, such as the "Eric" recording a beer commercial in *Drinking*, but for most of his work the basic distinction I've marked between Gray and Bogosian holds: Gray plays himself, Bogosian someone else.

This has changed in Bogosian's most recent works. In *Dog Show* (1992) and more fully in *Pounding Nails into the Floor with My Forehead* (1994), Bogosian appears as himself at key moments in the work. Interviews with the artist include clear references to his own understanding of at least one emerging problematic in his work since the success of *Sex, Drugs, Rock & Roll*:

> ... in the last couple of years, when I've come out and done something disturbing about a guy begging on the subway, it's like hardy-har-har-har. I hear horse laughs from the audience, and it troubles me. I figure the only way to get around this is to start talking a little more directly to the audience and dealing with the guy who stands behind the characters. (in Holden 1992: C13)

The effect, for Bogosian fans and critics at least, is considerable. When I saw *Dog Show* in Chicago in May 1992 (an early version that included some material from *Sex*, which had not toured there), the beginnings of this strategy disrupted the performance palpably. While this was partly about expectations being challenged, it was also due to the careful way in which Bogosian constructed his usual absence, only to break it. That break came in the form not of the "real" Bogosian, but of a persona who addressed the audience in real rather than fictional time. In the press, Bogosian described this as a development on earlier work.

> Dog Chameleon, the character Mr. Bogosian is presenting as a version of himself, is a variation on a character he invented many years ago, an "obnoxious comedian" named Ricky Paul. Dog is also a descendant, he said, of Barry Champlain, the abrasive talk-show personality who was the central character in his play and film *Talk Radio*.... "He's me, but he's also an alter ego." (Holden 1992: C13)

Dog Show evolved into *Pounding Nails*, and while the specificity of the character suggested by the above description waned, the structure of the piece around the breaks in character clarified somewhat.

The basic content is familiar, beginning with a show-stopping routine in which a reassuring doctor writes a prescription and nonchalantly cautions the patient about an incredible number of possible devastating side effects. There is a homeless man who fantasizes at length that he could "infect" a well-off commuter with a "molecule" of himself, a self-help therapist with a smarmy line of "inner baby" self-help, a drug dealer getting high with his stockbroker customer (this variation on the party-guy character has dogs named Harley and Davidson), a suburbanite barbecuing on an outrageously fancy grill.

Conveniently for critics in the audience, *Playbill* ran a feature on the unpublished show with extensive quotations and explanation about the metatheatrical moments:

> There is a moment midway through ... Bogosian, breaking character, advances toward his audience, a glass of water in his hand.... "This is also rehearsed," he remarks, picking up on an earlier announcement that "I say the same words every night—you're not special—if the place were empty tonight, I'd say the same." ... He sips the water. Slowly. "Very carefully rehearsed. Where I come out on stage and drink a glass of water—took a course in that years ago, at NYU." Sip, swallow. "Taught by Richard Scheckner [sic]." (Tallmer 1994: 33)

As discussed by the performer in this feature, "all that's about ... theatre. Going to the theatre. The show's an event, it's ineffable" (quoted in Tallmer 1994: 35). Bogosian is again quoted to the effect that the goal is to interfere with the easy laughter of some audiences, but the point seems to be as much to play with the conventions he has created in his own work.

Eric Bogosian's Multiple-Character Performance 115

> There comes a time in the show when everybody starts wondering: "what's he really like? ... I mean, he plays all these people. I don't even see any nails up there. When's he going to start pounding nails? Oh, maybe this is the real HIM." ... We passed that point just now. (Bogosian, quoted in Tallmer 1994: 32)

Other moments toy with the performer's identity within the frame, as in the character who introduces himself to a therapy group with "My name is Eric, and I'm a recovering male." Another instance is the young performance art fan who catches the star offstage and attempts to ingratiate his way into the business by fawning on Bogosian. The piece makes humor from his naivete, but also from his effective manipulation of the unseen artist (who is of course playing the fan).

All this estrangement of the performance contract, all these metatheatrical interruptions would certainly be expected to please critics with Brechtian predilections, such as myself. Bogosian has shaped the form and content of this work to create critical spectators. The water-drinking *gestus* both calls attention to the circulation of actorly presence and, in its reference to Schechner, ironizes the kind of performance theory that might inform that very moment. The later moment, with its observation of the passage of real time around the piece's theatrical time ("that moment has just passed"), calls the spectator away from passive identification with the characters and into the here-and-now of Bogosian's social commentary. The "recovering male" sketch, in its use of the performer's given name, implicates the content as to some degree his own, or at least reminds the audience that it is, after all, Eric who plays Eric. And the performance art fan segment foregrounds spectatorship, celebrity, and the risk that the political in Bogosian's work will be subsumed by its "cool."

From the point of view of what has become the common-sense view of politicized performance, then, this work is an improvement on the relative seamlessness of the earlier work. These specific instances of formal innovation, however, are not without a problematics of their own.

The easiest to observe is probably the not uncommon difficulty of unsecured irony, represented by the recovering male, Eric. As one who enjoys whining about how annoying the men's movement has become, I of course read this piece as a critique of the easy personalism of self-help style politics, and saw Bogosian's use of his own name as a complicated acknowledgment of his own susceptibility to such indulgent discourses. To my eye it was of a piece with the critique of liberal rhetoric to be found in many of his works. Simply reading the papers, however, reminded me that I have no privileged access to meaning. It's not men who are the ultimate butt of this joke, but feminism, at least according to the *New York Times*, which saw him as a "young man, battered by the women's movement," who is "seized" by "the forces of political correctness" and so even refers to his penis as "she" (Richards 1994: B6). If this reading is correct, then the use of "Eric" to name the character is troubling in the implication that Bogosian on some level feels emasculated by feminism.

This formation bears a structural resemblance to much talk radio performance, which in its recent form (far removed from the atmosphere in which Bogosian wrote *Talk Radio*) frequently uses "radical" personality as a sort of loophole to allow the expression of reactionary politics from a privileged position. Like many a straight white male "shock jock," Bogosian, bolstered by the hipness of performance art, is able to attack feminism from a much more secure position than the average straight white guy. In this sense, the monologist is positioned yet again as a social spokesperson; in this reading, however, Bogosian speaks not for the disenfranchised he represents, but for the privileged spectators he addresses.

I still prefer my first reading over that of the paper of record, and it is hardly fair to hold Bogosian responsible for the politics of his reviewers. Still, this example indicates that reflexive form is no guarantee of progressive content, and may even work against that content. Indeed, for those who read the moment as Richards did, Bogosian appears literally to have lent his name to the antifeminist backlash.

But this is just a simple case of a piece backfiring (I hope) and being inadvertently "signed" by the author.[12] The other reflexive and Brechtian moments are also of questionable effect, however, because they make visible a kind of gravitational pull around Bogosian reminiscent of the force pulling all that surrounds Spalding Gray into his own celebrity trajectory. Intimations of the "real person" behind the characters do not necessarily function in a Brechtian or even critical way.

For while the metatheatrical moments of *Pounding Nails* appear at first to foreground the construction of the work itself, they ultimately redound to the benefit of the performer. Rather than effective estrangements of the monologic apparatus, these are autobiographical moments that betray a seemingly condescending attitude toward the spectator.

Whether Bogosian "means" it or not, the water-drinking schtick ultimately seems to chastise the audience for hanging on his every move.[13] That is mild, however, compared to the critique he offers of an imagined audience member stupid enough to expect actual nail pounding—and to wonder, "what's he really like?" After that, the ridicule heaped on the aspiring performance artist, logically read as a stand-in for the implied spectator, seems to follow naturally. Bogosian may have wished to avoid apolitical consumption of his work as merely funny, but his response suggests the ultimate in hubris demonstrated by so many of the rock stars who are among the intertexts for Bogosian's work: contempt for the fans. Instead of making the work more political—his stated intent—the breaks in character make it less so. For instead of critiquing the audience for its attitudes and behavior outside the theater, he seems led to blame them for the apparent failure, as he describes it, of his own work.

This dynamic is made painfully clear in the video directed by Rob Klug in 1995. *Confessions of a Porn Star* frames footage of Bogosian in performance, doing material from a number of different shows, with a *faux* documentary in which Bogosian, in a dressing gown on a movie set, plays the part of a smug porn star taking a break in filming to talk to the camera crew. These sequences, in which the character is occasionally distracted by undressed women who leave the set's bed to fawn on the star, fall as flat as the weak narrative frames constructed around the concert films of Andrew Dice Clay (see chapter 5). However, they are significant as a further attempt on Bogosian's part to critique the structures of meaning established in his earlier work. In comparing his work as a performance art star to that of the porn star (who refers to himself as "Eric Bogosian," in case we're missing the point), he calls into question our prurient interest in "casualties declaring themselves" (Siegle's phrase), which I criticized in discussing his homeless characters. A twofold metaperformance is thus set up in his late work: the spectator's search for the author behind the work is mocked ("what's he really like?" Bogosian sneers sarcastically in *Pounding Nails*), and that very "content" is metaphorically labeled pornographic.

Unfortunately, these disruptive gestures do not significantly change the structure of the work. The spectator's quest for the author's intention is complicated by Bogosian's enigmatic self-reference, but that makes the search seem all the more important ("what's he really like?"). And while viewers of *Porn Star* will perhaps give a thought to the meaning of the fact that they are fascinated (or not) by Bogosian's content, the crazy-but-wise drunks, druggies, and street people are still there, just as are the seminude models hired to establish the porn star joke. Perhaps inadvertently (but perhaps not), Bogosian's attempt to undermine the easy laughter of his audience comes across as cynical rather than critical, the contempt of a "star" rather than the concern of a "real person." And the nudity and sensational title of this video suggest that this seemingly reflexive critique functions first as a marketing ploy.

This seems a harsh assessment of a formal move whose ostensible function I would applaud. Certainly even the self-interested metatheatricality described here has more potential and is less self-serving than the omnitheatricality maintained by Gray. When I saw the early *Dog Show*, I noticed a wealthy white woman in pearls nodding along enthusiastically with the sentiments of one of Bogosian's rationalizing liberals, and a reminder that the artist had a point of view seemed timely after that. Bogosian has yet to find a revision in his monologue form that really works, but the tactics of *Pounding Nails* are perhaps a move toward performative vulnerability or accountability that would address some of my concerns about the ironic structures of such monologues. The next chapter even more explicitly addresses the straightness, whiteness, and maleness of particular monologue performances. Among the issues addressed is the risk run by such work of creating a hypothetical "essential Bogosian" (fittingly enough, the title of a recent anthology—Bogosian 1994) who occupies the imagined normative straight white male center of performed representations. This particular difficulty certainly seems to call for a Brechtian response that includes the textual presence of the author (rather than the authorial "presence") on the stage. In my discussion of Danny Hoch in the concluding chapter, I look at some of the promising ways in which that multiple-character performer keeps at least partly visible his act of "writing" a work composed of difference.

Chapter Five

PERFORMING IDENTITY PRIVILEGE

This chapter extends my comparative study of monologue performance, with an even more explicit focus on identity. I briefly analyze key moments in solo performances at the "art" end of the spectrum by Josh Kornbluth and Wallace Shawn; I look as well at the differently situated identities constructed by stand-up comedians Andrew Dice Clay, Denis Leary, and Rob Becker.[1] My examples frame sections that compare these performers with Gray and Bogosian to explore how the performed identities construct and negotiate the interlocking factors of whiteness, masculinity, heterosexuality, and class positioning. The result is a chapter that seeks to know this constellation of single stars through alternately examining them individually and calculating angles of difference among them.

IRONIC NOSTALGIA FOR REVOLUTIONARY HETEROSEXUALITY: JOSH KORNBLUTH'S *RED DIAPER BABY*

A popular, if often lighthearted, critique of solo performance is that it is necessarily self-indulgent, autoerotic, "masturbatory."[2] This chapter will seek to arrive at "heterosexuality" by way of a specific performance of sexuality in a straight white male monologue: a moment of performance in the second act of Josh Kornbluth's *Red Diaper Baby* (1992).

Josh Kornbluth migrated from stand-up to build a relatively stable career out of solo theatrical performance, though he has not received the same popular and critical attention that stars such as Gray and Bogosian have enjoyed. His monologues are largely autobiographical and often clearly address his experiences as informed by his identity. In *Red Diaper Baby*, he constructs a mostly comic narrative of growing up in a New York Jewish family with strong socialist politics. While much of the humor arises from the conflicts between the young protagonist's desires and those of his communist parents, Kornbluth also suggests a nostalgic sympathy with his elders. Ethnicity and religion figure in *Red Diaper Baby* in a manner similar to Gray's early childhood monologues; communism and Jewishness provide material for Kornbluth to both embrace and ironize in a way similar to Gray's approach to his family's blend of dysfunctionality and Christian Science. Kornbluth's manner is less dry, more in line with a stand-up style of anecdotal narrative, and his attitude toward the material seems at once warmer and more aggressively sarcastic. Kornbluth's performance is also much more physical, at times achieving effects through gesture or enactment that Gray would construct verbally.

One interesting characteristic of *Red Diaper Baby* is the strong connection established between politics and sexuality. The following is excerpted from a passage in which Kornbluth describes how his naked, talcum-powdered father would wake him as a child by bursting into his room singing the "Internationale."

> My father, Paul Kornbluth, was a Communist. He believed there was going to be a violent revolution in this country . . . and that I was going to lead it. Just so you can get a sense of the pressure. . . .
>
> [I]f I didn't show the proper signs of life right away, my father would lean down over me . . . and he'd go, "Wake up, Little Fucker! Wake up, Little Fucker!" . . . For my dad, calling me Little Fucker was like calling me Junior . . . Beloved Little One. Little Fucker.

> I knew from a very early age that one day I must grow up and become a Big Fucker. And I assumed that would be about the time that I would lead the Revolution. 'Cause my dad had told me over and over that all of the great revolutionaries were great fuckers. But at this time I was just lying there in my bed, and my father would be looming over me with his—to me—enormous penis swinging around, spewing smoke, powder, whatever . . . while I just had this little, six-year-old . . . training penis. (quoted in Berson 1992: 18)

While Kornbluth clearly solicits laughter at his parents, just as he will later solicit laughter at the young Josh's attempts to both live up to his family's political values and construct his own—primarily sexual—identity, there are also subtle appeals to nostalgia in this work. The more available is the familiar coming-of-sexual-age nostalgia, in which some spectators are invited to compare their own early sexual experiences to Kornbluth's. For many, the nostalgia may be for a fantastic early sexual life for which Kornbluth is surrogate. Another potential nostalgia has its own clear division among hypothetical spectators; leftists are invited to indulge in a nostalgia for politics (their own or their parents') unavailable to those attending a "post-communist" performance in which socialist fervor is simply the central butt of the performance's jokes. Further, while there is no doubt that Kornbluth mocks his father's connection of fucking to revolution, the structure of the performance may create such a nostalgic fusion for straight male leftists in the audience: a longing for a time of uncomplicated sex and politics that never was.

Late in this story, Kornbluth recounts the lessons he received from Marcie, an unhappy housewife who taught him to crochet and have sex. Kornbluth mimes along with his narrative, performing sex acts on the body of the classically absent woman. This leads to the profoundly homosocial episode in which Kornbluth performs cunnilingus on the fourth wall; all that separates him from the guffawing men in the audience is the thinnest caricature of a woman's desire. He then enacts his lover's orgasm with his own body, creating a complex comic structure that seemed well appreciated by much of the audience at the show I attended (in New York City's Actor's Playhouse).

On the surface, the joke is how ridiculous Kornbluth appears while doing this impersonation. Beneath that is the misogynist humor at the woman's expense. Finally, I detect a shared laughter of male hetero/sexist community, for this representation, this solo performance of heterosex,

Andrew Dice Clay

Josh Kornbluth

Rob Becker

goes beyond the classic sexual structures of Hollywood film and realist dramatic narrative and manages to do away with the woman altogether. Because of this collapse, this performance cannot really be called heterosexual, though neither, of course, can it be properly termed homosexual. Finally, with no insult to masturbatory pleasure intended, this sex is best termed "monosexual" (though of course the movements of power through sexual, spectatorial, and theatrical apparati are of social rather than individual import). A central contention of my argument about this genre of white male monologues is that Kornbluth merely literalizes what his colleagues repeatedly enact metaphorically.

THE "DEVIANT" NORM OF "STRAIGHT" THEATER FORM

> [T]he "reality" of heterosexual identities is performatively constituted through an imitation that sets itself up as the origin and the ground of all imitations. In other words, heterosexuality is always in the process of imitating and approximating its own phantasmatic idealization of itself—*and failing*. Precisely because it is bound to fail, and yet endeavors to succeed, the project of heterosexual identity is propelled into an endless repetition of itself. Indeed, in its efforts to naturalize itself as the original, heterosexuality must be understood as a compulsive and compulsory repetition that can only produce the *effect* of its own originality; in other words, compulsory heterosexual identities, those ontologically consolidated phantasms of "man" and "woman," are theatrically produced effects that posture as grounds, origins, the normative measure of the real. (Butler 1991: 21)

Straight white male solo performers tend self-assuredly to demonstrate the self-reassuring stratagems of male heterosexuality. In the recent Dolly Parton film *Straight Talk*, in which Spalding Gray makes a cameo appearance as Parton's rival radio psychologist, Parton's character is seen as the superior, more helpful of the two, because she offers "straight talk" rather than psycho-jargon. In the two subgenres of solo live performance I discussed in chapters 3 and 4, Gray and Bogosian establish two distinct aesthetics of "telling it like it is"—Gray about himself, and Bogosian, in his most typical works, about the "other." They can be counted on for "straight talk" in another sense; Bogosian, Gray, and most of the performers discussed in this chapter articulate common ways for white bourgeois males to perform heterosexuality. Heterosexuality and het sex are not simply occasional topics of the monologues; these performers invariably speak heterosexuality and, through diverse formal means, construct different facets of straight culture's figure of white male normalcy. This figure of normalcy in part involves the construction of a (slightly) deviant chic, a gleam of difference. One can be "hip," they suggest, and still be "normal."³

On the other hand, the liberal doses of irony applied to all of their narratives and characterizations *imply* a critical stance on the part of the performers; these performances can "pass" for critical engagement with one's social position. This amounts to "inoculation," which consists, to paraphrase Barthes, in

> admitting the accidental evil of [a sexist or heterosexist] institution the better to conceal its principle evil. One immunizes the contents of the collective imagination by means of a small inoculation of acknowledged evil; one thus protects it against the risk of a generalized subversion. (Barthes 1972: 150)⁴

These monologues do invite the spectator to laugh at or even disapprove of some of the most glaring "evils" of heterosexism, but this has the effect Barthes cautions against: to conceal the founding inequities of heterosexual culture and their participation in it. And evil, of course, is too strong a term for what is "admitted" in these performances. Because their structure is primarily comic, such performances inoculate against a critique of heterosexist evil by introducing a humorous critique of the silliness of sex (almost exclusively understood as heterosexual).

Their pose of critical irony and their intriguing hint of deviance notwithstanding, these works fetishize and reify normative male heterosexuality. For well-behaved spectators (for hypothetical, or implied, straight white male spectators), the centering of heterosexual desire is determined by form, by function, by design, and by default.

The most telling formal qualities of performative male heterosexuality lie in the performer-audience relationship. These monologues take certain risks for dramatic effect, but always maintain the performer's body in a relatively invulnerable place, and offer that body to the audience in only the most restrained and convention-bound ways. This is partly because they deploy remarkable performative presence while simultaneously appearing to comment ironically on that presence. If "heterosexuality" is a bit too precise a term for this formal security, it might at least be called "straight." A bodily presence secured by both relatively conventional theatrics and a careful irony is necessary within the homophobic conventions of Western performance. As I will argue later, the implied audience for this work is universal and at the same time straight, white, and male.

One of Eric Bogosian's braggarts illustrates a heterosexual presence at once satirized and affirmed.

> Sometimes, when I'm in a bar, having a drink with some fellas, one will make an idle comment like "How does that guy do it? He always gets the girls!
>
> I remain quiet when I hear such remarks. I like to keep a low profile with regard to my "extracurricular activities." I don't need to advertise. I know what I've got. And the ladies . . . hell, they know better than I do.
>
> I'm not so good-lookin'. I was athletic when I was younger, but I'm no Mr. Universe. I'm medium height, medium weight. Never really excelled at anything, certainly not school. As far as my job goes, they can all screw themselves.
>
> But you know what? I don't give a shit. 'Cause I've got what every guy—and every woman—wants. And all the looks, brains, money in the world can't buy it. I'm "endowed."
>
> I've got a long, thick, well-shaped prick. The kind girls die for.
>
> You're laughing. So what? Fuck you. (Bogosian 1991: 27–28)

While the formal differences between this moment and the fragment of Kornbluth's performance cited above are considerable, both arguably participate in one familiar comic structure, which provokes laughter simply by a pseudoconfrontational centering of sex acts or genitalia. On the one hand, Bogosian's character is obviously comic, held up to ridicule for his fixation. On the other, the early Bogosian (unlike Kornbluth) never allows his performer's self to be visible, and so the attitude or intention of the performer must be reconstructed by the spectator. While his performance sets up complicated structures of irony and humor, for the most part Bogosian "plays it straight," and the characters speak for themselves. His work is governed almost entirely by theatrical convention; each scene, taken in itself, could come from any contemporary dramatic play in which the protagonist speaks to unseen characters. The thrill is provided in large part by the extent of Bogosian's mimetic grasp, which ranges in this piece from the mentally ill and homeless to voracious deal-makers to ethnic white street toughs; he can, the performance suggests, be anything. Bogosian possesses, as straight white man, an ostensibly universal body.

Spalding Gray, in contrast, always enacts himself in his monologues. Here the spectacle is one of vulnerability, of a performer who seems to invite us to know him completely. His mesmerizing gaze and voice are seductive in a theater, and even more so in cinematic close-up. For a time, his highly theatrical presentation of apparently actual experience tended to confuse drama critics. For example, there was some speculation in the New York press over whether, for Obie award purposes, the 1991 monologue *Monster in a Box* could be considered a "straight play." Nevertheless, even if Gray's powerful style escapes dramaturgical orthodoxy, it can still easily be classed as heterodoxy. A casual comparison with gay white male monologist Tim Miller's relationship with his audience—as when he enters the stage at the opening of *Sex/Love Stories* (1990) by climbing affectionately over the audience's laps—reveals what a relatively timid, if "straightforward," manner Gray adopts. In comparison, Kornbluth's mimed cunnilingus might seem theatrically "braver" than Gray's much less physical narration, but it nevertheless limits his own vulnerability to the comic facial expressions seen through the objectified nonobject (the imaginary woman between Kornbluth and audience).

In the following portion of *A Personal History of the American Theater*, transcribed from Gray's appearance on PBS's *Alive from Off Center*, Gray speaks with a charming, open smile, but also with a sense of reserve established by a very wry manner and rapid but carefully controlled delivery.

> I was having my first really sensual affair with my first sensuous girlfriend, during *The Misanthrope*.... We'd make love in front of the fireplace, and there was no furniture in the apartment at all, I just had a little mattress we'd put on the floor, two straight-backed chairs. We'd make love drinking sparkling rosé out of hollow-stemmed champagne glasses, listening to uh Samuel Barber's uh violin concerto. And I remember I guess I spent all my money on the sparkling rosé so I didn't have any money for firewood. So after *The Misanthrope* was over, I had them knock down the set and bring it over and pile it in the corner of the apartment and we made love in front of the burning *Misanthrope* set. And then one cold evening we ran out of *Misanthrope* set and I can remember jumping up, naked, and busting up the last two straight-

backed chairs and throwing them on the fireplace and we made love in front of the burning chairs. And shortly after that we uh, we broke up.

The mock-heroic narrative of sexual performance manages to be simultaneously both "mock" and actually heroic; Gray enacts both comic and "straight" man. Kornbluth's performance of het sex is structurally similar. Though he seems to emphasize further the apparent unlikeliness of his stage persona's heroic adventure, Kornbluth like Gray invites the hypothetical straight male spectator to see himself as sexually normal (yet heroic) through a simultaneous identification with and distantiation from the character on stage.

My examples show these performers in their most direct engagements with heterosex; they present an ironized heterosexuality that nevertheless establishes the het context of the performance and suggests that a more normative heterosexual understanding lies behind the performance. This deployment of irony allows the performer to sacrifice a certain excessive heterosexuality (in Gray's case, it is even his "own" excess) and still suggest a "normal" author-presence behind the act.

The oral sex soliloquy in Kornbluth's performance is part of a body of work much like Gray's, in that it is autobiographical and so "sacrifices" or ironizes his "own" experience. Kornbluth's work also resembles Bogosian's, however, in that it is more mimetic or dramatic than narrative. Bogosian uses no narration and so must provide the necessary exposition for each character piece through conventional dramatic means. While Kornbluth does use first person narration (like Gray, primarily in the past tense but occasionally in the present), he also enacts situations much more fully than Gray, tending to inhabit dramatic moments longer before resuming a narrative voice (while Gray's typical structure involves simple gestures and brief quotations). In one sense, then, Kornbluth is more theatrical than Gray and less theatrical than Bogosian.

In the abstract, this suggests a performance mode that is secured by neither set of conventions, that is structurally riskier in its use of both autobiographical narration and enactment. It is perhaps neither "straight" autobiography nor "straight" dramatic monologue.

It might be possible to construct a reading of Kornbluth's work as escaping my critique of monologue performance as predominantly "straight" in form. One might even speculate on his construction of a performance presence that oscillates between object and subject of the work, and muse on the politics of unstable performative identity. I find myself, however, with little interest in attempting such an argument because the moment of performance I cited, which I see as paradigmatic of this mixed form, so strongly refuses the critical potential of these performance dynamics. Rather than embracing the risk of performing one's own subjectivity and the danger of offering one's own (vulnerable, ridiculous) body to be seen, this scene firmly relocates the straight male soloist as the teller of the joke, importing the imaginary body of the woman and placing her literally between the performer's body and the spectator's. And if this spectator is amused by, invited to laugh at, the silly faces Kornbluth makes while licking his invisible partner, this is mere accompaniment to the primary laughter solicited at the behavior of the comic stereotype of the sexually aggressive older woman. And rather than mobilizing the liminal, fluid identity implied by this mixed form, Kornbluth exploits this potential to remain in the position of subject (he-who-tells-the-joke) while shifting his body briefly to represent the object (the comically climaxing woman displayed in the next moment).

Whether one accepts my analysis of conventional and/or cautious theatrical form as "straight," it is perhaps self- evident that these performers function as straight within straight popular or mass culture. Bogosian and Gray might be said to fulfill for performance two of the most predominant representations of masculinity in our culture: rock 'n roll bravado and PBS introspection, respectively. In spite of their considerable charisma and individuality, they nevertheless fit rather comfortably within a number of such preexisting discourses. For example, two responses are discernible in the audience laughter captured by the audio release of the Bogosian sample quoted above. One is the overtly intended one: ironic amusement at a man so fixated on his penis. The other is pleasure in hearing pride in one's heterosexual exploits spoken so brazenly. This is classic stand-up comedy laughter; the same analysis might be made of responses to the performances of Andrew Dice Clay. As noted earlier, in her retrospective essay on performance in the 1980s, C. Carr juxtaposes Bogosian and shock comic Clay (Carr 1990; see below).

A parallel structure in a more neurotically self-deprecating mode can be found in the Spalding Gray example, or perhaps even more clearly in the highly disturbing passage from *Monster in a Box* in which Gray plays his own AIDS hysteria for its comic value, reacting to an imagined symptom on the body of his female lover, Renée, with a rabid fixation on the perceived uncleanliness of a "stage-door Judy" with whom he had a one-night stand. On one comic level, Gray's self-centered fear and fixation on one moment in his sexual past are presented as to-be-laughed-at. On the second level is offered the perverse and offensive pleasure of seeing HIV rendered safely theatrical, safely (paradoxically) white and heterosexual—this because, finally, it is safely imaginary. The male white heterosexual spectator is offered the pleasure of having it both ways: with Bogosian, he is able to both laugh at phallic fixation and to indulge in it; with Gray, able to both mock another's fear of disease and indulge in and exorcize his own similar fear.

Even though such works seem obviously to belong within traditional and emerging modes of heterosexual culture, to function in familiar ways, that heterosexuality is nevertheless always insecure. These performances go to some length to establish the heterosexuality of the performer-presence; sooner or later it is demonstrated in an overt way. Most often these displays of heterosexuality occur through the semiotic mechanism of ostention: that is, when the thing itself is held out to represent itself. Like the shoes worn by a dramatic character, this heterosexuality is both merely and much more than itself. This is clearest in the case of Gray, since his text is his life, and the insistent mention of his "girlfriend" in many of the texts becomes almost a mantra: Renée, Renée, Renée. In his later work, in which he occasionally seems to address his audience in a first-person stand-up style, Bogosian at times includes a comic denial of homosexuality. In a clip included in *Porn Star*, he narrates a dream in which conservative figures Clarence Thomas and Jesse Helms are engaged in a gay orgy, and then wakes up: "I think to myself [pause] I'm a homosexual. . . . I can't be a homosexual. . . . I don't have the time, I don't have the time for all the parades and everything that ya gotta do." He thus sends up his own (feigned?) homophobia, mocks gay political activism, and establishes his own straightness in a single bit. More commonly, in Bogosian's menagerie of bragging tough-guy characters, the same het reassurance is attempted through a grotesque synecdoche, in which the part (sexism) is made to stand in for the whole (heterosexism, which is, in this logic, heterosexuality).

I am suggesting that heterosexuality, constituted by its performance, is offered up by these theatrical performances with great determination, as something familiar from real life in an aestheticized and dramatic frame. To borrow from Judith Butler, heterosexuality, in this anxious space, is not simply compulsory, but compulsive. And because it is "bound to fail," this performance that stands for itself must be exhaustively reiterated.[5]

At the same time, the paranoid signification of het-ness seems misplaced, for these performance art monologues operate within a general or dominant cultural presumption of heterosexuality. Seemingly unconcerned by the inevitable presence of spectators with good reasons to spectate differently, these works simply assume straight readings and readers. The mythic, assumed, well-behaved spectators have heterosexuality as the default setting for reading any text. This is not, of course, unique to these hypothetical audiences. Outside of lesbian and gay cultural contexts, heterosexuality, no matter how anxious, remains foundational to our culture's epistemology.

Heterosexual hegemony relies on twin contradictory gestures: assumption and assertion. The anxious need to teach, to repeatedly perform heterosexuality, of course deconstructs its supposed natural status, but ideology is not necessarily bound by logic. It is dependent, however, on the ability not only to exclude the most threatening others, but also to recuperate some apparent deviance into the same.

These performances, like much of our culture, teach heterosexuality; specifically, they demonstrate certain modes of behavior appropriate to white men of a certain class stratum. A key operation of this kind of cultural production is the containment of alternative desires within the "mainstream." These performances construe "appropriate behavior" within a strategically wide range. The simple "artiness" of performance recuperates "straight" from its synonymity with "boring." Although heterosexuality *is* performance, the performers' willingness to stage that performance frames this *particular* heterosexual maleness as something worth looking at, while also suggesting that a certain degree of variance from an absolute norm is not only acceptable, but desirable.

The heterosexual depicted by Spalding Gray is hardly idealized, perfect, or wholly normative. Sex figures in his monologues primarily as an occasion for anxiety or dissatisfaction, and a common trope of his performances is the moment of bemused contemplation of some newly discovered sensual quirk. *Swimming to Cambodia* catalogues Gray's accumulation of nearly "perfect moments" on a neocolonial swing through Asia. An earlier monologue, *Sex and Death to the Age 14*, details all Gray's experiences, many of them bizarre or amusing, with sex and death through his adolescence. Bogosian's multiple characters display a variety of straight male desires, from prostitutes' customers, to men leering after women on the street, to rubber fetishists. And Kornbluth hardly embodies a normative male heterosexuality, since the joke is so often that he is not. As one review put it, "since he resembles a friendly beach ball, to which have been appended stringy hair and flapping hands, these feelings of insufficiency are meant to be a continuing source of amusement" (Richards 1992: 8).

The effect is to open out normative male heterosexuality just enough to reassure male heterosexual spectators—none of whom, of course, match a normative model—that their own experience of sexuality is "inside" the acceptable or "cool" range. Much of the ideological work performed by cultural products aimed at relatively educated straight white men is the production of such systems of difference that present little threat to the foundations of white, bourgeois straight culture.

The great irony I encounter as a spectator of these performances is that the body most desired is my own. Certainly I am led to desire myself, at least to a desire for myself, for a self-identity that is the paradoxical prerequisite for male heterosexual narcissism. I want to "just be myself," and I desire myself as displayed in the body of the performer, who is, on one level or another, just being himself. In turn, I sense the performance's desire for me, for the captive body of the male spectator, gazing straight ahead at a supposed mirror that purports to be me. When these performances "work" most powerfully, when they succeed in maintaining the straightness of my gaze (which constantly threatens to erode, to slip into a deviant critical glare, or into something else at any rate not precisely "straight"), the pleasure of this connection is heady.

For me, the vital remaining question is the degree to which these works engage in the critical examination of heterosexual privilege. While I think the majority of them teach male heterosexuality, they are not particularly involved in teaching anything *about* heterosexuality. Gray may unabashedly enact the confusion of a liberal U.S. American facing the incomprehensible in southeast Asia, as he does in *Swimming to Cambodia*; Bogosian may publicly criticize the National Endowment for the Arts (see Bogosian 1992) and reserve his most acerbic characterizations for big-money deal makers; and Kornbluth may imply a lack of commitment in current left-liberal discourse through his nostalgic account of his communist parents and their friends. All, arguably, express particular situations of an identity in crisis, but none of their works risks a full investigation of the markers of class, race, gender, and sexuality that allow them to function as the subjects of those dilemmas in the first place. Certainly, when Kornbluth relates his childhood understanding of the imperative that he grow up from "Little Fucker" to be a "Big Fucker" like his father and other great revolutionaries, the transmission of heterosexist culture is ironized and ridiculed rather than validated. However, this is social analysis at the level of the joke, and it is developed not into a full critique but into a slightly ironic frame for the antihero's coming of age to the applause of the audience at his invisible sexual spectacle. While all three of these performers catalogue varieties of heterosexual experience, displaying them for amused consideration by the audience, they do not offer investigation into either the causes or the effects of a culture of male heterosexuality.

When uttered but not examined, the reiteration of male heterosexuality, even when couched in passive, unassuming charm, amounts to an aggressive insistence on the heterosexual imperative, and its implied male prerogative. Absent any critical self-examination of heterosexuality, these performances fall back on the support of mythic but still powerful dominant culture; just as whiteness and maleness are supposedly self-evident, so heterosexuality seems to be. And aside from those moments when such presumption can be amusingly seen as comedy, or even camp, critical spectators may find themselves bored or irritated by the monotonous monologue of straight masculinity. The heterosexism of assertion and the heterosexism of assumption are both heterosexisms of anxiety, and while the performances treated here may be said to illuminate aspects of white male heterosexuality, they must also be said to anxiously, compulsively reiterate and reinscribe them.

THE COMEDY OF GENDER ESSENTIALISM: ROB BECKER'S *DEFENDING THE CAVEMAN*

At the beginning of this study I said that Robert Bly's *Iron John: A Book about Men* haunted this text. It is representative of my fears that universalized straight white male identity will respond to its de-universalization (by multicultural, feminist, and queer activity) by constructing a specificity for itself that seems to admit its particularity, its place within as opposed to above difference, but in fact constructs a "new" self-congratulatory (straight white) man designed to maintain privilege. This is not the place for an extended critique of Bly's work or the "men's movement" (both of which, after all, are somewhat more complex than the preceding sentence). However, Rob Becker's solo comedy performance *Defending the Caveman* carries the simplistic logic of male essentialism to its puerile end.

Since 1991, Becker has produced *Caveman* in cities from San Francisco to Washington, D.C. The show opened at the Helen Hayes Theatre in New York in March 1995 and was still running more than a year later. *Caveman* presents itself as an extended argument for male and female as distinct cultures founded on biological and historical differences. It is a comic argument (the tongue-in-cheek biography of Becker in the playbill claims that in preparation for the show "Rob made an informal study of anthropology, prehistory, psychology, sociology and mythology, along with dramatic structure and playwriting"). It might even be argued that Becker, strictly speaking, does not "mean" it (some of his supporting arguments are patently absurd, to comic effect). Still, *Caveman* distills popular thinking about sexual difference into a continuous, if not entirely coherent, riff on the inevitability and even superiority of numerous supposedly male traits and behaviors.

While the show opens with a video in which Becker and his wife Erin Becker perform comic domestic situations to a soundtrack of Paula Abdul's "Opposites Attract," *Caveman* is essentially stand-up comedy with a set. Becker, dressed in a Midwestern "regular guy" uniform of work boots, jeans, and a t-shirt over his beer belly, is seen in a Flintstones-esque living room of "stone" armchair, table, and television. A spear is his only occasional prop. While framed as an argument for his vision of men and women representing two distinct cultures, the performance has as a second structure the topical organization of the standard stand-up routine, and Becker frequently employs classic stand-up devices, such as marking a transition between topics by simply pausing after a last joke and then continuing: "Another thing...."

Becker's performance style is founded on the antipresence common in recent stand-up; he slouches, shuffles, and delivers his lines in a distinctively nontheatrical voice that frequently gives an offhand quality to his pronouncements. Lest the audience miss his point, Becker mumbles a summation of the show's message: we need to honor "the caveman" and try to understand him, rather than dismiss male culture as simply laziness and tasteless bad manners. However, even in the mock-reverential portions of the performance, Becker's expressions of honor toward his primitive nature are lent humor by his unimposing voice, posture, and manner.

The jokes are mostly familiar material about differences between men and women, and they generally produce a laughter of recognition in the audience. At times I could see one member of a heterosexual couple laugh and elbow her/his partner, only to be nudged in turn moments later. Becker received applause early on from women and some men for the simple declaration that "all men are assholes." This was echoed later on by mostly male applause when he concluded that women "are not hindered by logic" in their thinking—a qualification in some endeavors, an impediment in others. The show is male-focused, and pseudoanthropological humor about "male behavior" is a staple. For example, Becker describes dirty underwear left on the floor as "sacred," and develops complicated explanations for the male need to manage television remote controls. In many instances, Becker clearly scores points by appropriating "feminist" humor strategies: "The penis: sex organ, or birth defect?" On the other hand, comments about masculine behavior are quite frequently paired with parallel jokes about women, many of which, from my perspective, seemed less charitable. For example, in arguing that male culture has evolved from hunting, women's from gathering, Becker seemed to achieve a "build" in the jokes about male hunting behavior through simple repetition, while his ascription of feminine activities such as shopping and having conversations to "gathering" instincts seemed to me to increase in dismissiveness.

Men's movement ideology would of course critique rather than celebrate Becker's show, since it praises extant male behavior rather than seeking to change it. For all its faults, the movement does ask men to change, while Becker merely ironically asks that attitudes about men change. Nevertheless, the show does represent a sort of worst case scenario for the emotionalist hypothesis that grounds men's movement rhetoric. In *The Inward Gaze: Masculinity and Subjectivity in Modern Culture* (1992), Peter Middleton, who avers his own "typical" involvement in and support of the men's movement (1992: 119), raises important questions about what he sees as its founding theory: the "impoverished emotional development in men" (1992: 118). The result is an individualist psychologizing outlook that has little capacity to engage structural social injustice. In Middleton's words,

> Emotion should be a valued part of our subjectivity. Not surprisingly there are now many self-help therapy books for men that try to teach how and why to feel more deeply. If the problem is a lack of psychological development, then men ought to be able to retrain themselves individually. Men can be encouraged by a rhetoric that stresses sexual difference to the advantage of women, and therefore fosters a new awareness of men's deprivation. (1992: 120)

Becker, of course, does not even stress the need for individual therapeutic change in men; instead he argues that men as they are should be viewed and treated differently: "instead of looking at a man as an asshole, why not think of him as different?" While he clearly misses the one theoretical element of men's movement theory with any potential for positive social change,[6] Becker still demonstrates one logical outcome of that theory: men's different "development" (Becker is more biologistic) excuses their behavior as the product of naturalized sexual difference, and even produces a male narrative of emotional victimization.

THE KING OF ASSHOLE COMEDY: ANDREW DICE CLAY

Becker's assertion that "all men are assholes" sets up his plea that women should actually think of men not as "assholes" but as "different." The founding observation, however, could almost be the motto of a subgenre of stand-up: (male) asshole comedy. This work embraces masculine confrontation and condescension as its central value, and produces "shock" comic effect by asserting rather than ridiculing the behavior of the male asshole. (Though I will discuss only white male "assholes," some non-white comedians also make use of this tactic.) Rob Becker's place in this movement is as its philosophical center, its intellectual element. The epitome of asshole performance, however, was Andrew Dice Clay. As Clay claimed in "Dice Rules," "they don't have a champion belt for comedians, but if they did, I'd be the undisputed King of Comedy." The widespread view of Clay's work as sexist, racist, and homophobic would place the comedian on the offensive defensive: such critics "can go fuck themselves," he told his concert audiences.

The infamous stand-up performances by Clay in the late 1980s and early 1990s make little pretense to the theoretical or scientific trappings of *Caveman*. Indeed, in many ways they could not be more different. In contrast to Becker's antipresence, Clay's body-builder physique and vocal aggression clearly assert dominance of stage and cinematic space.

And while Becker cites the essential division of male and female "cultures" as comic justification for quotidian masculine behaviors (fishing, failing to listen to one's wife in conversation), Clay seems to assert the privilege of the straight white man in every aspect of the form and content of his work. In fact, the central comic strategy in his performance seems to be to overstate this arrogance to the point of absurdity.

The apogee of Clay's "Diceman" characterization was his blockbuster "Dice Rules" tour of 1989–1990, which *People* reports grossed more than $4 million (Abrahams 1990: 57). His climactic performance at Madison Square Garden is preserved in a document that is a curious combination of "concert" film and poorly-made narrative feature. My citations from this film will be offensive to some, but I have in fact not needed to quote the most outrageous portions in order to give a sense of the material.

The narrative film frame, titled "A Day in the Life," purports to chronicle Dice's transformation from a sissy/kid character (who seems to be conceived as a Pee-Wee Herman imitation) into the powerful and successful Diceman. The wimp character (which illustrates Clay's acting at its worst) deals with a series of thinly characterized antagonists: he rises one morning to be henpecked by a fat white woman (a bizarrely mixed lover/mother image) and progresses through his "day," abused in turn by a hysterical white male bank teller, a Yiddish-speaking man who seems to take out his frustration at being unemployed on Andrew, an Indian or Pakistani storekeeper who is outraged when poorly executed slapstick resulting from Andrew's clumsiness trashes his store, and a hysterical black male filling station attendant who abuses young Andrew for his own racial victimization. In the end, however, Andrew buys a leather jacket from a gruff older storekeeper (also played by Clay in bad makeup, silver from his hair showing on his ears) and is transformed into the leather-clad Dice, who returns home and gets revenge by first overpowering and then kissing his amazed partner.

The underwritten direct-address segments that periodically interrupt the narrative—featuring Dice and a hoodlum sidekick—make painfully evident that the narrative frame is intended to pad the concert footage to feature length. The concert film that follows certainly succeeds by comparison in capturing Dice as a powerful comic figure. In larger-than-life hair and a stud-covered jacket, Dice lights a cigarette upon entering, savoring the wild cheers of the audience. The film continually returns to lingering shots of an enthusiastic white crowd that is more male than female, though as Dice notes, "we got some nice looking hoovers hangin' out. I'm all about pussy. I live it, I dream it, I fuck it."

These and similar pronouncements are typically followed by cheers, during which crowds of young white men scream approval and shake their fists in the air. Dice's power extends to the many women in the audience, as when he orders a woman in the front row to turn and face the audience: "show 'em those fucking tits."

Kornbluth's coming of age narrative and some of Becker's comments involve a thread of content clearly developed in some of Bogosian's braggart characters: the perception of demands placed on men to please women sexually. Clay takes up this theme even more explicitly: "Up to about six years ago, women didn't even know they're supposed to feel good in bed, and then some dumb, dummie dunge douche-bag bitch writes a book about some spot up their ass, and we been looking for it ever since." These sentiments are echoed with remarkable similarity by yet another asshole comedian, Denis Leary, discussed below. The Diceman's apparent anxiety about the topic would seem to be indicated by his alliterative fumbling for the right insult, but Leary makes essentially the same assertion, in slightly more refined language, emphasizing that, lately, "it's hard to be a macho guy." Sharing such thoughts verbally constructs the same homosocial dynamic I described earlier in reference to Kornbluth's performance, as different as he is from these stand-up performers in some other ways. While the anxiety about female orgasms and the performance of oral sex can be read in some instances as a display of male vulnerability and in other cases as an occasion to assert competence, it also seems to hold a key place in a subtle narrative of male victimization. Even though Clay uses this and related topics as an excuse to comically dismiss his lovers' desires ("shut up, bitch" he says in more than one instance), the discourse also functions within the broader cultural construction of the straight white male as victim of new demands. The fact that most of these performers seem at least tacitly to acknowledge some merit in female sexual desire may imply some "sensitivity" in them even as they somehow suggest they are doing "women" a favor.

In *Dice Rules* Clay's humor follows a progression from purely self-aggrandizing bragging to the display of his own insensitivity as an object of humor (featuring such jokes about his own stupidity as buying his girlfriend a broom for Christmas one year, a dustpan the next) and back again. At the core of *Dice Rules* is the recitation of a dozen or so nursery rhymes Clay has rewritten into crude narratives of female objectification. Some of the rhymes date from earlier performances, and the film emphasizes how many of the spectators know them by heart. This is humor at its most juvenile, involving profanity and crude sexual imagery for its own sake, and building on the simplest of deconstructive pleasures—that of defacing the canonical text. The effect on the crowd is electrifying, as Clay develops a thunderous call and response pattern with groups of die-hard fans.

Dice Rules is one of Clay's "mature" works, and it lacks the racist and homophobic vigor of some of his earlier performances. In this concert, explicit homophobia is missing, and the structure of hetero/sexist humor is punctuated by what feels like a perfunctory string of racist and otherwise offensive jokes, such as "Thank god for Donald Trump or the Japs would own everything," a mention of his own habit of parking in spaces reserved for "cripples," and a bit imagining the usefulness of midgets as sex objects who could be tossed in a drawer when not needed.[7] The act ends with an Elvis-esque musical number and what appears to be an attempt to imitate John Travolta doing the song "Greased Lightning" in the film version of *Grease*.

Clay's work seems almost to analyze itself, so plainly are its core elements constructed as the expression of the "Diceman's" character. While one reading might try to trouble Clay's discourse by playing off the weak framing elements (in the documentation, the narrative frames; in performance, the inferior rock and roll), Clay's fan base seems to tolerate these elements as part of the ritual of consuming what they pay for. What they pay for, the loosely organized stream of audience abuse and absolute objectification of the absent female character, is in fact so pure in its foul language and so defined in its abusive image-repertoire as to constitute its own amazing formalism.

Most critics, of course, have not seen Clay's work as worthy of such analysis, but it is ultimately unsatisfying to explain his popularity by simply insulting his audience (especially its large working-class component) through recourse to cliches such as the "baser instincts" to which "obscenity" such as *Dice Rules* is said to appeal. This essentialist explanation might even be Clay's own, or that of other comedy theorists. For example, in the otherwise useful account of the function of stand-up to which I referred in chapter 2, Mintz falls back on such a naturalized connection between performer and audience. While Clay may perform as the "negative exemplar" he describes, Mintz also states that "to the extent that we may identify with [a comedian's] expression or behavior, secretly recognize it as reflecting *natural* tendencies . . . he can become our *comic spokesman*" (1985: 74, emphasis mine). While Clay does play both sides of this dynamic, the appeal of his discourse is not natural and instinctual, of course, but ideological, and the Diceman is both the comic spokesman and the poet (remember the nursery rhymes) of hetero/sexism. When asked to judge Corneille's play *Le Cid* (1637), the newly formed French Academy claimed that the pleasure derived from "irregular" works must be explained not by error or bad taste on the part of the audience, but by finding some deeper transcendent regularity that in fact ordered the work. While I prefer to look for ideology where the Academy sought universal truth, we perhaps share an almost superstitious faith in the power of artistic formulae.

Clay's performance in this period is certainly irregular and indecorous by the standards of mainstream culture, but its secret order, its unseen organizing regularity, is hidden in plain sight. Like Kornbluth's *Red Diaper Baby*, Clay's performances tap into a "transcendent" (ideological) truth: the objectified woman is the site around which an audience of men (and women?) can be united. This site is not necessarily a sight, for this objectification can exist without all the machinations of "the gaze." In fact, objectifying the absent is an even more convenient operation, since any threat to the masculine hero is kept offstage (she's sometimes in the front row). Clay's performances are even more nostalgic than Kornbluth's, for he harks back to a humor exchanged among men in private, aggressively acting it out in mixed company. Like neoclassicism, this neo-hetero/sexism constructs and adheres to its own laws. In short, when male solo performance, both "high" and "low," unites its spectators around the female body the protagonist holds before them, it follows Dice rules.

ORBITING THE REAL MAN

> It is always necessary for a woman to die in order for the play to begin. Only when she has disappeared can the curtain go up. (Cixous 1984: 546)

In no other performance form is Cixous's statement metaphorically truer, for by definition solo performance eliminates the actual presence of any "other." Working in tandem with the anxious performance of straight male presence is a continuous representation of female absence. Women must still occasionally be imagined, however, both because masculinity is so efficiently distinguished by marking a difference from femininity, and because of the tendency for heterosexuality to provide the motive force for the narrative.

In straight white masculine culture, any difference between (male) gender and (hetero)sexuality is frequently elided. In many representations of straight maleness, heterosexuality is in fact constitutive of proper masculinity. Various gay male cultures of course understand masculinity as a more fluid and variable notion, and certainly for gay men no one masculinity can be said to encompass sexual practice or identity performance. In short, there is a difference between masculinity and heterosexuality, but that difference is typically invisible to straight male culture. The assertive heterosexuality I charted out earlier also functions as the gendered content of these performances. Put another way, the use of "male" in many contemporary (masculinist, heterosexist) contexts describes not only a gender, but a sexuality, and the anxious reiteration of heterosexuality should also be seen as the anxious enactment of a normative script of maleness. For this reason, there is considerable overlap in the works I am discussing between the performance of gender and the performance of sexuality. In focusing on heterosexuality I examined sexuality primarily as an attribute of the performers that the performances take pains to assert and naturalize. This section focuses somewhat more on (heterosexual) maleness in interaction with individual women and social structures.

The necessity of somehow representing the absent woman presents less difficulty for autobiographical soloists than for multiple-character solo performers. Gray's recollection of himself is a present-tense reporting of the past; within the frame of his Homeric form, the storyteller is the only character (performer?) necessary. His women are for the most part narrated rather than performed, and his brief impersonations of female characters are usually presented as straightforward quotations. Kornbluth's more mimetic enactment of Marcie in *Red Diaper Baby* nonetheless relies on narration to establish the dramatic situation. Becker does use video images of a female "character," but within the monologue proper, women are either offstage past-tense narrative objects or abstract present-tense figures ("women are . . ."). A similar structure holds true for Clay, though in some of his performances actual women spectators can become momentarily involved. To some extent content as well as form determines the place of women within these representations. For example, while Gray's stories often revolve around a heterosexual quest, and so must frequently refer to women, often through physical description (i.e., the Thai dancers described in *Swimming to Cambodia*), Bogosian's cast of characters requires only the slimmest ghost of woman to retain maleness as an identity. In Gray the "content" of women is most often their desirability and occasionally their threat; in Bogosian it is frequently their irrelevance.

Bogosian's performances are technically dramatic in their entirety: all of the action is impersonated, none narrated. Four scenarios result from Bogosian's use of the convention of portraying only one character per scene (the pure monologue): (1) the limitation of potential dramatic situations to those involving a single person (various street people in various performances who talk to themselves); (2) the use of the audience as a stand-in for the character who hears the monologue (the condemned prisoner speaking to a television audience at the end of *Funhouse*); (3) the use of theatrical devices such as telephones to account "realistically" for the absence of the hearer (the wife on the telephone and the secretary on the intercom in *Sex, Drugs, Rock & Roll*); and (4) the miming of the presence of invisible speakers (the violent "joy-riding" monologue in *Drinking in America* in which the speaker slaps hands with the imaginary Joe).

Probably the most common of these devices in Bogosian's work is the use of audience as stand-in. None of Bogosian's characters speak to an audience as a stand-in for a group specifically identified as women. When the hearer is "mimed" as present, the implied character is almost always a male buddy, though in *Men Inside*, the character in the "held down" vignette speaks to his invisible onstage lover, Cheryl, explaining that his perceived sexual inadequacy is the result of stress (1987a: 122). The most common use of female secondary characters places them on the telephone, the intercom, or, occasionally, offstage. "Woman" is perhaps most completely absent in the scenes in which (usually deranged) characters speak to themselves or in which any audience is clearly irrelevant. Rarely is an unseen female character actually vital to the character's story. While this perhaps adds another dimension to the contemporary alienation Bogosian might be said to chronicle, it also has the effect of depicting male narratives as self-sufficient, obscuring their embeddedness in hetero-structured financial, sexual, and representational economies.

Interestingly, women are central to Becker's anecdotes and pronouncements, though this is clearly attributable to the binary gender system foundational to his performance. The irrelevance of women in his work is not on the level of content, or even in the actual composition of his audiences (which at the performance I attended was largely made up of heterosexual couples and some families), but in the figurative address of the pseudoritual. In its appropriation of men's movement primitivism and masculine celebration, *Caveman* imagines (and stops just short of explicating) a masculinity under threat by a kind of popular feminism; its remedy, like many men's movement activities, is to construct a sanctified space that is conceptually (if not literally) "for" men. That this is a tongue-in-cheek gesture complicates but does not negate this conceptual separatism.

Becker's strategy is closely related to a pretended critique of masculinity that offers itself as a chivalrous defense of women. Andrew Dice Clay later asserted that his work involved the construction of a character, "the Diceman," who was distinct from himself and in fact an ironic commentary rather than what Clay himself believed (Clay now uses "Andrew Clay" in his acting work). A brief reference to another Clay performance easily refutes that claim. That his Diceman performance cannot function as masculine self-critique is made evident by "For Ladies Only," a special produced for HBO's Comedy Hour (1991). Instead of an opening narrative, "For Ladies Only" begins with a monologue Clay delivers in a theater auditorium surrounded by a film crew and half a dozen cameras. He tells a long story about the difficulties with writers and producers that made it impossible to finish a preconcert short narrative film, and briefly explains the point of the project: to answer his critics by switching to "ripping men apart now." However, "For Ladies Only" is only superficially different from concert performances such as "Dice Rules." Even the metaconcert devices are similarly anticlimactic. Here, they include Dice singing a love ballad after the audience has left, an audience plant whose excessive laughter seems to confuse rather than amuse the audience, and a wild dance between Dice and a woman who suddenly appears from nowhere in the middle of the act.

Clay's audience is perhaps a bit more even in its gender make-up in this performance (and look to be of a slightly higher socioeconomic class), and he addresses more comments to men in the audience (made easier by the setting, intimate compared to Madison Square Garden). What shifts toward the male spectators, however, is not so much the objectifying (feminizing?) anatomical comments—his jokes about the men's penis sizes are mild compared to the rapturous imaginary description he offers of a front-row woman's genitalia early in the same show (as in "Dice Rules," he later asks another to turn and display herself to the crowd). Rather, the outrageous male behavior claimed pridefully for himself in "Dice Rules" is projected a bit more sarcastically onto male spectators of "For Ladies Only." Thus Clay dwells on the same descriptions of hetsex under the pretense of analyzing and critiquing masculinity.[8]

These jokes are supplemented by one-liners and anecdotes; each of the humor types frequently couples a pseudocritique of men with misogynist, homophobic, or racist elements. "Ya ever see the look on a guy's face when he cums? I never did," he claims. His critique of masculinity continually returns to homosexuality: a spectator with one earring is "half a fag;" two men Dice reads as a couple are treated to a nursery rhyme about men turning gay. Introducing the racist portion of his act, Clay claims to have "turned black" some time ago. He then does a short series of jokes about black men and large dicks: "If I was a chick I'd only fuck black guys." At one point he seems to make a claim for the liberating potential of his discourse, since he ostensibly gives the same treatment to all groups. His humor is based in essentializing those groups, however, and in terms of gender difference and sexuality, women are still represented as the passive recipients (victims?) of men's essentially brutish nature. When women are not passive, they seem necessarily to be aggressive, as when Clay, *à la* Kornbluth, imitates a woman "slap-fucking" her husband—simultaneously beating, berating, and sexually "taking" him. This description should make clear that this work is not really any different from his other routines. Clay's revision of his asshole persona into the romantic defender of women (the show's backdrop features enormous pink hearts that say "Dice") is no more "for ladies" than the men's movement is "for women," and his "inclusion" of two female performers (with whom he dances) does not significantly change the structural maleness of this solo act.[9]

The isolation central to Bogosian's multiple-male works and to Clay's single-character male monologues can be instructively contrasted with

John Leguizamo's *Spic-o-rama* (1992), in which he impersonates both Latino and Latina characters, all members of the same family. I would normally expect this family structure to naturalize the family as an immutable social unit, but Leguizamo seems largely to avoid this pitfall. This is in large part because much of the work's humor comes from the seeming implausibility of that unit. Further, the multiple characters serve to provide a sense of cultural context for each other. Thus, while each of his solos suggests a certain isolation on the part of the character, this very isolation or alienation is presented relationally, and gender, race, and sexuality (as well as family, law, etc.) are present as factors that constitute and/or mitigate that isolation. Leguizamo both critically and sympathetically charts the "dysfunctional" family, including a patriarchal father, a preening, British-accented son who imagines himself as a "white" Anglo actor, and a young mother. Leguizamo's female impersonation both complicates his stage identity as a normative male (further complicated by the characters' range of ages and even attitudes about race) and creates a female character seen as central to the social and personal conflicts illuminated by the show as a whole.[10]

While Leguizamo's drag might be regarded as an example of the genre of straight male drag that plays gender for relatively reactionary humor, the suggestion of camp about all of his characters tends to involve his female characterization in a more analytic comedy of a family in its social context. Most importantly, even if female impersonation in such a context ultimately fails to "really" introduce "woman" to the solo male stage, the staging of that very failure arguably undermines the specifically masculine occupation of center stage by highlighting female absence. It certainly does so more than Becker's offstage wife, Gray's recollected female, Bogosian's displaced woman, or Kornbluth's crudely impersonated sexual partner. Perhaps only Clay's aggressive confrontations with real and imaginary women, constantly referenced by the antifeminist text and subtext of his work, more effectively estranges the masculinity of solo male performance—but that, of course, seems highly dependent on the spectator.

If only the narrowest depictions of femininity are usually admitted as content on the stage of the straight white male monologue, masculinity itself is somewhat more broadly examined. Earlier I spoke of a recuperative "opening out" of normative heterosexuality. Again, because straight male culture tends to see (hetero) sexuality as constitutive of proper (male) gender performance, that description applies as well to the works' exploration of masculinities that are not strictly normative. Becker perhaps comes closest to constructing a norm: common sense with a little dumb jerkiness. Clay by contrast is deliberately over the top, not normative in the sense of typical, but perhaps grotesquely idealized—a utopian/distopian masculine.

Kornbluth and Gray perform themselves as characters who do not precisely match an imagined norm; moreover, these characters are thoroughly aware of that deviation and frequently comment on it ironically. *Sex and Death to the Age 14* and *Booze, Cars and College Girls* both thematize "manhood" and generate much of their comic energy from Gray's descriptions of his boyhood and adolescent understandings of appropriate male behavior. In *Red Diaper Baby*, Kornbluth's comedy is constructed around the passage of a comically non-normative protagonist through masculine rites of passage seen as normal.

Bogosian enacts an array of male characters who likewise differ from the norm. Unlike Kornbluth and Gray's autobiographical characters, some of Bogosian's fictions behave as if they lived that normative masculinity, or even its utopian incarnation, as in "The Stud." Bogosian's characters—especially the sexual braggarts reminiscent of "the Diceman," the working-class tough guys, and the business-obsessed husbands—seem to orbit an imaginary "real" man. The presentation of the multiple characters often seems to invite comparison not to other characters, but to a missing center, readily filled, perhaps, by the imagined character of the performer.

I have argued that the "disappearance" of the performer is constitutive of Bogosian's work; he does not actually disappear, of course, but remains visible (if not tangible) as the authorial trace. At the same time, however, Bogosian's characters do represent him. They are *Men Inside*, and Bogosian frequently comments on the process of amplifying parts of himself to create the characters. The implied or interpellated "norm" represented by the imagined performer/author, then, is one who is in control of his differences from the norm and who can manipulate them. In this regard the imaginary Bogosian is comparable to the performative Gray, in that both deploy their own minimal deviance to create performance.

Kaja Silverman writes of "marginal male subjectivity" as a departure from a specific "ideological paradigm" she refers to as "the dominant fiction" (1992: 12). Bogosian's characters, who are almost all less marginal than the male subjectivities Silverman investigates, circulate around this dominant fiction and suggest its presence. As I have suggested, the author-presence "Bogosian" may be confused with this imaginary man at the center of these somewhat deviant men. Gray's persona similarly hovers around a fiction, not least because Gray seems so acutely aware of this paradigm. At times he clearly treats it as an imperative, as in his attempts at "normal" sex or normal home ownership. At the same time, the hint of an author-presence "behind" the performing self again suggests that the "real" Gray—the one who "knows" normality—might fulfill this imperative. Thus, while these depictions of minimal deviance certainly do revise the hypothetical "real" man, they must also be said to reify it.

But isn't this inescapable to the extent that deviation always structurally suggests normality? Mustn't this be weighed against the positive aspects of "opening out" the normative man? In his study of all-male realistic dramas, Robert Vorlicky suggests that some recent exceptional male-cast plays rethink rather than reinforce masculinity.

> The tension created by the paradox of man's dependence upon, rejection of, desire for, and desire to be an "other" provokes some of the most startling, though infrequently articulated, personal dialogue in male cast plays. It is also intrinsically linked to a man's urge to understand and to accept himself as differently masculine, and thereby to understand and accept difference in others. (Vorlicky 1995: 17)

Vorlicky stresses that such progressive efforts are hardly predominant in the male-cast canon, and notes that this revision is most common in plays with characters who are gay and/or of color. But shouldn't the multiple masculinities created in male monologues be viewed as encouraging the "differently masculine?" Is this possibility supported or critiqued by Judith Butler's contention that "the body becomes its gender through a series of acts which are renewed, revised and consolidated through time?" This suggests that the performance of variance from a "dominant fiction" of maleness might effect incremental change in the represented body of the male, which is, to borrow further from Butler, the "legacy of sedimented acts" (Butler 1988: 523).

Of course, the difficulty lies in distinguishing between the revision of gender and the recuperation of difference—the "ideological effort that goes into negating and defusing challenges to the historically dominant meaning of gender in particular periods," as Michèle Barret puts it (1985: 82). While Butler argues elsewhere that "it is only *within* the practices of repetitive signifying that a subversion of identity becomes possible" (1990: 145), it does not simply follow that all variant repetitions are subversive. Most male soloists' variations might be said to belong to a limited repertoire of repetition. If their characters seem to enlarge the territory of the norm, they also suggest its most central sameness by the orbits they trace around it.

SEX, DRUGS, ASSHOLES: DENIS LEARY

"I'm an Asshole" is the musical number with which Denis Leary opens his stand-up show, *No Cure for Cancer*. I will discuss Leary only briefly here as a third asshole comic. In this song he sings about himself as an "average suburbanite white slob" who makes intricate plans to irritate other people. For example, like the Diceman, he likes the idea of parking in handicap spaces.

While Rob Becker claims that "all men are assholes," Leary revels in his own superior abilities as one. Like Clay, he is a super-asshole; unlike Clay, he does not so much essentialize his behavior and attitudes as celebrate them as exceptional.

Leary's style is oddly positioned between the shock comedy practiced by Clay and the topical semi-demystifying critique of other contemporary comedians. The most striking quality of his performance is his creation of an implied spectator who will be wounded by his critique. This is not necessarily the real audience, but rather a hypothetical audience that would embody the cultural attributes Leary lumps together for ridicule.

This is clearest in Leary's construction of this audience as nonsmoking vegetarians. *No Cure for Cancer* is structured by Leary's relationship to cigarettes, and even more than Clay he uses the act of lighting up to punctuate his act. He smokes aggressively, luxuriating in its transgression and wallowing in the imagination of what it will do to him. This reaches its climax in an extended bit about the electronic voice boxes used by those who have had the larynx removed to treat throat cancer. (Clay does the same schtick—briefly and with little success—in *Dice Rules*.) Leary likewise rhapsodizes about meat: "meat tastes like murder, and murder tastes pretty damn good."

Many of Leary's topics are standard comedy fare: jokes about drinking, drugs, working out, the 1970s, music ("Bring me the head of Barry Manilow"). While his act is perhaps no more transgressive than most, he manages to make the sense of transgression—especially of mainstream cultural sensibilities and "political correctness"—constitutive of his style. His attitude suggests a self-righteous and quixotic attack on the niceties of contemporary culture; however, this attitude is grounded not in a stronger moral tradition, but in a hipper and in some cases more cynical performance of self. In part this is the standard transgressive attitude of stand-up, emphasized by other hoarse-voiced performers from George Carlin to Judy Tenuta, but it's a curious mix of almost-left and libertarian-conservative transgressive discourses, a cross between Lenny Bruce and Bill Maher, the host of the comedy talk show "Politically Incorrect." Leary relishes his own contradictory position, one minute mocking rock and rollers who have died choking on their vomit, the next celebrating alcohol and tobacco. The "promo" spots he did for MTV sometimes featured "progressive" bits such as antiracist humor, yet his act includes casual homophobia (he rejects the proper pronunciation of paté as depending on a "faggoty" accent) and misogyny (as when he responds to recent lawsuits blaming heavy metal music for teen suicides by asking "Does that mean I can sue Dan Fogelberg for making me a fucking pussy in the 1970s?"). And like Clay he plays disability for laughs, relishing the thought of parking in reserved spaces. On the whole, Leary's pursuit of transgression as an aesthetic takes on a Machiavellian feel, grounded in no other ethic than the accumulation of presence.

It is very possible to discuss Leary in terms of masculinity and sexuality: he makes a few jokes about the men's movement, the new pressure on men to give women orgasms, men's macho relationship to their children. To illustrate (and celebrate while critiquing) the masculine tendency to repress pain, he tells an anecdote about his father cutting his thumb off and refusing to let his wife drive him to the hospital—he taped his thumb together and drove himself. In response, Leary turns to his brother and says "forget about being able to cry . . . we're not ever gonna be able to cry."

But while his act is about masculinity and heterosexuality, it is also about whiteness, though less explicitly so. Leary does eschew the racist humor that is a Dice Clay staple, and his cynicism prevents him from indulging in liberal platitudes about race or universalist disavowals of its importance. Rather, Leary effects a "positive" construction of his own whiteness (meaning that it is neither fully repressed/denied nor constructed negatively in contrast to people of color seen to be "marked" by a "race" whiteness does not possess). I am not suggesting that Leary's construction of whiteness is somehow progressive, merely that the absence of racism as subject matter—and indeed the absence of references to racial otherness in general—makes him a clear example of whiteness as an attribute rather than a universalized absence of color.

Leary makes two explicit references to his whiteness in *No Cure For Cancer*. In the opening number, he is an "average suburbanite white slob." Later, that very averageness or generality is particularized somewhat, as Leary tells a series of jokes about his Irish father. The discourse of Irishness features some standard humor about drinking, but also more original material in which the desire to put up paneling is seen as a uniquely Irish-American obsession (the anecdote about his father's severed thumb features a paneling-related construction accident, and his father drives himself to the hospital in a wood-paneled station wagon). While Irishness is perhaps the ethnicity most often invoked by whites seeking to defuse/partake in claims of identity-based oppression, Leary's use of it here is much more matter-of-fact, seemingly grounded more in an understanding of his identity as in part specifically constituted by ethnicity.

Leary's act is also "white" in less explicit ways, though these are difficult to specify without problematic recourse to hypothetical performers-of-color. Certainly his cultural references are for the most part generically "white" (Barry Manilow perhaps most of all), but the racial constitution of his act is necessarily white. For example, humor about smoking and cancer is necessarily different for a white performer than one of color, whose references to cigarettes would inevitably reference (explicitly or not) the specific sociological facts of cancer death rates and tobacco company marketing campaigns in poor minority communities. Likewise, while he never mentions race, Leary's extended comparison of powder cocaine and crack is undeniably racially inflected. More generally, rock and roll, whatever its cultural debts, is at this point in time a white-defined aesthetic that Leary translates to solo performance (as Bogosian does more self-consciously).

The point is not to decide whether Leary is "racist," but to insist on the racialized operation of his performance and of white performance more generally. The next section focuses on a reading of race in performance that is in some ways more traditional, focusing in large part on the white construction of the racial other. My reading of Leary's racial construction is not the typical white reading of race, which construes nonwhites as "having" race and whites as universalized because they lack the "mark." Whiteness as such is more usually constructed negatively, over and against the "other," and solo performance by straight white men is on the whole not exceptional. Whether as a single white character defined against difference, or as a multiple-character performer whose whiteness is constitutive of the universal body, such soloists need the racial other in order to be themselves.

"ALL COLORS COMBINE TO MAKE WHITE"

> It seems . . . that white masculinity's ideological strength and weakness, which might in fact coincide almost completely, inheres in the simultaneous privilege and responsibility it grants its other of defining what it is. (DiPiero 1992: 133)

If the performance of maleness and heterosexuality is marked by anxiety and compulsive repetition, this at first glance seems not to be the case regarding whiteness. For one thing, race is commonly assumed to be a legible and obvious characteristic, so obvious that it can seem (in some contexts) invisible. Further, most white Americans are not subject to frequent challenges to their racial status or its meaning. In contrast, contemporary culture is obsessed with gender identity and (its perceived link with) sexual identity. Homophobia itself takes on the character of an interrogation of gender and sexuality. Its pervasiveness mandates, among other things, that straight men continuously monitor their own performance.

If straightness is, as I have asserted, both a naturalized assumption and a nervously guarded privilege, and if maleness is an attribute apparently visible but frequently in question (especially in its normative and heterosexual version), racial whiteness is a quality that is typically "read" rather than assumed, the interpretation of which, for most white "spectators," is rarely questioned. To approach the question from another direction, the performative Gray and the author-trace of Bogosian exhibit little anxiety about their whiteness. Heterosexuality is always in doubt and must be shored up by assumption and assertion. Normative maleness is an impossible idea and must be guarded by a preemptive liberalization of that norm. Whiteness, by contrast, has a self-evident meaning that seems to be accessible to any competent spectator. "We" "read" whiteness almost instantly, perhaps without noticing that we do so. The white spectator (and thus the white performer) can rest easy about race, since it is so casually assumed to simply and unproblematically represent itself.

Of course, racial self-representation is not so unproblematic. The apparently low level of anxiety about race manifested by these texts is if anything more politically problematic than the high level of energy they expend because of sexual anxiety. White silence about race simply rubber-stamps the status quo. As Timothy Maliqalim Simone states, "The maintenance of a racial apparatus, then, may depend on its relative 'silence'" (Simone 1989: 92).

In short, bounded by the liberal and humanist assumptions of white performance traditions, venues, and audiences, white performers have nothing "to gain" from noticing race, let alone investigating it. Because liberalism must admit the injustice of white privilege to assert a fundamental sameness between all people, almost any mention of race within a white performance event might be said to undermine the centrality of white experience—if only because so many whites are made "uncomfortable" by the admission of racial difference.

This formulation of the racial dynamics of white performance is of course a repression. White culture is never purely white and always expresses other cultural traditions. For example, what I refer to as white American culture is inseparable from African-American and other traditions. Toni Morrison's *Playing in the Dark* (1992) argues that "Africanisms" have been structurally indispensable in many classic white American novels. Ralph Ellison's essay, "What America Would Be like Without Blacks" (1986: 104–112), shows how unthinkable "American culture" is without not only African-American culture, but also cultural traditions of European-American dominance. Despite the isolation of these performers onstage, their cultural production is equally unthinkable without (1) traditions of white power relative to racial others, and (2) nonwhite cultural traditions.[11]

Some conscious or unconscious acknowledgment of racial difference must inevitably appear in white cultural genres. This often takes the form of ostensibly unintentional "mistakes," like racist Freudian slips.

For example, in video clips shown early in Becker's *Caveman*, footage of black Africans in traditional dress is included (not long after shots of apes) to represent "cavemen"—structurally highlighting the whiteness of his primitivized suburban setting and "just-a-regular (white)-guy" delivery by contrasting it with a blackness racistly assumed to be primitive. In contrast, in the works of Gray and Bogosian, "race" (that is, nonwhiteness) appears intermittently but explicitly, usually signifying the mobility and agility of the straight white male subject through whom, in monologue, all history must be read.

Swimming to Cambodia is the Gray text most structurally dependent on racial difference. In fact, in its concern with pleasure and the "perfect moment," *Swimming* makes the specific racial exoticism of Thailand not simply its setting but its topic. While Thai women are seen as compliant and desirable, Thai men are alternately buffoonish and indifferent. More than anything else, Gray the character is in Thailand to consume race, to construct a blissful white male experience around the encounter with a racial and sexual other. While ironizing his fascination with the Orient, Gray at the same time exuberantly shares the sexual and artistic war stories of an actor on exotic location. Again, white female spectators may have had different reactions to Gray's narrative, but imagining white male spectators at performances of *Swimming* in New York's Performing Garage, this storytelling appears as a grotesque version of a conservative ethnographic paradigm. It is, in Trinh Minh-ha's words, a conversation "of the white man with the white man about the primitive-native man" (Minh-ha 1989: 65).[12]

Gray, as stage heterosexual, is of course even more interested in "primitive-native" woman. But Gray is also a stage intellectual, and this joining of heterosexual narrative with an aesthetics that seems to treasure irony, complexity, and loss produces a kind of colonial tragedy—with, of course, a white male hero. One example of this is the story of Joy, Gray's "Pat Pong girlfriend."

> When we got back to the hotel I realized something was wrong—because two basic intentions in making love are pleasurable relief through sex, and some recognizable change in "the other." I could never really see the change in this particular other. And why should I expect change? After all, I was paying her. And I figured whatever she said or did was just an act. Also I think it had a lot to do with language. Eighty percent of erotic love for me is the language in and around the event. But she spoke very little English. (1985: 104–5)

Even a story that seems to explore the complex difficulties of intercultural communication turns out to be about Gray's loss, rather than about history, politics, or even Joy's specific economic and cultural circumstance. This desire to produce "change" in "the other" is one attribute of neocolonialism. In conjunction with Kornbluth's enactment of sex-induced "change in the other," this encounter comes to seem paradigmatic of straight white monologues' relation to sexual or racial "others."

Bogosian's different formal situation means that he does not recollect "others," but instead mimetically represents them. As I have suggested, much of Bogosian's appeal lies in his virtuoso depiction of a wide range of characters across lines of social class, ethnicity, and even race. As the Jewish protagonist of *Talk Radio* (the film) makes clear, Bogosian's universal body can cross lines of difference many performers would shy from. Indeed, Bogosian's later work does feature a "whiter" demographic in its characterizations, such that one critic mistakenly announced that performer Danny Hoch (discussed in chapter 6) was different because Bogosian "austerely confines himself to his own gender and ethnic group" (Feingold 1994: 83). Compared to *Talk Radio*, one of Bogosian's characters of color, a rapping, raving African American in the vignette "X-Blow" from *Sex, Drugs, Rock & Roll*, is a less complicated or nuanced presentation, if only because it is shorter. "Sucker dissed me, man, he dissed me! I had no choice. He showed me his gun, so I walked up to him, I stuck my screwdriver into his stomach, and I ran it right true his heart. He looked surprised, man" (1991a: 70). While this character is actually less violent (at least in terms of time spent discussing violence) than, for example, Ritchie in *Drinking in America* or the narrator of "Stag" from *Sex*, his racial identification invokes a history of white representations of Black life. While Bogosian's white "ethnic" characters might be said to play on (or complicate) stereotypes of ethnics, or of the working class, Bogosian "passes" as these characters much more smoothly than as a black character. He has to work overtime to represent dialect, physicality, attitude.[13]

Like Bogosian's depictions of homeless white men, this character talks a philosophical line, in this case concerned with the notion of a mischievous, playful god willing to visit destruction on humanity for his own amusement. The implication—reinforced by the structurally parallel intelligent madness of the homeless characters—is that the representation is unusual because this Black man is talking about God, fate, and humankind. This echoes the most condescending aspects of some white Americans' "celebration" of African American accomplishment, relying on a racist premise to establish worth. That is, value is located in the ability to produce culture despite all that African Americans have going against them.

Surely this is not Bogosian's intent. More likely, the representation of characters such as X-Blow is meant as a gesture of inclusion. In her essay "Representing Whiteness: Seeing *Wings of Desire*," bell hooks critiques that film's supposedly liberal gender politics and its use of people of color as a "backdrop" to the white narrative.

> Current trends in avant-garde cultural production by white people which presume to challenge the status quo regarding race and gender are ethically and politically problematic. While it is exciting to witness a pluralism that enables everyone to have access to the use of certain imagery, we must not ignore the consequences when images are manipulated to appear "different" while reinforcing stereotypes and oppressive structures of domination. (hooks 1990: 171)

Representations such as X-Blow arguably traffic in stereotypes, thereby reinforcing them. And while the heavy ironic frame of dramatic monologue performance would seem to suggest that spectators view such characters critically, what seems available for critique in this vignette is not Bogosian's act of representation, but the apparent irrationality of a black street character who rejects a white work ethic in favor of owning a bigger gun. It is all too easy to imagine a racist reading of the monologue. Like Caliban, metaphorically "of color" no less in Browning than in Shakespeare (see chapter 2), X-Blow appears as curious, like a talking oddity. Of course, this reading is not inevitable, and Bogosian's racial curiosity certainly seems both more courageous and more complicated than Gray's simple colonial Joy. Still, X-Blow illustrates how easily the universal body can fail, and how easily well-intentioned representations of otherness can slide into tokenism and fetishization.

Perhaps these works are, after all, as anxious about race as about gender and sexuality. Perhaps this anxiety is just harder to see (perhaps it's harder for me to see it). Morrison describes the appearance of people of color as pivotal elements in white fiction as the use of "metaphorical shortcuts" into which white writers compress significant psychological and/or narrative events (1992: x). This applies to Gray's quest for health in *Gray's Anatomy*, and to his encounter with Joy, in which the language that constitutes his existence becomes also the barrier to his ecstasy in a metaphoric tragedy of neocolonialism.

X-Blow, who enjoys violence in the same way he imagines God to do, can be read as the anarchist/nihilist "dark side" of Bogosian's image of society (this sort of literal metaphor is exactly the type of construction Morrison cites in her preface). The next, equally boisterous character in *Sex, Drugs, Rock & Roll* might be seen as the other side: he is the luxury-loving, life-affirming "gruff ethnic" (white) whose zest seems both mocked and endorsed. Morrison argues for the need to study "the strategic use of black characters to define the goals and enhance the qualities of white characters" (1992: 52–53), a criticism I think may be applied to this structure in *Sex, Drugs, Rock & Roll*. But the character who ultimately is enhanced, I think, is not so much the white character who follows X-Blow, but the hypothetical author-presence "Bogosian" at the center of this performance. As metaphors, these black and white characters stage this Bogosian's "open meditation on the conflicts in my life" (1991a: xvi). This suggests that X-Blow is more the author's projection of qualities in himself than the representational pluralism hooks describes.

This does, however, imply another explanation for such representations: Bogosian's attempt (conscious/intentional or not) to represent masculinity universally. Logically, a claim to all maleness is reinforced by the apparent inclusion of varieties of masculinity. In chapter 6 I examine the simultaneous deployment of male essentialism and an aesthetics of universalism in straight white male monologue performance. However, this study needs to raise class more explicitly as a representational question before turning to a performance that does not so clearly produce racial "comfort" for white spectators.

CLASS PRIVILEGE AND WHITE GUILT: WALLACE SHAWN'S *THE FEVER*

> As for the world portrayed there, the world from which slices are cut in order to produce these moods and movements of the emotions, its appearance is such, produced from such slight and wretched stuff as a few pieces of cardboard, a little miming, a bit of text, that one has to admire the theatre folk who, with so feeble a reflection of the real world, can move the feelings of their audience so much more strongly than does the world itself. (Brecht 1964: 187)

Class privilege has of course been at the center of the performance works I've examined here, and particularly in discussing Bogosian I have raised class as an issue in performance, because he so explicitly illustrates the disparity between his wealthy and poor characters. However, because these representations arguably appeal to masculine sameness across class difference, they can be said ultimately to conserve masculinity without necessarily forwarding any class critique. Further, however "moving" the representations of other classes may be, they are still bound by the problematic Brecht discusses, in which representation matters more than reality.

Might my critique of the politics of straight white male monologues be answered by performance that directly treats politics as its content? A brief analysis of Wallace Shawn's monologue *The Fever* (1991) offers an example of political content and emphasizes class as a fourth identity variable that has so far been least important in my discussion of these monologues.

Shawn is not as "famous" as Bogosian or Gray, and this performance has not been made into a feature film. However, *The Fever* has been published as a paperback, and the performance moved from La Mama to Lincoln Center. Shawn has written several controversial plays, and is himself a popular culture figure, though not as a monologist: he has appeared in such diverse films as *Annie Hall* (1977), *My Dinner with Andre* (1981), and *The Princess Bride* (1987). His performance in *The Fever*, then, involves celebrity aura and other extratextual information in a manner similar to Spalding Gray's performance.

Shawn's monologue, which he began performing in the living rooms of his wealthy friends for crowds of ten or twelve people, is a rambling narrative of a traveler, vomiting into a hotel toilet in a poor Central American country, recalling his recent past: "I'm travelling—and I wake up suddenly in the silence before dawn in a strange hotel room . . ." (Shawn 1991: 3). A charmingly insecure figure relates his history of privilege and the contradictions in it. These are revealed to him through the anonymous gift of volume one of Marx's *Capital* and a trip to a "revolutionary country" (apparently Nicaragua) and surrounding poor countries facing civil wars.

Shawn's performance has the strict simplicity, the "doing without" of the archetypal performance art monologue. While Brecht marveled at the emotional effects produced by dramatic theater's "few pieces of cardboard, a little miming, a bit of text," Shawn uses almost nothing but text. Like Spalding Gray in his most typical monologues, Shawn remains seated in a plain chair throughout. Unlike Gray, Shawn has no table, no notes, and no water glass. He simply sits and speaks. This speaking has an ambiguous addressee, for while Shawn could correctly be said to be speaking "to" the audience, there is a hint of distance involved. In watching, I was reminded of the difference between the performance of "asides" and that of many soliloquies. The former, as rupture, often contact the spectator more directly than the latter, in which actors often seem to speak to the "house" rather than to the audience. The introspective tone of Shawn's material coupled with a difficult to describe quality of his focus in performance left me feeling as if I were being addressed metaphorically but not literally. This sense of not quite being touched by Shawn's gaze contributed to the hypnotic quality of the performance; the text has a seductive rhythm and a near-stream-of-consciousness structure that works surprisingly well with Shawn's somewhat self-conscious mannerisms.

This performance style supports the work's ability to draw an audience into it as story, without limiting its effect as real event. While the text is structured like first-person fiction, the performance is largely coded as autobiographical confession. This intimation of autobiography was strongly supported by the intertext of the New York theater press, which tended to stress the similarity between Shawn's privileged background and that of the narrator.

The basic structure of *The Fever* is its weaving together of three contrasting strands. Shawn's narrator contrasts beautiful, epiphanic moments from his esthete's life with anecdotes about the suffering and hardship experienced by the poor and the politically radical. The third source of material is political theory, especially that provided by the gift of *Capital*. In fact, Shawn's "play" would be of interest to cultural critics and activists if only because he literally explains Marx's concept of "commodity fetishism" in clear and memorable language. "For two days I could see the fetishism of commodities everywhere around me. It was a strange feeling. Then on the third day I lost it, it was gone, I couldn't see it anymore" (1991: 21).

In turn, the first two types of content, the narrator's experience and that of the poor and/or radical, serve as examples supporting the basics of marxist economic analysis. For example, a confrontation with the "book" of his life's mundane facts serves to illustrate the systematic historical process of the accumulation of wealth. "For God's sake—did I have to travel to a poor country where no books are printed in my own language—did I have to be cast down onto a bathroom floor in a strange hotel—in order to finally be forced to open that dull volume, the story of my life?" (1991: 8). Later, the systematic torture described early in the text is recalled near the end as the means by which "those who do not fear death" are controlled. Throughout, the narrator's growing discomfort and alienation—based in new experiences as well as political theory—are chronicled.

> I went home and I resumed my regular life. But I couldn't help noticing that something awful was happening to me. At first I tried to ignore it, or dismiss it, like some symptom you hope will go away by itself, but it didn't go away. What was it that was happening? I'd always said, "I'm a happy person. I love life," but now there was a sort of awful indifference or blankness that was coming from somewhere inside me. (1991: 25–26)

As the play continues, Shawn analyzes and harshly critiques his (character's) position of privilege in a way that is both refreshing, because so little contemporary performance is meaningfully informed by marxism, and disappointing, because his marxism is simplistic and because ultimately the emotional conflict that keeps the critique interesting overpowers that same analysis.

The Fever is a "white" text in many ways: in the race of its author, performer, and character, and in the race of the majority of its spectators and critics. Its whiteness is constructed in contrast to people of color, such as the revolutionary "follower of Marx," Juana, whom the narrator meets in a cafe in a "poor country" (1991: 24–25). But *The Fever* might be discussed as a "white" text in other ways as well. Its minimalist avant-garde "performance" aesthetic, for example, might be regarded as "white," as might be the development of the character from dry economic analysis to desperate feelings of guilt, of being implicated. Finally, in this country at least, the structural position of interrogating class privilege from the inside is easily thinkable only as a "white" position. Ironically, in his attempt to explain the arbitrariness of his class privilege, the protagonist seems to naturalize "race" as a factor that may, but should not, have anything to do with economic privilege.

> I say, It's not my fault that I was born with a better chance in life than the chambermaid. It's not my fault that I have a little money and she

doesn't. But I don't "have" the money the way I "have" two feet. *The money's not a part of me, the fact that I have it isn't a fact about me like my coloring or my race.* . . . Keeping the money is just a choice I'm making, a choice I'm making every day. (1991: 66–67, emphasis added)

While Shawn does not explicitly connect his racial and economic privilege (in fact, he seems to separate them), surely for most spectators the "choice" of privilege ultimately produces a guilt that is also structurally white. This is not to say that economically advantaged minorities might not feel a similar guilt. Rather, I am arguing that the class guilt experienced by whites is alloyed with their racial privilege in a unique way. The aspect of *The Fever* with the most radical political potential is its attempt to reframe privilege as an active rather than a passive state, but Shawn's audience is in danger of falling into the position of his "character," in that this vague and pervasive guilt comes to feel like an element of identity (hence unchangeable) to be forgiven rather than a symptom of injustice to be confronted.

One element that does seem to implicate the audience actively is a doubling of the character, signaled by a shift in Shawn's pronoun usage in this piece, from an "I" that refers quite clearly to the narrator to an ambiguous "you" that seems to include the narrator but might include the audience as well.

And it's as if a voice like vomit is coming up slowly from my throat. Stop! . . . No. Listen. I want to tell you something. . . . I'm trying to explain to you about the people who hate you. . . . You understand your situation. Without a place to live, without clothes without money, you would be like them, you would *be* them. (1991: 54–56)

This tactic seems in some ways most problematic, but it is also this willingness to include members of the audience in his critique that might make Shawn's work potentially critically effective—for some spectators. As a white male child of privilege watching this piece, my experience was that my history was inescapable (in a strangely pleasant way) and that the fundamentals of marxist analysis were shown to apply to my life directly and consistently.

That experience points toward the failure and the potential in Shawn's work. Because there is no recognition in the piece of who his audience is, Shawn makes the classic universalist error of assuming a spectator constructed fully by the performance. In fact, on the night I attended, I would guess that less than a fourth of the audience at La Mama really fit the "you" employed in the piece. At the same time, the universalist frame of this piece—sadly, the frame around most straight white male performance—allows those whom the shoe does "fit" to enjoy the complicated pleasures of identification the piece offers while not feeling explicitly "named" as the subject of the work.

On the other hand, that "you" did fit me to a certain degree, and had I not been so distracted by the incongruity of its general application, my interpellation as the subject of this discourse might have been all the stronger. Perhaps, too, I was distracted from the critical edge in the work by the concluding lines, which seem to both resolve and wallow in a sense of historical guilt: "Forgive me. Forgive me. I know you forgive me. I'm still falling" (1991: 68). At this moment, if "you" are following the trajectory of the piece, it is not even a question of whether the theatrical depiction of suffering "can move the feelings of their audience so much more strongly than does the world itself" (Brecht 1964: 187), but instead of what value lies in a seemingly cathartic sharing of more self-indulgent emotions. Of course, the ironic tone of the piece as a whole implies a critique of that very indulgence....

Could Shawn's performance offer a starting point for straight white male performers to begin to use their points of identity with other straight white men in a politically critical way? Could a hypothetical model for such performance be constructed by imagining a work like Shawn's, with the addition of a self-conscious and conscientious recognition of performative and spectatorial identity privilege as a matter of both form and content? With the subtraction of guilt as the inciting incident in the emotional drama of its centered protagonists? In chapter 6 I present my arguments for a pessimistic outlook in this regard. I want to emphasize, however, that I am not simply dismissing all straight white male performance as politically hopeless. I have pointed to potentially critical or resistant moments in a number of works, and *The Fever*, for all its flaws, is at least remarkable for the rigor with which it keeps privilege on stage as the topic under discussion. My pessimistic last chapter begins with an optimistic discussion of another performer, Danny Hoch, whose work is class-conscious, politically explicit but not guilt-driven, gender inclusive in an interesting if perhaps not perfect way, relatively nonheterosexist, and, above all, racially complicated.

Chapter Six

THE UNIVERSAL, THE ESSENTIAL, THE PARTICULAR, THE POLITICAL

THE UNIVERSAL BODY, PART TWO: DANNY HOCH'S *SOME PEOPLE*

D anny Hoch's multiple-character solo performance is marked by an urban hip (or even hip-hop) style and a highly contemporary pop-cultural sensibility. His work is also marked by both an explicit political commitment to the material and an implicit ethics of representation. I introduce *Some People* here not to offer a simple answer to my question in the last chapter about the political potential of straight white male monologue, but to raise the same question as complexly as I know how, about a performer whom I am inclined to respect but who is still caught in certain problematic dynamics of monologue performance.

Hoch is a young Jewish performer from New York, whose multiple-character solo show, *Some People*, was presented at P.S. 122 and then restaged at The Public Theatre. I saw it there in December 1994, under the direction of Jo Bonney (who directed Eric Bogosian in several of his pieces). HBO broadcast an hour-long version of the show in the fall of 1995. The work includes eleven characters of varied race and ethnicity, two of whom are women, in a work that presents a cross-section of contemporary urban life.

I went to the performance on the recommendation of a theater scholar I respect. As we entered the theater, the audience (mostly white and middle-class the time I was there, with a few younger hip whites) listened to Spanish-language music and sat in front of a mostly bare stage crossed by a clothesline holding a few costume pieces. The playbill offered some quotations. From Hoch:

> The street was there, right outside, so that's where I grew up. In a neighborhood where there were a hundred different languages, accents, cultures and foods, everyone seemed to be a "minority," even white Jewish kids like me. There was no real sense of prevailing "white America" because nobody had ever been there.

From Studs Terkel's *Race*, someone named Myles Horton:

> You have to be careful not to think you're somebody else. I have to say to myself, "Look, Horton, get as close to people as you can, but don't get things mixed up: you're white." You've got to recognize that you can never fully walk in other people's shoes.

And from Cornel West's *Race Matters*:

> In these downbeat times, we need as much hope and courage as we do vision and analysis; we must accent the best of each other even as we point out the vicious effects of our racial divide and the pernicious consequences of our maldistribution of wealth and power.

I found myself, as usual, wary of good intentions, but these early signs seemed promising.

The first character in *Some People* begins speaking in a near-blackout, little more than a silhouette. He is the Caribbean Tiger, a DJ. He's a sweet, funny man who gently mocks a male caller, then flirts with the second, a sexy-voiced woman (both are played by Hoch on tape). The Tiger's rapid-fire broadcast washes out over the audience in a lilting Afro-Caribbean dialect that's completely convincing to my white Southern and Midwestern ear. In the dark, even though I know he's white, Hoch offers me illusion if I want it, but when the lights come up there's little sense of shock or Brechtian alienation at the whiteness of his skin.[1]

Danny Hoch as Blanca.

Danny Hoch as Flex.

The next character is a Latino rapper. Hoch wears a baseball cap backwards and thumps out a beat on a black cube, part of the neutral transformable space crossed by that clothesline. The rap is a crowd-pleaser; the audience is both amused by and engaged in the bravura of unpredictable rhymes. The singer stops to talk to his imaginary "crew" of friends about where the musical "sample" should fit into the verses, what a record contract would mean to them, and about his girlfriend. Hoch illustrates the strong pull the sexist camaraderie exerts on the character, but also shows him subtly resisting it, expressing a more romantic, and perhaps progressive, appreciation of the young college woman and her goals. She inspires him to go to college, and he imagines showing up at Harvard with his record advance and being easily admitted.

The next character is Kazmierczack, a Polish handyman who persists in making laborious social conversation with an unseen customer as he fixes a stove. The conversation is trivial, and the basic humor structure is the familiar one of the immigrant's comic attempts at English, but Hoch projects a strong sense of the man's pleasure in stringing together words, in making contact. This issue is thrown into relief by Bill, a later white male character who might be put up against the best of Bogosian's obnoxiously privileged men. Like Bogosian, Hoch creates the comedy out of letting slip the stupidity that is the foundation of the man's very smugness. In arguing that all immigrants should in effect be quarantined until they learn English (so as not to inconvenience him when they drive his cab or do his laundry), Bill notes that some immigrant groups seem to learn English more reliably. "American Indians . . . they learned it when they came over!"

Other characters include Tono, a suave Latin dancer in a spangled jacket who chooses a partner from the audience; Al Capon, a Spanish-speaking DJ; Doris, a Jewish mother who struggles to maintain a liberal decorum while scolding her son on the phone for the danger she sees in his work and friendships with people different from them; and Flex, a young Black man who seems sympathetic because of his aspirations, but who mocks the workers at a Chinese take-out restaurant with the same nastiness Bill showed earlier. The last character listed in the program is Cesar, an older Puerto Rican man uncomfortably discussing with a therapist the death of his son at the hands of the police. This piece is the quietest of the evening, emphasizing the character's dignity and sadness.

I find myself much more appreciative of Hoch's work than a simple description such as this would have led me to expect. The structure of the performance reminds me to think about the same questions I have raised about Eric Bogosian, but somehow pursuing them seems less important. The desire simply to like the performance is strong enough to make me suspicious.

Why do I (want to) like Danny Hoch's performance? Many of the reasons recall the appeal of Bogosian's work. Hoch is personally charismatic and attractive. *Some People* couples intelligent and intricate character writing with virtuosic and compassionate character acting. Leaving aside for the moment the "politics of" the work, both Bogosian and Hoch include politics and political questions in their work, especially questions of race, gender, and class difference to which I am critically predisposed. Both are "cool."

There are important differences between the two. Hoch is young, up-and-coming, and this perhaps leads me to be less suspicious of the cultural appropriations required to sustain the "universal body." On the other hand, Hoch performs that body "more" universally, incorporating greater racial, ethnic, and gender diversity. Blanca, a young Latina, is developed subtly in a long piece that might be compared favorably with Leguizamo's female characterizations, of which I spoke approvingly above. Other content issues stand out as well. While there are no pointedly gay or lesbian characters onstage, there are frequent references that go some little way toward complicating the picture of society Hoch anthologizes.

There is also an intangible attitude I sense behind the performance about the performer's relation to his characters. While I have little doubt that a progressive and skeptical politics grounds Bogosian's construction of characters, and that he consciously works toward complexity and against stereotype, there is some difference that makes Hoch's work seem less finite or packaged, perhaps in part process- rather than product-oriented. I am not sure I can totally account for this perception, but I have identified three key aspects of the politics of Hoch's show.

The first is a function of the greater diversity of characterization, coupled with an attention to linguistics where some performers might concentrate on accent. Bogosian clearly has something to say about society that he communicates through the juxtaposition of characters. However, *Some People* offers greater inclusiveness and flirts with illegibility for some of its audience. Al Capon speaks almost exclusively Spanish, and while the sense is available to the attentive nonspeaker, the density of this and many of the other fast-talking characters' lines challenges almost anyone's ear at some point. This seems to suggest that Hoch's relation to the material differs. While he obviously has "something to say" as much as Bogosian, these qualities suggest that the multiplicity of urban speech controls Hoch as much as he shapes it. In other words, the typical act of the solo performer (especially when straight, white, and male) is the performance of speaking; Hoch certainly performs this, but foregrounded as well is the performance of having listened.

It is difficult to say how much of this perception is conditioned by the marketing of the show. The press was prone to fetishizing Hoch's background even further than did the program, as if to authenticate the representations; the *Voice* indulged in two separate feature articles (Stone 1993; Russo 1994). Still, the performance itself included Polish, Spanish, and slang English in amounts sufficient to suggest that no one person (certainly not a "mainstream" straight white male) could be the sole implied auditor. In contrast to "realist" details that convince by metonymically suggesting a larger whole (and Hoch's work, like Bogosian's, is full of such signs), these actually work against the construction of dramatic irony so central to many character solos; in those moments I, at least, no longer know more than the characters.

To sharpen this distinction, I would say that multiple-character work like Bogosian's is the performance of cultural virtuosity, while Hoch's is often the performance of cultural fluency. But I will return to this in my third point of difference.

My second distinction lies in the structure of the individual character pieces: frequently, Hoch's do not have the "shape" one expects, do not quite "add up" or "pay off" in the comic structure that might be built on the very funny foundation established for most of the characters. One critic expressed a related observation this way:

> Mr. Hoch is cooler than Mr. Bogosian, meaning only that his monologues don't have Mr. Bogosian's narrative shapeliness. Instead, they seem free-flowing, as if improvised on the spot. They are like musical riffs, like jazz. They also have something of the same effect. You respond in a purely emotional way to what you're hearing, while getting an extra boost from your awareness of the artistry involved. Good theatre works that way. (Canby 1994)

While I should take this depoliticized consumption of "pure emotion" as a caution against my own valorization of *Some People* as political performance, the lack of "narrative shapeliness" is in my reading a strategy for avoiding the reactionary laughter characteristic of so many of the comedy performances I've discussed.

A good example of Hoch's use of alternative structure is Blanca, who talks to her girlfriend about her black gay roommate in a very complicated moment. She wants to kick the roommate, Lemmington, out of the apartment because he doesn't clean up after his dog, "but he'll think it's because he's gay." Further, Blanca believes he has AIDS: "'cause he's all skinny.... Manny's skinny too but Manny's just skinny. Lemmington's gay and skinny.... Them people be getting that shit anyway, right?" As she leaves, Blanca returns to the topic of her boyfriend Manny's suggestion that they use condoms: "And let me tell you something. If Manny comes to me with that whole condom thing, I'm gonna be like 'excuse me, you think I'm dirty? Who do you think I am? Do you even know who you are?'" The sad irony is what Blanca doesn't know.

By the end of this monologue, Hoch has created strong sympathy for the character in large part because she is both intentionally and unintentionally funny. Some small additional element of humor results from the drag involved, and more because "the talkative Latina" has been comically characterized before. To whatever degree the audience is invited to laugh at her, however, it is taken aback by the subtle emotional transition near the end. Sympathy *for* her is retrospectively heightened, almost replacing any comic distance *from* her, by the sadness of her exit. Hoch's voice softens and deepens somewhat at the end of the speech, truer almost to the declining mood than to the character.

The peculiar sadness results from the somewhat abrupt departure of a character one feels warmly toward (through a mix, perhaps, of "original" and stereotypical responses) at the very moment she is least sympathetic. Hoch creates a moment in which a traditional theatrical disappointment (the departure of a well-liked character) coincides with a disappointment characteristic of his writing: the discovery of the workings of prejudice, ignorance, or self-interest in a character previously made likeable. Hoch creates this discovery repeatedly, and uses it in several ways, but it operates most strongly in the sense of absence created by simultaneous human failure and departure: someone you like is no longer there, and no longer precisely who you thought they were. In the Blanca monologue, the intimation of the danger she might face is a third emotional strand. Rather than a "rising" narrative structure with mini-climax near the end, or a conventional dramatic "twist" in the plot or characterization punctuated by a blackout, Hoch evokes a waning of the character, a slow but unexpected sense of loss.

A different example is provided by Doris, the Jewish mother talking to her politicized son on the phone. Some of the humor is familiar: she is, after all, a Jewish mother character. There is also familiarity in the structure of catching someone who has a liberal self-image in a less-than-liberal moment, heightened by the fact that mother and son seem to be having a political argument: "I am not a scared liberal complaining reactionary. [Pause] What does that mean?" But its use of familiar elements does not limit its complexity. Doris is caught several times between her prejudice and the liberal language she has clearly adopted to deal with her son. "I should be worried enough that my son doesn't get shot by some black kid—or white kid. . . . I know white people shoot people with guns, David, but—not in the train, David." And while Doris is shown speaking from a position of privilege, she is also shown reflexively invoking the Holocaust in order to excuse herself ("Six million, David. Six million.")

Hoch's implied critique is enmeshed with affection (as are most of his characterizations), and beyond Doris's likeable qualities, her implied connection to the white Jewish performer, in a show with no other Jewish characters, gives the monologue a quality, if not of self-critique, at least of questions that hit close to home. Indeed, it's easy to imagine that "David"—who is described by his mother as doing work with a "group" that "goes to all the bad neighborhoods" in the city "like the Peace Corps, only in New York"—listens to her with an attitude close to that of Hoch himself, whom the program describes as having worked with an NYU theater program "bringing conflict resolution through drama to adolescents in New York City's jails and alternative high schools." And David is clearly infuriated with his mother by the end of their phone call—Doris says, "I love you. Stop shouting."

The character of Doris thus involves both sympathy and a recurring critique of her politics. This content is part of a structure that actively includes her among the "some people" the piece cares about. In this regard, the role of Bill is crucial, for the straight white guy, while clearly amusing to Hoch, occupies the structural niche of unsympathetic character. While many of the others are shown to be "human" and thus on some level disappointing (Doris, Blanca, Madman, Flex), Bill is without self-critique or doubt about his own privilege. This structure positions Doris with the other characters, suggesting by extension Hoch's placement not among white men looking in, but on the inside of the work, among the "colorful" New Yorkers he is celebrated for bringing to the stage. In standing center stage with these characters, Hoch perhaps decenters the straight white male authorial and spectatorial presence.

The place of the performer's self in the work is the third aspect of Hoch's show I want to emphasize. I have just argued that Hoch is in effect listening to Doris on the phone, and I said before that Hoch performs the act of listening as much as the act of speaking. I think much of my admiration for the show comes from the way Hoch is constituted as a character on the stage.

In discussing Bogosian, I emphasized how his author-presence was suggested by the characters that orbit him, that the work necessarily positioned the observer as norm against which characters were measured. This dynamic may be at work to some degree in *Some People*, and Hoch does not address this in the direct way Bogosian seems to be investigating. That is, there is no "Danny" in the piece as there is an "Eric" in *Pounding Nails*. But Hoch is "in" the piece in other ways. The first is the dynamic set up by the Doris and Bill vignettes. Another may be the very fetishization of the "authenticity" of his experience allowed by the show's publicity. However problematic that notion, it does aid in suggesting to the spectator a critical presence behind the construction of the work, along with the program quotations and the brief rap encore that closes the show: "I know some of you people / have never seen Brooklyn or Bronx / that's very funny to me, ha ha ha ha-ha ha-ha...." Hoch sings in a Caribbean accent, wearing a knit hat and sunglasses. At first glance, this is a contradictory moment, in which the identity of much of the audience is acknowledged, but in which Hoch creates yet another character. Yet this song, which offers a caution about the words "us" and "them" and a comic parable about the downfall of the chickens, who once ruled the earth and now are eaten, is clearly framed at the same time as "Hoch" speaking to "us." The last of the listed "characters in order of appearance" is Cesar, the lights have changed, we have applauded.

By those signs, this is the "real" person in curtain call, or in a liminal characterization for an encore. Yet we are addressed directly by a character in costume and dialect, a metaphor for how Hoch has been speaking throughout the performance. This character might be read as an impersonated "not-Hoch," but might also be seen as a performative construction on the real white Jewish male body of the actor. One intertext for this moment, then, is the white "wannabe" rapper (though neither precisely the ludicrous Vanilla Ice nor the more "real" personae of the Beastie Boys). In the performance of character astride the edge of the theatrical frame, Hoch perhaps keeps both his own identity and the identity he and we desire playing across the same body. Curiously, it is the very "imperfection" of this impersonation that makes it the most promising passage of the performance.

Hoch seems to struggle in this piece to keep himself and his audience in the here and now. Arguably, any performer who traffics in "presence" (which is to say most) attempts to maintain present-tenseness as part of that presence. And a brief moment of direct address at the end cannot undo that power. But Hoch also remains in the work as another kind of presence, which I would call "writerly" as opposed to performative, in the audacity of his choice of characters, in the implied act of listening to urban multivocality, in the unexpected anticomic structure of often funny pieces. In the midst of an apparatus efficient at universalizing experience, Hoch's construction of his work and direct/indirect appeal to his audience seeks to particularize the experience of the performance itself.

This is an author-presence quite different from that created when an artist speaks through the construction of proximate others, yet it is not simply the fetishization of difference created through appropriationist avant-garde caricatures of those seen as truly other.[2] Hoch uses his cultural fluency to speak with his characters, to become like them while of course not becoming them. He has said that "What I do is almost minstrelsy. I'd like to try blackface" (quoted in Stone 1993: 82). If such a fraught experiment were to succeed it would be because Hoch attempts to avoid caricature (even sympathetic caricature) in favor of the best of the "wannabe" aesthetic; Hoch seems to perform not just virtuosic transformation, but the very desire for that transformation.

Hoch is "not" white—and not only because he is Jewish. First of all there is the argument Thomas DiPiero sums up in the title of his article, "White Men Aren't" (1992). As I have tried to keep in mind throughout, identity terms like white, heterosexual, and male produce the same instability in my critical discourse they produce in all lived and represented discourses of identity. The difficulty is most acute in the attempt to define the limits of this study. The U.S. government classifies many "Hispanics" as "white," but I cite John Leguizamo's work above with the sense that I am referring to work by a (non-"white") Latino in order to contrast it to the work of "white" men. There are Jews of many skin colors and nationalities, and many "white" Jews would both acknowledge a degree of white "skin privilege" and maintain that their lived experience is of an identity more "of color" than white. Among performers in this study, Jewishness is textually specific in the work of Kornbluth and Hoch—and specificity itself runs counter to the supposed "universality" of whiteness. Specificity within "whiteness" has different meanings for different performers: Andrew Silverstein's use of the stage name Andrew Dice Clay suggests one meaning, while Eric Bogosian's Armenian looks are arguably an asset in his creation of "ethnic" characters of many kinds.

According to my own argument, in fact, none of the performers discussed here "is" white, and I must acknowledge varying degrees of violence in discursively making them so. DiPiero's title sentence also marks a convergence of gender theory and critical race theory: without their active construction within discourse white men aren't white or men (or straight, for that matter). Such identity terms mark not ontological essence but historical subjectification. Straight white male identity is necessarily unstable, constantly undermined by its own generality.

But more specifically in the case of Hoch's performance, there is a rigorous attempt to give up whiteness momentarily—not to escape it, which Hoch surely understands as impossible, but to put aside (the privileged vision of) one identity and to learn rather than appropriate others. Of course, the success of this attempt is open to debate, but the rigor of the endeavor is what accounts for the unique quality of the work. And despite the attempt to unlearn identity privilege, Hoch does not aspire to a fully universal body; he does realize that he "can never fully walk in someone else's shoes."

Another question to ask of the attempt is whether white spectators are prepared conceptually to allow whiteness to be performatively dismantled, or, indeed, what it takes to get privileged spectatorship to see a general critique of privilege in any full way. What George Lipsitz (1995) describes as the "possessive investment in whiteness" held by most whites—the literal material interest whites share in the continuation of the status quo—might be metaphorically applied to the interest straight white male spectators hold in continuing to spectate from that position. The exchange of meaning, presence, pleasure that shapes the way privilege talks to itself is not easily altered by a shift in a single component. Because straightness, whiteness, maleness are a way of seeing—in the theater as much as in culture at large—and because that way of seeing affects even those not interpellated by its identity descriptors, the subtle critical dimension of Hoch's piece, and his own "writerly" appearance in the text, may not function as I might wish for all spectators. For many, it may still function in a negatively "ethnographic" way.

Further, my positive reading of Hoch's work constantly threatens to slide into the platitudes of liberal humanist criticism. For example, in one of my sentences, the only difference between my discussion of the work's critique of each character's place in a culture of prejudice and ignorance and a universalist discussion of those characters is that I use quotation marks in saying that all are shown to be "human." More disturbing still is the fact that my desire to read Hoch's near-minstrelsy as political and critical perhaps ignores the potential for an obviously racist appreciation of the humor of any particular moment only because of my indoctrination into anti-essentialism. In any event, I will resist the temptation simply to stamp my meager critical approval on the piece, obscured as it must be by my own privileges. Further, there is no question of simply holding Hoch up as a model that "good" straight white male soloists should emulate; not only are his skills and working context available to few performers, but the proliferation of imitative performances would surely weaken the specific identity politics of his efforts. Instead, having noted the promising tactics Hoch employs, I will turn to a broad dynamic of universalism and essentialism that threatens the viability of *any* critical work in the monologue of identity privilege.

ESSENTIALISM AND UNIVERSALITY

With a little imagination, the form of solo performance might be described as "essentially" male, even though it metaphorically denies even biological specificity in asserting its universal value. One might, for example, describe the single body as the ultimate phallic symbol. This argument constructs the erect body as isomorphic to the penis and allows

The Universal, the Essential, the Particular, the Political 173

for a sort of reverse synecdoche in which one (mis)takes the whole for the part. This reduction of the male body to a genital signifier seems, for the moment, more amusing than useful: it is difficult to argue for Gray's seated body as an example of phallic physicality, for example. On the other hand, such an account might explain why masculinist culture perceives solo female performance as threatening, as it would represent women's acquisition of both the linguistic phallus and the visual (and kinesthetic?) "phallic symbol." Too, the specific erotic of Danny Hoch's *Some People*, the arrival and departure of presence and identity of a chimerical author who both does and does not offer "his" voice, might be accounted for as a "play" with phallic presence, rather than its assertion/insertion in the domesticized space of Hoch's stage.

At any rate, there is precedent for regarding the occupation of center stage as traditionally, if not essentially, masculine. Feminist critics and historians have frequently pointed out that conventional dramaturgy often replicates a social gendering of public and private spheres. Nancy S. Reinhardt, for example, notes that

> Traditionally, in tragedies or serious dramas, stage-center (the open neutral acting space) is reserved for men—for the protagonists, the tragic heroes, the "doers" of the main action. The sides, background, niches and balconies function as the inner domestic space where the women usually are kept. (Reinhardt 1981: 363)

Again, this might be used to construct an argument for the historical subversion of this scenic regime by female performers. Certainly it highlights another way in which solo performance by men is traditional rather than avant-garde. Further, the "neutrality" of the central acting space is important. For one thing, the distinction Reinhardt notes between a neutral center stage and the domestic specificity of the background invokes the traditional gendered opposition of masculine universality and feminine specificity.

"Neutral" settings amplify the universalist, "everyman" status accorded Gray and Bogosian in different ways. For Gray, the undifferentiated space allows his winding narratives freedom of movement across the time and space of his autobiography, which fills the space with his all-encompassing narrative-in-progress. For Bogosian, the bare stage (or such abstract, if almost urban, settings as that for *Sex, Drugs, Rock & Roll*) allows him to slide from character to character with his trademark ease, using at most a few pieces of quickly changed furniture to suggest a locale (most frequently a street or office, only occasionally a domestic scene). And since true stand-up, like that practiced by Leary and Clay, ostensibly happens in the here-and-now of the performance event, these works typically do without representational setting and construct even more forcefully the notion that, if the stage space is not actually universally representative of all space and time, it is at least the only place to be, the center of a geography of presence, surmounted by the soloist who is king of all who survey him.

Becker's *Defending the Caveman*, which I described in chapter 5 as "stand-up comedy with a set," would seem to be an exception, since it involves a representational faux-Stone Age living room. In fact, the overlay of "prehistoric" materials on twentieth-century Western bourgeois furniture creates an ahistorical anywhen, suggesting the universal truth of the comic anthropology Becker offers. Like *The Flintstones*' prehistoricization of the bourgeois domestic comedy of *The Honeymooners*, *Caveman* naturalizes by primitivizing. It is worth noting that what is represented is not the whole of the domestic sphere, which would seem to contradict my use of Reinhardt's observations above, but the male preserve within that sphere, the television and easy chair whose cushions still bear the impression of that earlier pseudo-outrageous, semi-ironized philosopher of white masculinity, Archie Bunker.

A further comparison with Leguizamo's *Spic-o-rama* clarifies the distinction. Leguizamo's depiction of an entire family uses a set that could be adapted to suggest different locations, but which always involves signifiers of shared domestic space (kitchen appliances, beds, etc.). Leguizamo's characters are literally embedded in a setting that suggests actual material relations and historic specificity. In contrast, Bogosian presents multiple characters as if their significance is not dependent on unseen others, while Gray presents a single character as if it were the only one. In short, these straight white male works reiterate straight white maleness as the central theatrical experience, without need of context and of universal importance.[3]

To some observers, recent solo performance has witnessed an inversion of sorts in another gendered binary: that of extroversion versus introversion. In an essay looking back on performance in the 1980s, C. Carr notes the emergence of a "rude girl" network (including performers such as Karen Finley and Lydia Lunch) as evidence of female performers' encroachment on traditionally male territory. She then points to an opposite movement.

> Certain men, meanwhile, began to do the introspective work that males have never been encouraged to pursue. For example, Spalding Gray's popular monologues (*Swimming to Cambodia, Sex and Death to the Age 14*, etc.) are part of the "personal," "confessional" tradition women supposedly have a corner on. Gray is a reporter bearing witness to his own everyday life. *Swimming to Cambodia*, for example, draws on his experiences as a bit player in the Hollywood movie, *The Killing Fields*. But exposing his own expectations, temptations, and pretensions became the core of his narrative. (Carr 1990: 205)

While I doubt the ostensibly introspective character of Gray's career, since his performance frame consumes everything around it, Carr is certainly correct that the idea, at least, of (white?) male introspection enjoys a certain currency in contemporary U.S. culture. However, introspection and self-examination are not neutral performative qualities that signify identically on differently marked bodies; male display of introspection, I argue, all too easily acts to shore up the identity privilege it might appear to examine.[4]

The valuation and valorization of solo performance seems to me to have consistently involved gendered premises. Much solo performance by women has been analyzed by feminists in a manner that has made the importance of gender explicit. One dominant theme especially applicable to autobiographical performance is the value of experience, particularly of women's experience in a cultural context that has devalued it in favor of male narratives. As Carr and others noted, this makes (or made) the autobiographical monologue a useful feminist tactic (though by no means the only one). Performers such as Holly Hughes and Annie Sprinkle tell stories based on their own experience. Even the more ambiguous narratives of Karen Finley seem somewhat based in fact and usually draw some of their power of persuasion from the trance-like manner of her delivery: the suggestion of interiority functions to ground her words in a sense of truth.

The frequent citation of Carolee Schneemann's 1975 performance, *Interior Scroll* (which involved, among other things, the artist extracting the text of the performance from her vagina), testifies to the popularity of interiority as a metaphor for much women's performance. For example,

Lenora Champagne refers to the work in her introduction to an anthology of texts by women performance artists: "Like Carolee Schneemann's interior scroll, the writing by these women comes from a deep, dark place" (Champagne 1990: xiii).

Broadly speaking, masculinist culture works to repress certain experiences, and the resistant art of those the center would exclude often focuses on the telling of nearly lost stories, especially telling one's own truths. One of the emphases of this tactic is on the value of the gesture of telling; the fact that one's story is uttered at all is a victory. The political, aesthetic, and epistemological value of "experience" has been the subject of lively discussion among feminist critics and theorists for some time, but the production and reproduction of knowledge alternative to the "mainstream" remains a key concern of feminist cultural production and of much current feminist criticism. Breaking cultural silence remains for many a vital tactic in agitating for social change.

In contrast, (straight white bourgeois) male discourse about the self does not so overtly value the gesture of speaking experience. It is true that in the classic dichotomies of masculine and feminine qualities, both doing and speaking fall on the masculine side. It is equally true that male autobiography has long been part of established canons of art and literature. The emphasis, however, is different. While this culture sees male self-absorption as commonplace and expected, the vulnerability of public introspection and the gesture of a man speaking of his personal experience is not marked as particularly valuable. Value may, however, be located in the manner of expressing that experience, in the speaker's attitude. The form is in some ways more important than the content. The qualities of bravado, modesty, eloquence, and simplicity may be judged appropriate for various narratives (bravado is common in sports narratives, for example, while modesty is often preferred for tales of courage in war, etc.).

For the stories told by many straight white male monologists, bluntness and irony are among the most valued of formal qualities. Both qualities can act to protect the unexamined self rather than exploit its vulnerability. Kornbluth and Gray's ability to render fascinating the mundane details of their lives depends on a heavy sense of irony. In the "monopolylogues" of performers such as Bogosian, what is specifically highlighted is not an ironic relationship to the self, but usually an outspoken depiction of the contiguous other—"men inside." Rather than speaking themselves in their maleness, these performers speak a sort of maleness-in-general. The illusion of speaking a "general" or typical maleness is achieved in large part through the blunt display of a variety of male characters who are obviously, outrageously *not* the performer, yet just as obviously might be. Bogosian's character "The Stud," whose blunt assertion of his heterosexual prowess I cited earlier, is an example of this outspoken "other" maleness. The piece is structured so that the performer is credited with a certain insight into maleness, but the performer is at the same time insulated from that attribute, protected by the ironic distance on which the piece is predicated.

It is again edifying to return to Carr's comparison of Clay and Bogosian, which she offers immediately after describing Gray's "personal" and "confessional" performance:

> Meanwhile, in pop culture, the word "taboo" was sometimes misappropriated to market obscene, hate-mongering comedians like Andrew Dice Clay, who screamed out the racist/sexist/homophobic feelings many had at least learned to hide. Perhaps the popularity of these Shock Comics reflected mass culture's response to the "crisis in representation." For whose crisis had it become, really? The macho white man had to reassert himself somehow. Ironically, such men could be case studies for the work of another performance artist who "crossed over" in the eighties, Eric Bogosian. (Carr 1990: 205)

At this point, the important thing about this passage is Carr's identification of a specific cultural moment in or from which Bogosian's work develops. If Gray might be said to "chronicle" the emergence of the neurotically introspective male, then Bogosian, Carr suggests, charts the reassertion of the "macho" (read "heterosexual") white man (a reassertion Clay enacts less critically). While this distinction is a little too neat to cover the breadth of their work, these artists nevertheless may be seen as articulating two possible responses to that "crisis of representation" I read Carr as (sarcastically) suggesting is the straight White Man's Burden. Gray's cool assurance and Bogosian's virtuosic ability to disappear behind a wide variety of extreme examples of male identity mean that their relation to the performative production of knowledge about the self remains characteristically distant and "male." Both performers remain on the abstracting, analytical side of the treatment of gendered experience, and both approaches might loosely be called ironic, implying as they do a distance of one kind or another between the speaker and the spoken.

Women's autobiographical performance—emphasizing the value of speaking (the self) itself—can be seen as at the least corrective, and perhaps as subversive of masculinist assumptions about the values of different experiences or the telling of different stories. Since male experience has historically been universalized, the telling of that experience tends to function in representation not as a real physical action but as abstract and rational cognition; "reason" remains in a privileged position relative to "feeling." (I emphasize again that this is due to a social misreading of these two instances of performance; it is not, of course, that women's autobiographical performance is necessarily more about feeling and experience while men's is more about reflection and examination of experience.) Until the powerful theatrical, critical, and other cultural apparatuses that hold this hierarchy in place are fully dismantled, narratives of the underrepresented may continue to carry a sense of liberatory speech. Equally, narratives of the chronically overrepresented (such as the stories offered by straight white male monologists) will continue to sound like monotone reiterations of masculine irony.

A crucial problematic for straight white male bourgeois culture is an inversion of one facing the activist gesture of liberatory minority discourse. When the performance of experience (autobiographical in the case of Gray, "ethnographic" in the case of Bogosian) speaks of identity it tends to authorize this speech through essentialist assumptions. The very idea that experience "as" a man can validate speaking (performing) as man/men assumes an irreducible core of maleness available only to men. Of course, these performances rarely if ever explicitly claim to speak for the category of man, or any other category for that matter. Nevertheless, it is an effect of the reception of these works that categorical representations appear in the event of performance.

This is clearest in the case of Bogosian, whose collections of exclusively male characters come to seem like catalogues of masculine possibility. The cover of *Drinking in America* triumphantly quotes a *New York Times* review: "A breakneck comic tour of the contemporary American male psyche." This essentializing effect only increases with time, as each new work contributes to the encyclopedic structure of his *oeuvre*. The obtrusive heterosexuality of Gray's performances also poses the question of what it is to "be" a man, and invites the male spectator to compare his performance of masculinity (heterosexuality) to Gray's. All this is to argue for an essentializing tendency on the part of a hypothetical spectator of the work. The degree to which critics invest these performers' works with veracity regarding male experience would seem to bear out this assumption of a popular essentialism.[5]

Further, because the only body present onstage is male, and the texts performed so often stage heterosexual drama through that single body, the works themselves imply that they should be read as representing one "side" of a necessary and inevitable identity boundary. What this means for the female spectator of this work remains unclear to me, but it suggests that the white male heterosexual spectator is asked not simply to identify with the character presented, but to align himself with the class of characters the work references. Considered in the context of the men's movement's successful valorization of essentializing about male experience, the example of male monologue suggests that male cultural production that purports to investigate maleness now always runs the risk of building up an experience barrier around the field of male subjectivity.[6]

Diana Fuss concludes *Essentially Speaking* with a discussion of essentialism in the classroom, focusing especially on the privileging of experience as the grounds for speaking. While she is concerned that a theoretical antiessentialism might remove experience as valid "evidence of a sort for the productions of ideology" (1991: 118) and as a motivating and empowering force for students who might otherwise be institutionally silenced, I think essentialism in the service of already empowered social identities must be considered differently. For example, male cultural production about men—men speaking about the experience of manhood—can function to isolate the examination of masculinity as a male preserve, to suggest that the experience of "being" a man is necessary to any critique or revision of masculinity. This is a bit like suggesting that an occupying army should have a monopoly on the analysis of colonialism.

Of course, this should prove no problem for feminism per se, as it has never needed male permission for its work. Rather, the risk posed by even implicitly essentialist male cultural production is that it may make it more difficult for men to hear any critique of their male power, and may be deployed as a defense against the challenges posed by various "de-colonized" subjects. If essentialism is a hotly debated topic in contemporary feminism, lesbian and gay studies, and in the study of "race," no such debate seems worthwhile in (straight white) "men's studies," if we are to have such a thing. In short, cultural production that tends to essentialize male identity seems necessarily reactionary.

Essentialism in the service of privileged identities works to secure that privilege. Straight white bourgeois men do perhaps face a crisis of identity and of representation, as Carr suggests. If so, the reconfiguration of straight white male discourse as but one essential and impermeable discourse among many may paradoxically reinforce the very straight white male cultural power that has so resisted its own de-universalization. The monologues considered here often manage to traffic simultaneously in both high art universalism and (straight white bourgeois) male essentialism. This essentialism results from the assumption of heterosexuality and the invocation of an unexamined male commonality, creating what may be the most serious flaw in monologue as a strategy for straight white male self-examination: to the extent that monologism limits the presence, even ghostly, of other "texts," it may tend to seal off the identity that is its subject.

IDENTITY PRIVILEGE AND BOURGEOIS AVANT-GARDE COMMUNITY

The aesthetic foundation of what I call the "bourgeois avant garde," especially as manifested in (straight white male) monologic performance art (or "arty" performance, at least), renders it incapable of clearly acknowledging its own historical specificity. That is, the bourgeois avant garde can neither recognize nor admit its own positioning in a cultural topography in which location is measured by yardsticks of race, gender, sexuality, and class, because its founding aesthetic concepts depend on ahistorical conceptions of creativity and genius. For such performance to acknowledge its formation of anything other than a universal community of spectators would be to admit failure.

Performance is a vital component of contemporary avant-garde art. Henry Sayre, for example, identifies the "postmodern avant-garde" practices described in his book *The Object of Performance* as rooted in a strain of modernism "oriented, in one way or another, to performance" (1989: xi). One hackneyed observation about performance is that it is "always new," and Rosalind Krauss describes avant-garde aesthetics as typified by a desire for and valorization of originality.

> The avant-garde artist has worn many guises over the first hundred years of his existence: revolutionary, dandy, anarchist, aesthete, tech-

nologist, mystic. He has also preached a variety of creeds. One thing only seems to hold fairly constant in the vanguardist discourse and that is the theme of originality. . . . The self as origin is safe from contamination by tradition because it possesses a kind of originary naivete. . . . The self as origin is the way an absolute distinction can be made between a present experienced *de novo* and a tradition-laden past. The claims of the avant-garde are precisely these claims to originality. (Krauss 1986: 157)

The self is the origin of originality. And if self as origin allows an escape from a tradition-laden past, this gesture of avant-garde originality is also an escape from a history-laden present. In a way, this is the same old story of individualism as a strategic evasion of the social. Personalism serves to excuse the offenses discussed in the previous chapter, placing value on expressing the original truth of the self rather than understanding that self as a social outcome. The genius of the artist produces objects, utterances, that are at once individual and unique, and at the same time history-free and of universal value.[7]

Because the self is the origin of transcendent artistic production, avant-garde aesthetics are both universalist and personal. The privileged status given transgression by the avant garde comes from its individualism. In the common avant-garde *agon* of genius-versus-convention, or genius-versus-audience, the struggle takes the form of artistic genius transgressing the ideology of the second term. Transgression, produced to fulfill a claim to originality, may be called the defining characteristic of the avant garde.[8]

This transgression of social or artistic convention often takes as its target the "average" or "center" of society, as expressed in the avant-garde battle cry, "épater les bourgeois." Because in performance the audience so often stands in for the society the artist wishes to confront, avant-garde performance tends to attack its own audience (this may take the form of indifference, condescension, or outright assault). This hypothetical avant-garde performance, then, does not invoke community, reflect community, or attempt to construct community; rather, it attacks community out of aesthetic necessity. In this regard, while Andrew Dice Clay and (to a slightly lesser extent) Denis Leary encourage audience complicity in their views (Clay's male spectators pump their fists in the air, screaming approval of his more outrageous heterosexist narratives and pronouncements), stand-up comedians' habit of attacking spectators

(Dice details the imagined masturbation routine of one male, and refers to front-row women as "hoovers") places them within this avant-garde tradition. In comparison, while Hoch seems slightly distrustful of his audience, he also solicits their clap-along participation in his final direct address.

The apparently defiant originality of the avant-garde self has proved attractive to a broader market than the term "avant-garde" would suggest. In fact, when it becomes possible to speak of "mainstream performance art" (as one might when discussing the careers of Gray and Bogosian), then "avant-garde" arguably describes a quality (of, perhaps, "originality") rather than a position (in the literal sense of avant-garde as "ahead"). This bourgeois avant garde does not take up a position in front of (or outside of) mainstream culture; it can only mark off a locale within it. Like a specialty boutique in a shopping mall, it is not operating in an alternative market, but marketing an alternative product.

I am obviously not talking of an avant garde, then, in a precise historic sense, or in terms of movement and chronology. Rather, this describes a performative quality marketed by a certain sector of the art/entertainment industry. If historical avant gardes have been marked by the gesture of breaking with tradition, convention, good taste, etcetera, then the bourgeois avant garde is the selling of that gesture back to an audience against which it was presumably directed in the historical or mythic first place.[9]

For example, Bogosian's transgressions are primarily on the level of content rather than form; they lie in the act of speaking the unspoken, or appearing to. In *Drinking in America*, he presents a lecture on torture techniques alongside a testimonial to the pleasures of black rubber clothing. His language is foul, and many of his characters abrasive. Bogosian's "transgressions" are in fact packaged, contained, in part by the episodic structure of his works, in which any potential for a developed critique or analysis is cut short by a change from one character to another, and in part because his topics are not truly unsaid. Rather, they are what Barthes might call the "stereotype" of the outrageous, that which is continually reiterated as exemplar of the repressed.

Spalding Gray codes transgression in the explicitly confessional tone of his work. This is especially evident in *Sex and Death to the Age 14*, which might almost be a transcription of early sessions of psychoanalysis. This continues in *Booze, Cars and College Girls*, his next monologue,

The Universal, the Essential, the Particular, the Political   183

though there the seeming transgression occurs not so much in his willingness to tell the audience about himself as in his gleeful recounting of his sexual adventures, including the peculiarities of anatomy and desire of the women involved. The performance by Kornbluth often functions in the same way. The avant-garde thrill, however, does not come simply from this sexual frankness; it involves the seeming vulnerability of men who remain capable of ironizing that very vulnerability.

Shawn's transgressiveness might seem more promising, since it is explicitly political. He engages in a direct and theoretical way with marxist social analysis. While his discussion is simplistic at times, he does focus on political theory in a manner usually excluded from mainstream performance. Shawn claims to have developed the monologue in the living rooms of his wealthy friends, but even in the theater (especially once *The Fever* moved from La Mama to Lincoln Center) there is something that seems dangerous in this act. The irony in *The Fever* is more complex than in Gray, Bogosian, or Kornbluth's heterosexual narratives, both because of its more "fictional" or "dramatic" status and because the vulnerability is constructed around participation in class privilege rather than heterosex. Still, the thrill of *The Fever* is in part that of watching a "vulnerable" man pick his psychic scabs.

Further, even Shawn's more interesting gesture of transgression does little to alter the centered nature of the performer. All are still at the center of their stages and their narratives, with (speaking) privilege intact and unquestioned. In addition, none of them are transgressive formally. Shawn's narrative is mildly discontinuous, at times resembling a modernist stream-of-consciousness, but rather than challenging narrativity, this structure seems simply to offer the mental pleasures of decoding and rearranging his discourse. Most importantly, none of the transgression is "on" the body. Bogosian's mode is acting, while Gray's is storytelling, but the implied body-presence of these forms is left unaddressed, leaving the tiny visual field of the performance dominated by the single body, which is thus magnified rather than diminished or decentered.

When Gray, Kornbluth, and Shawn blur the boundaries between fiction and autobiography in performance, or when Bogosian depicts a philosophical homeless man who confronts the audience with angry, ranting social critique, and even when Clay repeatedly punctuates his monologue with the exclamation "you gotta fuck her like this!" a bourgeois avant-garde aesthetic is at work. The implied audience for this aesthetic delights in the hint (or declaration) of transgression—in Gray's intimation that the concepts of truth or identity are being undermined, or Bogosian's teasing of spectatorial privilege.

The bourgeois avant garde, then, unlike the "real" avant garde (if there is such a thing), does not actually assault the spectator. Rather, it allows the spectator to duck the attack, to imagine instead that it strikes another. After all, to thrill to Gray's seeming confessional vulnerability and transgressive, assertive autobiographism, one must imagine oneself inside his aesthetic, not out. To appreciate Bogosian's passionate representation on his own body of a flawed social order, one must be aligned with the artist. Someone *else* is discomfited by Gray's openness or satirized by Bogosian's impersonation. With the exception of their few actual targets, someone *else* is the "pussy" or wimp victim of the shock comedian's sarcasm. The motto of this avant-garde spectator might be "épater les autres bourgeois." (The spectator who could utter such a slogan arguably represents a failure for political works such as those of Bogosian, Shawn, and Hoch.)

The environment in which this exchange of transgression occurs constitutes what I would call an "avant-garde locale"—a performative environment filled with this bourgeois avant-garde aesthetic. But avant-garde locales do not exist only within obscure, "arty" performance venues. They are metaphoric sites, fabricated in performance. The straight white male avant-garde performer, at once unique and universal in his expressiveness, constructs within even the most bourgeois, season-ticket-holding audience an avant-garde space of artistic noncommunity, or perhaps anticommunity. In fact, so thoroughly disseminated is the avant-garde ideal (among artists and audiences) that its invocation as a transcendent value may be said to create an avant-garde *virtual* community. In this locale, common-sense notions of community (shared geography, politics, preference, etc.) are submerged beneath an ostensibly universal identificatory model: the artist stands (or sits) before "us," allowing the projection of our own sense of self-as-origin onto his superior expressive apparatus. If our identities provide us access to this identification, then multiple, similar selves can experience the giddy sensation of community without the nitty-gritty of community: its politics and its daily pleasures. Identity privilege in avant-garde locales can create a powerful coherence of one performer's identity privilege and presence with some spectators' identity privilege and desire.

The virtual community of the bourgeois avant garde, whose primary pleasure is the reassurance it offers its members that only "les autres" are flabbergasted or affronted, cannot really afford the actuality, the historicity, that I offered earlier as the defining element of what I consider performance art. The straight white male bourgeois avant garde, if I may combine so many "loaded" terms, is unable to admit a central aspect of its "actual space"—that is, the history of the bodies inside it. This is because the virtual community it constructs, founded on an aesthetic system of "greatness" and self-as-origin, collapses under the weight of history.

This is not to say that straight white male monologue might be "repaired" simply through acknowledging that it is straight, white, and male. The problems of this individualist form as practiced from a position of identity privilege cannot be swept away by suddenly turning back from universality and claiming straight white men as a "community." For one thing, as Michel Benamou said in 1977,

> for all the *participation mystique* which demands fulfillment in our alienated lives, the distance between actor and the public cannot be abolished willfully. It is the hard-won achievement of reflexivity through the history of consciousness which has separated us into an actor and a spectator. Techniques of participation [which I would say in the bourgeois avant-garde aesthetic are reducible to techniques of identification—M.P.], short of restoring *communitas* in society by some advance to Anarchy, are bound to fail outwardly; but more important, they are resisted inwardly by the postmodern reflexivity: structure is of our mind as well as of our society. (Benamou 1977: 6)

In other words, "we" cannot think ourselves as one. But even that very desire may be suspect. Iris Young, in her provocative essay "The Ideal of Community and the Politics of Difference" (1990), offers a critique of the binary opposition of individualism/community in much current political theory. She describes this opposition as related to similar binaries, notably masculine/feminine, and notes that placing new emphasis on the second term "can have some critical force with respect to the dominant ideology and social relations" (1990: 307). But she suggests that the very opposition "is integral to modern political theory and is not an alternative to it" (1990: 306). The point is not, then, that straight white male avant-gardists should trade in a universalist/individualist conception of artistic value for an essentialist/communal conception. "The oppositions themselves," Young notes, "arise from and belong to bourgeois culture, and for that reason merely reversing their valuation does not constitute a genuine alternative" (1990: 307).

It is perhaps good that it is so difficult for the straight white male avant-gardist to acknowledge his own identity group, let alone facilitate its sense of "community." The possible outcomes of such "community" might include a general postmodern nostalgia, casual arty misogyny, or outright white supremacism. Or perhaps really admitting history into the space of performance would reduce such a performer to a stunned or sheepish silence?

The aesthetics of the straight white male avant garde are clarified by comparison with a performer such as Tim Miller, famous as one of the so-called "NEA Four." Miller's program note for *My Queer Body* states that "all his various performance art agitating goes toward articulating a queer cultural identity and trying to find an artistic, spiritual and political response to the AIDS crisis," and Miller does seem to create for his audience the sense that identity is being articulated in the performance space—an identity that bears some relation to a politics that reaches beyond that space. In performing his autobiographical narratives, Miller speaks *to* the spectators, at times touching them, always implying the possibility of the touch. They are bodies in the same space and time, and the performer is able to recognize this present tense, to point to his sameness with regard to some spectators, his difference with regard to others, notably lesbian spectators and some presumed to be straight. These bodies are in the same space and time, then, not because of a homogeneous white gay male audience, but because of a present-tense white gay male politics.

This is not to fetishize gay performance, or any "other" performance, or to suggest that straight white male performance is inevitably and essentially "bad." I think there are moments in Hoch's performance (and perhaps even in Shawn's own performance of his monodrama) that ask after the space and time of the event. I do think, however, that the problematics of identity privilege cannot be resolved by ignoring, smoothing over, or simply ironizing privilege. Nor can they be resolved in the construction of hypothetical communal harmony. Straight white male performance can be neither "real performance art" nor "real identity politics" while it remains circumscribed by bourgeois avant-garde aesthetics.

While it does at times invoke the present and actual for aesthetic effect (as in Gray's autobiographical, direct-address performance), this straight white male performance art cannot invoke a more broadly conceived "present and actual" because the avant-garde conceptual system founded on universality collapses under the weight of actual history. Avant-garde manifestations of the traditional center (the historically constructed center) cannot support a reordering of a centric conception of space and value into a noncentric, juxtapositional one—like the "unoppressive city" described by Young (1990: 317). These aesthetics of the center cannot handle a politics of difference, and it is too frightening to imagine an overt rather than implied politics of the same.

Instead, the straight white male bourgeois avant garde creates a fictive actual space—a virtual community—an avant-garde locale constituted around shared identity privilege. Most ironically, this shared identity privilege is in most cases covert, unacknowledged, produced instead through identification, implicit identity. This locale structurally parallels the stereotypical men's movement scene of a circle of men drumming, with the exception that the men's movement explicitly proclaims identity even as it tends to ignore power in favor of psychologism or "spirituality." Straight white male bourgeois performance art, like the community constructed by stereotypically "aware" men, creates a mythic space of male value outside history. If straight white male bourgeois performance art seems absent from its audience, this is because it is caught in the contradiction between its identity privilege and an actualist art form that would tend to undermine that privilege. These performances of necessity transpose themselves into a fictive scene of self-knowing, even while they "pass" as present-tense performance art.

CONCLUSION

This project has outlined a genre of performance and enumerated its faults. This is all well and good, and I suppose I think of it as useful critical labor. But it is hard to say if I have produced "new" knowledge about this straight white man to whom I keep referring. This is not to say that the category is somehow not accurate or useful. While I am of course interested in destabilizing such categorical markers of identity, I also think that straight white men are more likely than most to inhabit their supposed identities with a boring steadiness, an arrogant nonchalance. This is particularly true of bourgeois straight white men, since they (we) occupy the position least affected by economic or transcultural challenges to established identity.

But this is, in a way, simply a restatement of a theme so recurrent it threatens to become numbing: here is the center, see how central it is, notice how we orbit around it. The trap here is that the critic must report this legendary centrality in order to make clear the power invested in these men and their representations. However, this always risks reinforcing the hegemony it purports to analyze. What can be all too easily lost is the vital fact that in the daily lives of many people in our society (many lesbians and gay men, for example, and many who live in largely non-European-American communities), male white bourgeois straights are far from central elements. White straight male power really does exist first and foremost in the realm of (particular) representations, and if we must never forget that this representational regime is of course backed up by very real force, it is perhaps just as accurate to suggest that this force is in fact supported only through the exercise of representation.

To return to my earlier point, I'm not confident that this study has always succeeded in holding before its gaze both the reality of this power and its highly arbitrary and artificial constructedness. I do hope it has usefully analyzed some of the representational strategies that make that constructedness so difficult to keep in view. In fact, I would argue that this approach in general is the politically necessary one for "straight" "white" "men" who are interested not just in keeping quotation marks around these words, but also in rewriting the language they contain. At the same time, I recognize the irony of my own project, of writing a monograph about monologue.

I have mentioned the recent popularity of a number of loosely connected cultural activities commonly referred to as the "men's movement." Particularly the poetic and pop-intellectual wing of this movement seems invested in promoting introspection as a means of social reform, or at least of "healing" part of society—men. I want briefly to restate my opposition to this point of view, which the movement shares with some performance art. Narcissist self-examination (what does it mean to be male [straight, white]) instantly becomes a part of a representational hegemony. If "men" or any other privileged class really want

The Universal, the Essential, the Particular, the Political 189

to work for change, a better place to look is the complex of representations that bring that class into existence.

I have argued that a straight white male bourgeois avant garde cannot admit the reality of identity into the space of the performance, and have hinted that this means it cannot offer "real" performance art under my provisional formal definition. Does this mean straight white male performance art is impossible? No, but it is very hard to imagine, if only because it is so difficult for me to conceptualize such performance apart from those other two terms: "bourgeois" and "avant garde." And to escape those words, this performance would probably have to participate in dismantling the remaining three. Idealistically then, perhaps straight white male performance art *is* impossible.

Notes

CHAPTER ONE

1. For example, a widely used general history of theater lists an evolution from single narrator storytelling to group enactment as a strong alternative to the theory of ritual origin. Advocates of this theory suggest a pattern of development in which the recalling of an event (a hunt, war, or other feat) is gradually elaborated, at first through the use by a narrator of pantomime and impersonation, and then through the assumption of each of the roles by a different person. According to this theory, then, drama and theater originate in the narrative instinct (Brockett 1987: 6).

2. In this particular pronoun construction, I mean to include myself in a mythic group of "well-trained theater-goers" addressed by the monologist. It will become clear, I hope, that no such unified "us" can really exist; in fact, one critical difficulty of this project lies in these performers' assumptions about the audience, or in some cases their failure to make any specific assumptions. For now, "us" indicates my complicity in a cultural construction, a mythic theater audience, a ghostly community glimpsed in traditional Eurocentric constructions of performance history.

3. For example, Jill Dolan begins a chapter on "Materialist Feminism: Apparatus-Based Theory and Practice" by restating the notion that "the address of the traditional representational theatre apparatus constitutes the subjectivity of male spectators and leaves women unarticulated within its discourse" (1988: 99). While Dolan and feminist performance critics more generally go on to complicate this description of the traditional apparatus, in particular by exploring the implications of the active or resistant spectator, I think much remains to be learned about the way forms constituted through

theatrical apparati pursue a preferred addressee of the sort this construction implies.

4. Consider "Why I Wear What I Wear," the *GQ* interview with Bogosian (Mansfield 1989). While similar but less fashion-conscious publications are less likely to feature dress in titles and headlines, the most common Bogosian costume—black jeans, t-shirt, and sneakers—consistently attracts attention. I would venture a consensus reading of his all-black uniform as indicating a certain stylishness and at the same time expressing a streak of "rock-and-roll" nihilism for which Bogosian is known.

5. Barthes discusses the uses and dangers of "method," and states in the following way the "two demands to which the work of research must reply. The first is a demand for responsibility: the work . . . must constitute a *critique* (remember once again that to criticize means *to call into crisis*). Here method is inevitable, irreplaceable. . . . The second demand, however, is of a quite different order; it is that of writing, space of dispersion of desire, where Law is dismissed. *At a certain moment*, therefore, it is necessary to turn against Method" (1982: 389). My argument makes use of some critical, interpretive "methods" to analyze the performances under discussion and uses others to treat the discourse or metatexts that surround them. At certain moments, however, I am less disciplined, allowing myself to "disperse desire," indulge in "irresponsible" associations of texts, wax impressionistic, speculate on "unreliable" evidence, and so forth. These are moments of a performative engagement with the text through which I hope at least occasionally to trouble my own critical monologue, to introduce the salutary heteroglossia of "desire."

6. I am playing here on the term "outing," a sometimes controversial tactic whereby some lesbian and gay activists identify "closeted" gay men or lesbians to increase "visibility." Whether one approves of this practice or not, "in-ing," as I use it, is clearly counterproductive from a pro-visibility point of view—though the anxious gesture of in-ing oneself as heterosexual does point to the presence of homosexuality.

7. Recall that "straight" can still mean an identity in contrast to drug use or criminality, or simply to countercultural movements. I hope my use of "straight" will invoke for some its earlier contrast to "hip." Since this distinction emerged in the African American and appropriationist practices of mid-century jazz and beat cultures, "straight" in my usage might suggest one both attached to conventional heterosexuality and marked as very (culturally) "white."

8. "What we need is a theory of sexual borders that will help us to come to terms with, and to organize around, the new cultural and sexual arrangements occasioned by the movements and transmutations of pleasure in the social field" (Fuss 1991: 5).

9. Bly in a sense haunts this study because he is among the most visible of those who have recently worked at defining maleness. Bly seems to either intrigue or annoy most "progressive" men, and I am firmly in the second category. His and related efforts tend to abstract the "male" in an ahistorical way that ignores most issues of race, class, and sexuality. This logic is played out in the stand-up comedy monologue by Rob Becker, *Defending the Caveman*, which I discuss in chapter 5.

10. It is perhaps also important to make clear what should by now be a commonplace: the performed identity in any of these pieces is not the same as the performer's identity, even in work like Gray's that is strongly coded as autobiographical. On the other hand, one of the features of this work (some would say of performance art in general) is that the artist is assumed to have a very close tie to the material. Gray, for example, is apparently narrating events from his own life; in work such as Bogosian's, this tie is manifest more in the performer's assumption of most or all of the traditional theatrical roles—performer, director, author, even designer.

11. There is little precise language for discussing these works. Monologue is usually defined in rather general terms: "1. a prolonged talk or discourse by a single speaker. 2. any composition, as a poem, in which a single person speaks alone. 3. a part of a drama in which a single actor speaks alone. 4. a form of dramatic entertainment by a single speaker." "Monology" ("the act or habit of soliloquizing") and even the French verb *monologuer* ("to soliloquize, to talk to oneself") have the same problem as "soliloquize"; these performers do not usually speak in true soliloquy, speaking to themselves as if no others were present (though a few of Bogosian's pieces are so structured). Wallace Shawn's *The Fever* is ostensibly a single-character play, or monodrama ("a dramatic piece for a single performer"). None of these pieces can be truly called an "aside" ("a part of an actor's lines supposedly not heard by others on the stage and intended only for the audience"), since there is not really any text for the works to be aside from. The term I apply to Bogosian's performances, "monopolylogue"—derived from "monologue" and "monopoly" ("the exclusive possession or control of something")—is accurate but very rarely used. The prefix to many of these words is, however, provocative, especially the associations evoked by such words as "monochromatic" ("of or having one color") and "monotonous" ("lacking in variety; tiresomely uniform; unvarying"). (English definitions are from *The Random House Dictionary of the English Language* [New York: Random House, 1979]. The French definition is from *Harrap's New College French and English Dictionary* [Lincolnwood, Ill.: National Textbook, 1982].)

12. This discussion of the effect of "presence" insistently raises the issue of the spectator's agency—or lack thereof. Of all that is not included in this

examination of performance art monologues by white heterosexual men, I most feel the absence of a focused discussion of actual audiences. While I refer at times to my own spectating practice, discuss the abstract, implied spectators of these works, and at times cite the observable reactions of the audiences in which I sat, I do not examine in any detail the ways in which spectators may be using these performances, rather than being passively used by them. I certainly do not think a text wholly determines its reader. On the contrary, my own experience aligns me with reader/spectator theory that emphasizes the way readers make use of texts, resist them, remake them.

This study of straight white male performance is, then, something of a worst-case scenario. Straight white men are not wholly made or made over by these works, nor are spectators who are not straight white men flatly excluded or erased in actual spectatorship. Ideology is not brainwashing, and pleasure is not (always) irrational submission.

CHAPTER TWO

1. Or, in a slightly different mode, when Danny Hoch or Bogosian impersonates disk jockeys, speaking relatively directly to the audience, although both do so through an imagined technological mediation and a heightened fictionalization of the spectators' imaginary role as radio audience.

2. The same ironic structures that seem to clarify the spectator's task in dramatic monologue performance could be seen as creating an ambiguity fundamental to autobiographical performance art monologues. Similar cues may indicate that ironic distance is appropriate, but the coincidence of "character" and "author" demands a complex appreciation of this irony rather than a simpler judgment of the character. See chapter 3.

3. Although I cannot speak as an insider to the world of literary criticism and the academy of literary study, my sense is that dramatic monologues and dramatic monologue poetry occupy similar places in the respective cultural hierarchies of which they are a part. That is, a slightly defensive tone on the part of some Browning scholars suggests that the dramatic monologue is less "high" than other forms of poetry, while certainly ranking higher than truly "low" cultural forms such as song lyrics, etc. Multiple-character monologue performance also seems caught between the high art of formally experimental, nondramatic performance art and popular/low culture forms such as stand-up comedy (discussed below).

4. The emphasis on "community" can also be phrased to recognize the commodity value of an author's seductive "presence" at a reading. In a feature article about the erotics of promotional readings (chiefly by novelists), Esther B. Fein quotes the literary equivalent of a booking agent: "Jay

Walker, who organizes readings for Brentano's, says readings are a mix. 'A little bit of networking,' he said, 'and a little bit of romance' " (Fein 1992: 7).

5. I should emphasize again that I am drawing on Bauman's phrasing of an ethnographic observation about performativity in general in order to construct an ethical observation about only one aspect of performance, which might be distinguished as "cultural" performance, "events for which performance is required" (Bauman 1977: 27)—as opposed to the appearance of performative speaking in other realms of life. In other words, because performance in all cases implies an assumption of responsibility (Bauman's point), "intended" performances, framed as "art," imply a responsibility for competence that goes beyond entertainment (my application).

6. In an essay critical of the "personal" aspects of Sylvia Plath's poems, Dutta argues that the "basic assumption of traditional confessional literature is that of a generally accepted religious frame of reference. What the moderns have, instead, is an existential concern with the problematic of the self" (Dutta 1981: 3). As the work of Spalding Gray illustrates, Plath's postmodern confessional successors have available as a frame of reference the endless representation and mediation of the self—its extension and amplification. In chapter 3 I will argue that Gray's performance is not simply a modernist display of the "problematic of the self," but a postmodern obsession with the representation of that problematic.

7. Speech, of course, is often considered not as failed phallic shit, but as a successful originary plenitude. As Régis Durand notes, the voice is at times viewed through nostalgia for a missing origin: "The voice has to do with loss, fall from the body. Yet it also has to do with the return to origins, to the dream of an *Ur*-language, a corporeality of language.... The voice, in this respect, is regressive. Mythically, it aspires to an original state, that of the "first men," before they became enslaved by words.... Individually, being an expansion of the body and a metaphor of fantasy, the voice follows fantasy's regressive pattern, and gives expression to traces of unconscious desires and constructs dredged up from the past" (Durand 1977: 102). On the other hand, that which is "dredged up" might be said to remain metaphorically excremental. In any case, the concept of voice aspiring to origin or retrieving the unconscious can serve as a precursor to my discussion in chapter 6 of avant-gardist originality.

8. Readers seeking general historical information on performance art should consult Goldberg 1988; a basic critical anthology is Battcock and Nickas 1984.

9. See Parnes 1985. This issue of *TDR* focuses on club performance.

10. This would seem to be in opposition to the strand of performance

Fuchs discusses in terms of "the revenge of writing." This strand is influenced by Derridean deconstruction, and while it must necessarily trade in performative presence to some degree, it takes as its project the dismantling of such ideas as "the simultaneous presence of audience and performers." In summarizing this other trend in performance, Fuchs suggests, we "might say that we have been witnessing in contemporary theatre, and especially in performance, a representation of the failure of the theatrical enterprise of spontaneous speech with its logocentric claims to origination, authority, authenticity—in short, Presence" (1985: 172). Perhaps much contemporary performance might be divided into a pseudo-Barthesian critique of authorship (which uses the perpetual "here-and-now" of the text against the "Author") and a Derridean critique of presence (using "writing" against "presence"). In practice, I think, these two deconstructive impulses may overlap and even operate together.

11. Carroll's argument about the "convergence" of art performance and performance art in the mid-1980s is actually that "both are preoccupied with the subject of representation" (1986: 78). While I give somewhat greater emphasis to the continuation of a preoccupation with "the real," I agree with this analysis. In chapter 3 I stress self-representation as both the strategy and the topic of Gray's performances. In chapter 4, my analysis of Bogosian's work begins from the assumption that spectators are cued to read his authorial presence as that which constructs the multiple representations in his performance anthologies.

12. In chapter 6 I will suggest that some "mainstream" performance art constructs a virtual or simulated community within a hypothetical "authentic" space that comes to overlay the actual performance space.

CHAPTER THREE

1. I thank Tracy McCabe for this insight.

2. There are multiple accounts of the transition from The Performance Group to The Wooster Group, many of which conflict; they are not directly relevant to this discussion. David Savran provides some information in *Breaking the Rules: The Wooster Group* (1988). Richard Schechner offers his view, in part, in *The End of Humanism* (1982).

3. I am familiar with Gray's early monologues primarily through the collection published under the title *Sex and Death to the Age 14*. Gray is shown performing material from these monologues in the Yonemotos' videotape, *Spalding Gray's Map of LA* (Gray 1984a); while he is presumably offering his usual performance for the camera, I should make clear that I did not see these early works in live performance.

4. A discomfort by no means unproblematic. In fact, the outrage expressed by many might be seen to arise from the same fascination and condescension that motivates enthusiastic participants. As representation, the tavern "sport" might even be seen as foregrounding the structures of power that inform even most "liberal" representations of bodily difference. Further, the metaphoric applicability of one activity to the other is a function of my own privilege as critic relative both to other spectators and to the tavern employees.

5. McCabe also pointed out to me that while grammatically the title of *Interviewing the Audience* "foregrounds" or privileges the audience, it is better considered, in my analysis, as the "object of a missing yet controlling subject."

6. In chapter 2 I discussed the typical poetry reading as related in some way to autoperformance in that both forms suggest a heightened vulnerability in the coincidence of author and performer. This has particular relevance for Gray and for this piece. The spectating experience I am describing here is in some sense about the intensification of this heroic stance through direct audience involvement. It points to the economy of performative danger at work in such self-offerings: the powerful presence of the star is constituted by his very willingness to risk that status publicly.

7. Prinz makes essentially the same argument in her article on gesture in *Swimming to Cambodia*, though in a more sophisticated, less blatantly "-centric" fashion; her analysis of his body language goes some way toward explaining how the performed perspective can come to seem like the naturally received one.

8. Demastes apparently doesn't see the position of representation and class privilege occupied by even the most avant-garde "art" theater companies; he certainly oversimplifies the Wooster Group's murky politics as "revolutionary."

CHAPTER FOUR

1. While theoretical and ethnographic concern with the activity of spectators, including their tendency to produce completely unintended editorial components, is an important aspect of contemporary performance studies, it should be stressed that audiences reconstruct performance meanings from the available materials. The fact that intention cannot be considered the ultimate determiner of received meaning actually heightens, rather than dismisses, the "assumption of competence" inherent in performance. I argued in the first chapter that the "assumption of accountability to an audience for the way in which communication is carried out, above and beyond its refer-

ential content" (Bauman 1977: 11), includes or ought to include political accountability for form. The use of charismatic presence in presenting what Banes calls "privileged, thus sympathetic interior views" represents a complex problem for critics and other active spectators.

2. However, Bogosian's creation of multiple characters carries a stronger implication of ironic distance than do Clay's single-character works. I will return to this analysis in my discussion of Clay in chapter 5.

3. It is not clear whether Bogosian at this moment performed a male character; he may have briefly performed the female sex worker. Reviews note that this speech was followed, apparently without a break, by "an androgynous figure writhing under a jaundiced spotlight," but also describe Bogosian as "grinding *his* hips furiously while rubbing *his* thighs and buttocks . . . coming on to the audience with the persistence of a hungry call girl" (Grubb 1984: 80–81; emphasis mine). At least in the published text and broadcast video, however, this character is not given voice.

4. Even when it appears in theatrical spaces, most critics find no reason not to call performance art performance art; one writer has even said that "there's no significant difference between Bogosian in a theater or in an art gallery" (Tatransky 1983). While I feel that the site of performance, and its implied audience, make a very significant difference, I would agree that Bogosian's work remains performance "art" in any venue (even cinema) for the reasons that follow.

5. Many critics have used the concept of shamanism metaphorically to describe the works of various performance artists. Some in performance studies, including Richard Schechner, have examined shamanic and avant-garde performance practice simultaneously. Still others have attempted to suggest that contemporary Western avant-garde performance artists are equivalent to shamans. All three uses have their particular problematics, but it is the last that seems to me to have the greatest potential for offensiveness. Levy, for instance, analyzes the works of Yves Klein, Joseph Beuys, and Karen Finley precisely as shamanic practices. Levy does not, of course, analyze the works of actual practicing shamans, nor are they offered a critical voice within the body of his text. Shamanism is simply assumed to be available to the Western avant-garde, including, apparently, Levy himself: "although I cite statements by prominent scholars of shamanism in support of my claims, I have tested the validity of these statements against my own practical experience and that of other shamans" (Levy 1988: 55 n. 1). I emphatically make no such claim to authority about "real" shamanic practice. In discussing Bogosian's performance, I invoke shamanism metaphorically, as an element of the hypothetical reception of his work.

6. Note here the emphasis on "doing without," which, as I suggested in chapter 1, is central to the reception of monologue performance.

7. Interestingly, there are moments when Bogosian's work looks like Gray's. While this is clearest in his later works, even some of his "classic" pieces seem to include the artist's "real life"—for example, the opening section of *Drinking in America*, titled "Journal" (1987a: 21-23), in which a man reads a written narrative amusingly describing the deep insights gained from his first experience with LSD; some critics interpreted this as a portion of Bogosian's own journal from the 1970s. John Howell, in his *Artforum* review, also read this as the intended meaning, but identified it as a "forgery" (1985: 108). The published text contains a stage direction that calls for an "improvised patter to the effect that this journal was found in an attic with some old college memorabilia" (1987a: 21), but no suggestion that the "character" is Bogosian.

8. It should be clear that I make a somewhat abusive use of Dollimore's terminology. He is engaged in a lengthy and subtle analysis of homosexuality, transgression, and containment, while I borrow his terms for the rather simpler argument that, for a hypothetical white bourgeois audience, representations (especially comic ones) of "street" characters both other the lower classes and imply their similarity to the spectator. Further, Dollimore's use of vocabulary such as "Other" is part of a philosophical argument, while I attempt only a rather "common-sense" description of the day-to-day practice of the figurative defenses of privilege.

9. It should be noted that the application of the auto/allographic binary to theater or music relies on a degree of prejudice precisely against performance: to see the drama as allographic is to devalue the performance of that drama, even if that labor is, as an afterthought, granted autographic status as an "instance" of the dramatic work.

10. This coincidence of performance art aesthetics with common theatrical vocabulary ("in the moment" is a hackneyed acting-class phrase) is further evidence that, formally speaking, the aim of much modern and contemporary theater can be said to be the same as that of much performance art. Or, perhaps, that allographic drama seeks autographic status in the theater while autographic performance often desires allographic reiterability.

11. In this sense it might be compared with *Suburbia* (1994), a conventional stage play by Bogosian produced at Lincoln Center. While the writerly aspects of his style were apparent, the production's basically realist aesthetic (including a detailed reconstruction of a suburban convenience store) operated on an actorly presence rather than an "art" one—even though one of the characters is a "wannabe" performance artist.

12. The ambiguity I noted in the live performance of this segment is considerably lessened in its inclusion in the video discussed below, *Confessions of a Porn Star* (1995). In this performance, "Eric" is still ridiculed, but the

suggestion that he has been brainwashed by PC feminism (the *Times* critic's opinion) is more clearly present.

13. Unless the water-drinking (and the reference to Richard Schechner) are a competitive dig at Spalding Gray, whose performances are frequently punctuated by meditative sips of water. This reading would still support my argument that any Brechtian effect on the show is secondary to self-aggrandizing reflexivity.

Chapter Five

1. The first two performers have relatively little connection with the world of the visual arts; I mean to suggest here a spectrum running from "arty" to popular, or perhaps from performance art monologues to stand-up comedy routines. Again, I think of my topography of the field of solo performance as sketching the marketing and perception of these works rather than arguing for their relative value or for essentialized formal distinctions.

2. Richard Schechner offers a serious consideration of the danger of narcissism in solo performance and the larger "personalistic" avant garde (1982: 44–54), but I am thinking also of offhand comments I have heard by theater people and others that most solo work is "masturbatory."

3. To be rigorous, Gray's narratives are not invariably *about* heterosexuality. In his novel, *Impossible Vacation*, "Brewster" explicitly describes a sexual encounter with a man in an Amsterdam bathhouse (1992d: 133–38). The moment closest to this in performance, however, is a "failed" encounter in Athens in the monologue *47 Beds* (1986: 97–98)—and the humor in that passage is actually homophobic (about homophobia) in Gray's preoccupation with its meaning: "what would the *Village Voice* say?" (1986: 98). Both moments construe a bit of "deviant" bisexual cachet without fully risking a nonfiction confession of "completed" homosexual acts.

4. Barthes actually writes that inoculation "consists in admitting the accidental evil of a class-bound institution the better to conceal its principle evil."

5. I am well aware that Butler's analysis is for the most part not of self-conscious, theatrical performance, but of sexual and gender identity as deeply performative in their social construction. In much of her work, Butler takes pains to clarify that this performativity is not volitional self-construction but the process of subjectification. I am not suggesting the contrary (that the performance of identity in the "real world" is theatrical, willed, conscious self-creation); rather, I am suggesting that acts of theatrical self-

creation should be read as subject to the same dynamics of social construction/subjectification as "real world" identity.

6. And this potential is limited. Middleton notes that "few men have been able to use this insight as the basis of an active political intervention, especially one which supports the struggles of the oppressed, whether gay men, women or Third World countries" (1992: 130).

7. This reference reminds me that while I want to try to understand the similarities between this popular and obviously offensive performance and performances that are "high culture" and ironize any offense, I also do not want to erase all differences. In the chapter on Gray, I compared his interviewing to "dwarf tossing;" Clay not only explicitly insults midgets, but his treatment of spectators *is* abusive in a completely different way. On the other hand, he could be said to accomplish in an offensive aside what Gray achieves only after a twenty-minute interview: the accumulation of presence at the "voluntary" expense of the audience.

8. The closest Clay comes to a critique of masculinity is when he perhaps accurately describes one function his act may have for men in the audience: to displace their crude thoughts onto him. "You figured you'll bring in your girlfriend you've been datin' for five years, Dice'll handle it. Dice'll call her every fuckin' thing you ever wanted to say . . . you'll laugh your ass off, you walk outta the fuckin' theatre and [say to your girlfriend], 'that Dice is a fuckin' jerkoff.' You go home, you get laid, and what do I do?"

9. While I think it is clear that Clay's performance here is neither feminist nor even chivalrous, I have left unanswered a question from the previous chapter: what is "the difference" between Bogosian's use of ironic distance in constructing multiple characters and the construction of a single offensive persona claimed by Clay? As my accounts of Clay's routines have demonstrated, the performer-audience dynamic, if nothing else, is completely different. When large segments of an audience pump their fists in the air and chant along with the "character," their approbation clearly accrues to (and was solicited by) the performer as much as the character. Whether Clay "is" Dice or not, and whether his audience makes a distinction or not, Clay himself "scores" for saying those things. Bogosian, on the other hand, "scores" for establishing his work's ironic structure. While I've questioned that structure, that critique is relatively distinct from my reading of Clay.

10. I am not quite as ready to describe positively the use of drag in Leguizamo's subsequent television (Fox's "House of Buggin' ") and film (*To Wong Fu . . .*) career, and I find especially regrettable (if hardly unprecedented) his (non-drag) role in the racist 1996 terrorist-thriller film *Executive Decision*. Leguizamo, along with noted stage actor B. D. Wong, aids the white hero's attack on Arab terrorists. This good-guys-of-color ensemble thus serves as the racial alibi for the film's revenge fantasy.

11. This does not mean that the point is to "prove" immediate and explicit models for white solo performance in, say, African American cultural traditions, but that deep patterns of cultural influence mark all contemporary "white" culture. Jazz aesthetics may be considered a cultural prerequisite to the performance poetry movement among white and black poet/performers (an influence on the development of monologue performance); bravura displays of identity, such as much rap music, inform the production and reception of other such displays (and are explicitly quoted by performers like Bogosian and Hoch); numerous oral traditions inform the contemporary "revival" of storytelling as an art form—an obvious reference in much performance art.

12. Becker's performance might be thought of, then, as a conversation of the white man with the white man about how his primitive nature distinguishes him from the white woman at the same time that his white "civilization" distinguishes him from the primitive-native man.

13. Apparently more so with the passage of time. As captured in the 1995 video *Confessions of a Porn Star*, X-Blow's updated urban black dialect is so strongly presented that it might appear a simple racist parody if taken out of context.

Chapter Six

1. As readers know by now, I am one who loves to read ideology in adaptation, and HBO both thrilled and disappointed me when it revealed its corporate anxiety, not by simply failing to duplicate the lighting, but by including in an opening montage several extreme closeups of Hoch's white mouth performing this character.

2. I'm thinking of the white Wooster Group's use of blackface in some performances, but also of Clay's claim to have "become" black, or Kornbluth's momentary cross-gender ridicule.

3. It is worth noting that Hoch's stage space is specified/domesticated by several factors: female characters, the recurrent references to stoves in both the repairman's and the mother's monologues, and the costumes hung on the clothesline across the space.

4. This is surely always in part due to something Peter Middleton notes in *The Inward Gaze: Masculinity and Subjectivity in Modern Culture*: "Reflexivity works imperfectly for men because they don't see what they are seeing when they see themselves" (1992: 11). But this sentence would often apply if the word "won't" were substituted for "don't."

5. This might be thought of in contrast to the use of "strategic essentialism" for feminist and antiracist ends (see Spivak 1987: 205), though straight

white male essentialism can certainly not be "blamed" on the critical use of essentialist tropes in feminist, anticolonial, and antiracist cultural production.

6. Whatever the pitfalls of cross-gender solo performance by men, the self-essentializing tendency of all-male solos appears as another argument for the value of female characters in work like Hoch's.

7. A propos of monologue and originality, recall Durand's discussion, cited in chapter 1, of how voice "mythically . . . aspires to origin" and "individually . . . gives expression to traces of unconscious desires and constructs dredged up from the past" (1977: 102). This is to say that the avant-gardist who aspires to originality—an originality grounded in the self—does well to choose a form in which the voice is so prominent.

8. It is tempting to borrow the language of Butler's description of heterosexuality for an account of the avant-garde: "as a compulsive and compulsory repetition that can only produce the effect of its own originality" (Butler 1991: 21).

9. My use of "bourgeois" is no more precise in a sociological or marxist sense than my use of "avant garde" is precisely art-historical. Rather, my adjectival "bourgeois" refers to a more generalized smugness or sense of comfortable privilege. The working-class youth segment of the audiences in Clay's "Diceman" phase spectated from a "bourgeois" smugness constructed largely from whiteness and male-identification.

References

Abell, Jeff. 1987. "A Process of Commodification." *New Art Examiner* (March): 29–31.

Abrahams, Andrew. 1990. "Andrew Dice Clay Rattled *Saturday Night Live* and Turned the Spotlight on His Favorite Person—Himself." *People Weekly*, 28 May, 57–58.

Auslander, Philip. 1987. "Toward a Concept of the Political in Postmodern Theater." *Theatre Journal* 39 (1): 21.

———. 1992a. "Media Theory as a Ground for Performance Analysis." Paper presented at the Association for Theatre in Higher Education Conference, Atlanta, August 2.

———. 1992b. *Presence and Resistance*. Ann Arbor: University of Michigan Press.

Bakhtin, Mikhail. 1986. *Speech Genres and Other Late Essays*. Translated by Vern W. McGee. Edited by Caryl Emerson and Michael Holquist. Austin: University of Texas Press.

Banes, Sally. 1983a. "Truth in Advertising." Review of *Devil's Advocate*, by Eric Bogosian. *Village Voice*, 4 January, 67.

———. 1983b. "Bits and Pieces of Bogosian." *Village Voice*, 19 July, 70.

———. 1990. "Will the Real . . . Please Stand Up?" *TDR* 34 (4): 21–27.

Barret, Michele. 1985. "Ideology and the Cultural Production of Gender." In *Feminist Criticism and Social Change: Sex, Class, and Race in Literature and Culture*, edited by Judith Newton and Deborah Rosenfelt. New York: Methuen.

Barthes, Roland. 1972. *Mythologies*. Translated by Annette Lavers. New York: Noonday Press.

———. 1977. *Image, Music, Text*. Translated by Stephen Heath. New York: Hill and Wang.

Battcock, Gregory, and Robert Nickas, eds. 1984. *The Art of Performance: A Critical Anthology*. New York: E. P. Dutton.
Baudrillard, Jean. 1983. *Simulations*. New York: Semiotext(e).
Bauman, Richard. 1977. *Verbal Art as Performance*. Prospect Heights, Ill.: Waveland Press.
Belsey, Catherine. 1980. *Critical Practice*. New York: Methuen.
Benamou, Michel. 1977. "Presence and Play." In *Performance in Postmodern Culture*, edited by Michel Benamou and Charles Caramello. Milwaukee and Madison, Wis.: Center for Twentieth Century Studies/Coda Press.
Benjamin, Walter. 1968. "The Work of Art in the Age of Mechanical Reproduction." In *Illuminations*, edited by Hannah Arendt. Translated by Harry Zohn. New York: Harcourt.
Berson, Misha. 1992. "Bay Sayers: When These Solo Performers Start Talking, San Francisco Audiences Listen Up." *American Theatre*, July/August, 13–19.
Blau, Herbert. 1983. "Universals of Performance; or, Amortizing Play." *Substance* 37–38: 140–61.
Bly, Robert. 1992. *Iron John: A Book About Men*. 1990. Reprint, New York: Random House.
Bogosian, Eric. 1987a. *Drinking in America*. New York: Random House.
———. 1987b. *Eric Bogosian's Funhouse*. Produced and directed by Howard Silver. Broadcast on PBS, *Alive From Off Center*.
———. 1988. *Talk Radio*. New York: Random House.
———. 1990. "Making Art, Making Money." Interview with Lilly Wei. *Art in America* 78 (July): 132–41.
———. 1991a. *Sex, Drugs, Rock & Roll*. New York: HarperCollins.
———. 1991b. *Sex, Drugs, Rock & Roll* (film). Directed by John McNaughton. Avenue Pictures.
———. 1992. "Un-American Activities." *New York Times*, 10 February, A15.
———. 1993. *Notes from Underground*. New York: Hyperion.
———. 1994. *The Essential Bogosian*. New York: Theatre Communications Group.
———. 1995. *Confessions of a Porn Star* (videotape). Directed and produced by Rob Klug. Ararat Productions.
Borns, Betsy. 1987. *Comic Lives: Inside the World of American Stand-Up Comedy*. New York: Simon and Schuster.
Brecht, Bertolt. 1964. *Brecht on Theatre*. Translated by John Willet. New York: Hill and Wang.
Brockett, Oscar G. 1987. *History of the Theatre*. 5th ed. Boston: Allyn and Bacon.
Bruce, Lenny. 1966. *The Lenny Bruce Performance Film*. Produced and di-

rected by John Magnuson. Performance recorded at Basin Street West club, San Francisco. Columbus Productions.

Butler, Judith. 1988. "Performative Acts and Gender Constitution: An Essay in Phenomenology and Feminist Theory." *Theatre Journal* 40 (December): 519–31.

———. 1990. *Gender Trouble*. New York: Routledge.

———. 1991. "Imitation and Gender Insubordination." In *Inside/Out: Lesbian Theories, Gay Theories*, edited by Diana Fuss. New York: Routledge.

Canby, Vincent. 1994. Review of *Some People*, by Danny Hoch. *The New York Times*, 30 October. Reprinted in *New York Times Theater Reviews 1993–94*, 409.

Carleton, Frances Bridges. 1977. *The Dramatic Monologue: Vox Humana*. Salzburg Studies in English Literature, vol. 64. Salzburg: Institut für Englishe Sprache und Literatur.

Carr, C. 1989. "This is Only a Test: Chris Burden." *Artforum* 28 (September): 116–21.

———. 1990. "Rehearsals for Zero Hour: Performance in the Eighties." In *The Decade Show*. Exhibition catalogue. New York: The Museum of Contemporary Hispanic Art, The New Museum of Contemporary Art, and The Studio Museum in Harlem.

Carroll, Noël. 1979. "Amy Taubin: The Solo Self." *TDR* 23 (March): 51–58.

———. 1986. "Performance." *Formations* 3 (1): 63–79.

Carter, E. Graydon. 1987. "Talk Man (Why Everyone in the Know Wants to See the Electric Eric Bogosian)." *Connoisseur* 217 (November): 166–69.

Chaikin, Joseph. 1991. *The Presence of the Actor*. 1972. Reprint, New York: Theatre Communications Group.

Champagne, Lenora, ed. 1990. *Out from Under: Texts by Women Performance Artists*. New York: Theatre Communications Group.

Cixous, Hélène. 1984. "Aller à la Mer." *Modern Drama* 27 (4): 546–48.

Clay, Andrew Dice. 1991a. *Dice Rules* (film). Produced by Fred Silverstein. Seven Arts Productions.

———. 1991b. "For Ladies Only." *HBO Comedy Hour*. Directed by Gary Halvorson.

Curry, S. S. 1908. *Browning and the Dramatic Monologue*. Boston: Expression Company.

Demastes, William. 1989. "Spalding Gray's *Swimming to Cambodia* and the Evolution of an Ironic Presence." *Theatre Journal* 41 (1): 75–94.

Derrida, Jacques. 1978. *Writing and Difference*. Translated by Allan Bass. Chicago: University of Chicago Press.

Dika, Vera. 1988. "Cinema: Critical/Mass." *Art in America* 76 (January): 37–41.

DiPiero, Thomas. 1992. "White Men Aren't." *Camera Obscura* 30 (May): 112–37.
Dolan, Jill. 1988. *The Feminist Spectator as Critic*. Ann Arbor, Mich.: UMI.
Dollimore, Jonathan. 1991. *Sexual Dissidence*. Oxford: Clarendon.
Drabble, Margaret, ed. 1985. *The Oxford Companion to English Literature*. 5th ed. New York: Oxford University Press.
Durand, Régis. 1977. "The Disposition of the Voice." In *Performance in Postmodern Culture*, edited by Michel Benamou and Charles Caramello. Milwaukee and Madison, Wis.: Center for Twentieth Century Studies/Coda Press.
Dutta, Ujjal. 1981. "Poetry as Performance: A Reading of Sylvia Plath." *Literary Criterion* 16 (3): 1–11.
Dworkin, Norine. 1989. Review of "Selections," by Eric Bogosian. *High Performance* 48: 68.
Dwyer, Rich, and Ralph Vittaccio, producers. 1988. *Performance—The Living Art*. Zootuch Productions.
Elam, Keir. 1980. *The Semiotics of Theatre and Drama*. New York: Methuen.
Ellison, Ralph. 1986. *Going to the Territory*. New York: Random House.
Fein, Esther B. 1992. "The Reading As an Occasion for Romance." *New York Times*, 6 March 1992, B1.
Feingold, Michael. 1994. "Moral Better Blues." Review of *The Scarlet Letter* and *Some People* by Danny Hoch. *The Village Voice*, 1 November: 83.
Finley, Karen. 1988. "The Constant State of Desire." Performance text. *TDR* 32 (1): 138–51.
Foucault, Michel. 1973. *The Order of Things*. New York: Vintage.
Frank, Peter, and Ken Friedman. 1984. "Fluxus: a Post-Definitive History." *High Performance* 27: 56–62.
Fried, Michael. 1968. "Art and Objecthood." In *Minimal Art: A Critical Anthology*, edited by Gregory Battcock. New York: Dutton. First published in *Artforum* 5 (summer 1967): 21.
Frieden, Ken. 1985. *Genius and Monologue*. Ithaca, N.Y.: Cornell University Press.
Fuchs, Elinor. 1985. "Presence and the Revenge of Writing." *PAJ* 26/27: 163–73.
Fuss, Diana, ed. 1991. *Inside/Out: Lesbian Theories, Gay Theories*. New York: Routledge.
Gaggi, Silvio. 1986. "Sculpture, Theater and Art Performance: Notes on the Convergence of the Arts." *Leonardo* 19 (1): 45–52.
Gates, David. 1993. "White Male Paranoia." *Newsweek*, 29 March, 48–53.
Geis, Deborah R. 1993. *Postmodern Theatric(k)s: Monologue in Contemporary American Drama*. Ann Arbor: University of Michigan Press.

Goldberg, Roselee. 1984. "Performance: the Golden Years." In *The Art of Performance: A Critical Anthology*, edited by Gregory Battcock and Robert Nickas. New York: E. P. Dutton.

———. 1988. *Performance Art from Futurism to the Present*. Revised and enlarged ed. New York: Harry N. Abrams.

Goodman, Nelson. 1968. *Languages of Art*. New York: Bobbs-Merrill.

Gordon, Mel, ed. 1987. *Dada Performance*. New York: PAJ.

Gray, Spalding. 1984a. *Spalding Gray's Map of LA* (artist's videotape). Produced by Bruce Yonemoto. Directed by Norman Yonemoto. Available at the Video Databank, School of the Art Institute of Chicago.

———. 1984b. "Excerpts from *A Personal History of the American Theatre*." *PAJ* 8 (2): 36–50.

———. 1985a. *A Personal History of the American Theater*. Directed by Skip Blumberg. Broadcast on PBS, *Alive From Off Center*.

———. 1985b. *Swimming to Cambodia*. New York: Theater Communications Group.

———. 1986. *Sex and Death to the Age 14*. New York: Random House.

———. 1987. *Swimming to Cambodia*. Directed by Jonathan Demme. Produced by R. A. Shafransky. Cinecom Pictures.

———. 1992a. "Vogue Arts." *Vogue*, June, 70–72.

———. 1992b. "Gray's Anatomy." *The New York Times Magazine*, 17 May, 43–48.

———. 1992c. *Monster in a Box*. New York: Random House.

———. 1992d. *Impossible Vacation*. New York: Alfred A. Knopf.

———. 1994. *Gray's Anatomy*. New York: Random House.

Grubb, Kevin. 1984. "Dancetera: Broadway and Beyond." Review of *Funhouse*, by Eric Bogosian. *Dance Magazine*, January, 78-83.

Gussow, Mel. 1986. "Spalding Gray." Review of *Terrors of Pleasure*, by Spalding Gray. *The New York Times*, 15 May. Reprint in *New York Theatre Critics' Reviews 1986*, 47.12 (September 22, 1986): 216.

Hall, Donald. 1981. "Reading Form." *Precisely* 10-12: 11.

———. 1984. "The Poetry Reading: Public Performance/Private Art." *The American Scholar* 54 (winter): 63–77.

Hoch, Danny. 1994. *Some People*. The Public Theatre, New York City.

———. 1995. "Some People." *HBO Comedy Hour*. Produced by Robert Small. Directed by John Fortenberry.

Holbrook, Chris. 1992. Review of *Interviewing the Audience*, by Spalding Gray. *TheatreWeek*, 3–9 February: 32–34.

Holden, Stephen. 1992. "Eric Bogosian Parodies Humanity's Dark Side." Review of *Dog Show*, by Eric Bogosian. *The New York Times*, 20 July, C13.

hooks, bell. 1990. *Yearning: Race, Gender, and Cultural Politics*. Boston: South End.

———. 1992. *Black Looks: Race and Representation*. Boston: South End.
Howell, John. 1979. "Solo in Soho: The Performer Alone." *PAJ* 10/11: 152–58.
———. 1985. Review of *Drinking in America*, by Eric Bogosian. *Artforum* 24 (November): 108.
Jameson, Frederic. 1988. "Postmodernism and Consumer Society." In *Postmodernism and Its Discontents*, edited by E. Ann Kaplan. New York: Verso.
Janoff, Barbara Letofsky. 1989. "The legend impersonated in solo performance: The history, development, and function of a contemporary dramatic form." Ph.D. diss., Columbia University.
Kirby, Michael. 1979. "Autoperformance Issue: An Introduction." *The Drama Review* 23, no. 1 (March): 2.
Kirkpatrick, Melanie. 1990. "Off-Broadway Offerings." Review of *Monster in a Box*, by Spalding Gray. *Wall Street Journal*, 30 November. Reprinted in *New York Theatre Critics' Reviews 1990*, 51.16 (17 December): 129.
Koziski, Stephanie. 1984. "The Standup Comedian as Anthropologist: Intentional Culture Critic." *Journal of Popular Culture* 18 (fall): 57–76.
Krauss, Rosalind E.. 1986. *The Originality of the Avant-Garde and Other Modernist Myths*. Cambridge, Mass.: MIT Press.
Leary, Denis. 1992. *No Cure For Cancer* (videotape of performance). In series *Showtime Comedy Superstars*. Directed by Ted Demme. Produced by Forrest Murray. Paramount.
Levy, Mark. 1988. "The Shaman is a Gifted Artist." *High Performance* 43 (fall): 54–61.
Lipsitz, George. 1995. "The Possessive Investment in Whiteness: Racialized Social Democracy and the 'White' Problem in American Studies." *American Quarterly* 47 (3): 369–87.
Mansfield, Stephanie. 1989. "Why I Wear What I Wear: Eric the Dark." *Gentleman's Quarterly* 59 (December): 94.
Markham, Edward Archibald. 1989. "Which Poem Am I Reading?" *Visible Language* 23 (winter): 112–22.
McDonagh, Maitland. 1991. "Laughter in the Dark." Review of *Sex, Drugs, Rock & Roll* (film), by Eric Bogosian. *Film Comment* 27 (April/May): 68.
Middleton, Peter. 1992. *The Inward Gaze: Masculinity and Subjectivity in Modern Culture*. London and New York: Routledge.
Minh-ha, Trinh T. 1989. *Woman Native Other*. Bloomington and Indianapolis: Indiana University Press.
Mintz, Lawrence E. 1985. "Standup Comedy as Social and Cultural Mediation." *American Quarterly* 37 (spring): 71–80.
Morrison, Toni. 1992. *Playing in the Dark: Whiteness and the Literary Imagination*. Cambridge: Harvard University Press.

Nelsen, Don. 1986. Review of *The Terrors of Pleasure*, by Spalding Gray. *New York Daily News*, 23 May. Reprinted in *New York Theatre Critics' Reviews* 47: 220.

———. 1990. "Gray: On the Front Lines of Life." Review of *Monster in a Box*, by Spalding Gray. *New York Daily News*, 15 November. Reprinted in *New York Theatre Critics' Reviews 1990*, 51.16 (17 December): 128.

Parnes, Uzi. 1985. "Pop Performance in East Village Clubs." *TDR* 29 (1): 5–16.

Phelan, Peggy. 1988. "Spalding Gray's *Swimming to Cambodia*: The Article." *Critical Texts* 5 (1): 27–30.

Prinz, Jessica. 1992. "Spalding Gray's *Swimming to Cambodia*: A Performance Gesture." In *Staging the Impossible: The Fantastic Mode in Modern Drama*, edited by Patrick D. Murphy. Westport, Conn.: Greenwood Press.

Quinn, Michael. 1990. "Celebrity and the Semiotics of Acting." *New Theatre Quarterly* 7 (22): 154–61.

Reinhardt, Nancy S. 1981. "New Directions for Feminist Criticism in Theater and the Related Arts." *Soundings* 64 (winter): 361–87.

Rich, Frank. 1982. "Preferring the Dark." Review of *Men Inside* and *Voices of America*, by Eric Bogosian. *The New York Times*, 10 September. Reprinted in *New York Times Theatre Reviews 1981*: 384–85.

———. 1983. "Serious Comedy." Review of *Funhouse*, by Eric Bogosian. *New York Times*, 3 July. Reprinted in *New York Times Theatre Reviews 1983–84*: 107.

———. 1990. "Bogosian Illuminates Life in the City." Review of *Sex, Drugs, Rock & Roll*, by Eric Bogosian. *The New York Times*, 9 February. Reprinted in *New York Times Theatre Critics' Reviews 1990*, 51.2 (5 Febuary): 385–86.

Richards, David. 1992. "The Minefields in Monologues." Review of *The Night Larry Kramer Kissed Me*, by David Drake, and *Red Diaper Baby*, by Josh Kornbluth. *New York Times*, 12 July, H5.

———. 1994. "Tales of the City from Eric Bogosian." Review of *Pounding Nails into the Floor with My Forehead*, by Eric Bogosian. *New York Times*, 4 February, B1.

Rosenberg, Scott. 1990. "Sex and the Solo Artist." Review of *Sex, Drugs, Rock & Roll*, by Eric Bogosian. *Mother Jones* 15 (January): 49–50.

Rosmarin, Adena. 1985. *The Power of Genre*. Minneapolis: University of Minnesota Press.

Roth, Moira, ed. 1983. *The Amazing Decade: Women's Performance Art in America 1970–1980*. Los Angeles: Astro Artz.

Royko, Mike. 1989. "Tossing of Dwarfs Raises Bigger Issue." *Chicago Tribune*, 17 July, Sec. 1: 3.

———. 1990. "Right to Have Their Own Weight Thrown." *Chicago Tribune*, 6 July, Sec. 1: 3.

Russo, Francine. 1994. "Discomfort Zone." Review of *Some People*, by Danny Hoch. *The Village Voice*, 1 November: 93–94.

Savran, David. 1986. *Breaking the Rules: The Wooster Group*. New York: Theatre Communications Group.

Sayre, Henry M. 1989. *The Object of Performance: The American Avant-Garde Since 1970*. Chicago: University of Chicago Press.

Schechner, Richard. 1982. *The End of Humanism: Writings on Performance*. New York: PAJ.

———. 1988. *Performance Theory*. Revised and expanded ed. New York: Routledge.

Schmidt, Paul. 1985. "Some Notes on Russian Futurist Performance." *Canadian-American Slavic Studies* 19 (4): 492–96.

Shank, Theodore. 1982. *American Alternative Theater*. New York: Grove.

Shawn, Wallace. 1991. *The Fever*. New York: Farrar, Straus, Giroux.

Siegle, Robert. 1989. *Suburban Ambush*. Baltimore, Md.: Johns Hopkins University Press.

Silverman, Kaja. 1992. *Male Subjectivity at the Margins*. New York: Routledge.

Simone, Timothy Maliqalim. 1989. *About Face: Race in Postmodern America*. New York: Autonomedia.

Sinfield, Alan. 1977. *Dramatic Monologue*. The Critical Idiom, vol. 62. New York: Barnes and Noble.

Snitow, Ann. 1990. "A Gender Diary." In *Conflicts in Feminism*, edited by Marianne Hirsch and Evelyn Fox Keller. New York: Routledge.

Spivak, Gayatri Chakravorty. 1987. *In other Worlds: Essays in Cultural Politics*. New York and London: Methuen.

Sterrit, David. 1990. "The Taming of a Radical Monologuist." Review of *Monster in a Box*, by Spalding Gray. *Christian Science Monitor*. Reprinted in *New York Theatre Critics' Reviews 1990*, 51.16 (17 December): 130.

Stone, Laurie. 1993. "Out of Hoch." *The Village Voice*, 30 November, 80, 82.

Tallmer, Jerry. 1994. "Bogosian in Your Face." *Playbill* 94 (3): 32–36.

Tatransky, Valentin. 1983. Review of *Advocate*, by Eric Bogosian. *Arts Magazine* 58 (September): 40.

Vorlicky, Robert. 1995. *Act Like a Man: Challenging Masculinities in American Drama*. Ann Arbor: University of Michigan Press.

Watt, Doug. 1990a. "Gray on Target." Review of *Monster in a Box*, by Spalding Gray. *New York Daily News*, 23 November. Reprinted in *New York Theatre Critics' Reviews 1990*, 51.16 (17 December): 129.

———. 1990b. "Sex." Review of *Sex, Drugs, Rock & Roll*, by Eric Bogosian. *New York Times*, 16 February. Reprinted in *New York Times Theatre Critics' Reviews 1990*, 51.2 (5 February): 384.

Winer, Linda. 1990. "A Darker Shade of Spalding Gray." Review of *Monster in a Box*, by Spalding Gray. *New York Newsday*, 23 November. Reprinted in *New York Theatre Critics' Reviews 1990* 51.16 (17 December): 131–32.

———. 1991. "A Thrilling Room of One's Own." Review of Virginia Woolf's *A Room of One's Own*, performed by Eileen Atkins. *New York Newsday*, 5 March. Reprinted in *New York Theatre Critics' Reviews 1991* (10 June): 277.

Wittig, Monique. 1980. "The Straight Mind." *Feminist Issues* (summer): 103–111.

Wright, Elizabeth. 1989. *Postmodern Brecht: A Re-presentation*. New York: Routledge.

Young, Iris Marion. 1990. "The Ideal of Community and the Politics of Difference." *Feminism/Postmodernism*, edited by Linda J. Nicholson. New York: Routledge.

Young, Jordan R. 1989. *Acting Solo: The Art of One-Man Shows*. Beverly Hills, Calif.: Moonstone Press.

Index

Absent woman: in performance art monologues, 139–40; in Clay, 138; in Kornbluth, 121
AIDS, 186; in Gray, 75, 128–29; in Hoch, 167
Alcohol, in Bogosian, *Drinking in America*, 94
Allographic art, versus autographic art, 107–08, 199
Anderson, Laurie, 39, 49, 84
Anderson, Mark, use of mundane detail, 37
Anthology, as structure in Bogosian, 94
Arcade, Penny, 44
Artaud, Antonin, 35
Atkins, Eileen, 24–25
Audience, 191, 193–94, 197–98; and the bourgeois avant-garde, 184; hostility to, 181–82; for performance art monologues, 14; and presence, 19; and whiteness, 171–72; in Bogosian, 100, 116–18; in Clay, 136–37, 138, 142–43; in Gray, 63–65, 67; in Hoch, 164; in Leary, 147; in Shawn, 159–60
Authenticity: of art objects, 18; as cultural construct, 47; in poetry performance, 29; in Bogosian, 109
Author: as artist prior to performance, 19; contrast to scriptor, 19; identity of, 193; and performance art, 12–13, 20; as present in poetry reading performance, 30; in Bogosian, 90, 95, 111–13, 145–46; in Gray, 54, 145–46; in Hoch, 169–70
Autobiography: in performance art, 48; in performance by women, 175, 178; in poetry readings, 30; in stand-up comedy, 33; in Bogosian, 113–18; in Shawn, 157; in Hoch, 168–69
Autographic art, versus allographic art, 107–08, 199
Autoperformance, 41
Avant-garde, 53, 58; as bourgeois, 184; "locale," 184; and audience, 184; and community, 184–86; and originality, 181, 203; and performance, 180–81; and race, 154; and the self, 181; and transgression, 181; in Bogosian, 83, 106; in Gray, 77

Bogosian, Eric, viii, 18, 24, 43, 44, 80–119, 120, 143, 144, 149, 155, 161, 166, 194, 202; alcohol, 94; allographic versus autographic art, 107–08; anthology structure of works, 94; audience, 100; as author, 13, 19, 90, 95, 111–13, 145–46; authenticity, 109; autobiography in, 113–18; avant-garde, 106; the body, 105; celebrity, 91, 96, 98, 106, 115; class, 81; condescension toward spectator, 116–18; consistency of characters, 98–99; costuming, 192; deviance, 131, 145; direct address, 17; disability, 86; documentation, 106; early career, 83; event, 114; female character, 198; film adaptation, 106; food, 92–93; frame, 84; feminism, 116; heterosexuality, 123, 125; homelessness, 97–98, 100, 104, 106; homophobia, 87–88, 129; homosexuality, 129; intention, 91, 117; irony, 89–92, 96, 112, 115–16, 177; laughter, 99–100, 128; masculinity, 88, 176–77; monopolylogues, 14; as performance artist, 100–03; as proximate other, 103–04; postmodernism, 111–12; presence, 84–85, 96; racism, 87–88, 153–54; the real, 102–03, 109; realism, 100; Ricky Paul (character), 83–84, 91, 114; roots in avant-garde, 83; setting, 173–74; shamanism, 100–03, 108, 111; television adaptation, 109–11; transgression, 182; typical work, 81; universality, 88, 113, 125–26, 154, 155; virtuosity, viii, 85, 89, 98, 108; whiteness, 150, 153–55; women, 141–42

Works:
—"Art World Underground" (article), 83
—*Confessions of a Porn Star* (video), 118–19, 129, 199–200, 202
—*Dog Show*, 113–14
—*Drinking in America*, 93–95, 141, 153, 178, 182
—*Funhouse*, 92–93, 141; reviewed by Rich, 93; television adaptation, 109–11
—*Pounding Nails into the Floor with My Forehead*, 114–17, 118
—"7 Americans," 85, 102
—*Sex, Drugs, Rock & Roll*, 96–100, 102, 125, 141, 153, 155, 173–74; characters reappearing in, 97; homelessness in, 97–98, 100; laughter, 99–100; objectivity, 100; reviewed by Rich, 98, 100
—*Suburbia*, 199
—*Talk Radio*, 95–96; irony in, 96, 116; *Talk Radio* (film), 153
—*Voices of America*, 86
—*Men Inside*, 86, 141, 145; masculinity, 88; politics, 88
Bonney, Jo, 161
Brecht, Bertolt, 155–56, 160; Lehrstuck compared to Gray, *Interviewing*, 62–63
Browning, Robert, 26, 28, 154; "Caliban upon Setebos" compared to Bogosian, 91–92; in hypothetical poetry reading, 32
Bruce, Lenny, 84, 148; compared to Bogosian, 98; similarity of comedy to performance art, 38
Burden, Chris, 39, 101; challenging art gallery conventions, 40
Butler, Judith, 123, 129–30, 146, 200–01

Cage, John, 66
Cale, David, use of mundane detail, 37
Carroll, Noel, 196; definitions of performance art, 39–40, 42, 43
Carroll, Pat, 25
Carson, Johnny, 34
Celebrity: in Bogosian, 91, 96, 98, 106, 115; in Gray, *Personal History*, 69; in Gray, *Monster*, 71; in Shawn, 156
Chaikin, Joseph, definition of presence, 16
Cixous, Hélène, 139
Class, 155–56; in Bogosian, 81
Clay, Andrew Dice, viii, 117, 119, 135–39, 177, 181, 183, 198, 203; absent woman, 138; and feminism, 144; as comic spokesman, 139; audience, 136–37, 138, 142–43; compared with Becker, 135–36; compared to Bogosian, 90–91, 201; compared to Gray, 201; compared to Kornbluth, 143; compared to Leary, 137, 147; devi-

ance, 145; disability, 138; frame, 138; defense of his material, 34; homophobia, 143; homosociality, 137; intention, 91; Jewishness, 171; laughter, 128; masculinity, 201; masculinity and heterosexuality, 143; nostalgia, 139; objectification, 139; racism, 138, 143; relationship of comedy and performance art, 14–15; women, 142–43, 144

Works:
—*Dice Rules*, 136–38
—"For Ladies Only" (television), 142–43

Colonialism, in Gray, 57, 76, 108, 152–53
"Comic spokesman," 33; in Clay, 139
Commercialism: and performance art, 42; in Gray, 70
Community: and bourgeois avant-garde, 184–86; and poetry readings, 194–95; of straight white male subjects, viii; in Gray, *Interviewing*, 63–64; in Gray, *Personal History*, 68; male, in Kornbluth, 121–22
Confession, in Gray, 56
Costuming, as part of monologic apparatus, 4; in Bogosian, 192
Curry, S. S., criteria for performing dramatic monologue poetry, 31–32

Demastes, William, 197; defense of Gray, 77
Derrida, Jacques, 46; speech falling from body, 35
Deviance: in heterosexuality, 124; in masculinity, 144–45; in Becker, 145; in Bogosian, 131, 145; in Clay, 145; in Gray, 130–31, 145; in Kornbluth, 131, 145
Disability: in Bogosian, 86; in Clay, 138; in Leary, 147
Documentation of performance art, 106; as methodological problem, 20
Dollimore, Jonathan, 199; the proximate, 103–04

Drag, in Leguizamo, 144
Dramatic monologue poetry, 26–28; defined, 26–27; and cultural hierarchy, 194; as oral medium, 31–32; compared to Bogosian, 89–90
Dwarf tossing, 197; compared to Gray, *Interviewing*, 64–65

Elitism, 22; in distinguishing comedy and performance art, 36
Essentialism, 10, 16; and heterosexism, 9; and maleness, 178–80; and solo performance, 172–73; in straight white male monologues, viii; in Becker, 132–33
Event: in performance art, 47; in poetry performance, 29; in theatrical performance art, 43; poetry reading as, 31–32, in Bogosian, 114; in Gray, 55, 62, 71–72, 79; in Shawn, 157
Experience: and feminism, 175–76; and male autobiography, 176

Feminism, 7, 9, 132, 200; and apparatus theory, 191; and autobiographical monologue performance, 175; and essentialism, 202–03; and male essentialism, 179; and performance art, 39; in Becker, 134; in Bogosian, 116; and Clay, 144
Film adaptation: of Bogosian, 106; of Clay, 136–37; of Gray, 57–60
Finley, Karen, 6, 44, 174, 175; shamanism, 101
Fluxus, 39, 107
Food, in Bogosian, 92–93
Form, and heterosexuality, 123–28
Frame: in Bogosian, 84; in Clay, 138; in Gray, *Personal History*, 68–69
Fried, Michael, 40
Frieden, Ken, *Genius and Monologue*, 46–47
Fuchs, Elinor: definition of presence, 16; writing undermining presence, 18

Gay men, visibility as pressure on straight male identity, 7
Gaze, 131
Genius: as construction, linked to monologue, 46–47; as part of monologic apparatus, 5
Genre: as critical fiction, 11–12; as discursively constructed, 37; of performance art monologues, vii
Gesture, 197; in poetry performance, 29; in Gray, *Swimming*, 58–59
Goldberg, Whoopi, 95
Goldthwait, Bob, on stand-up comedy and performance art, 35–36
Gomez-Peña, Guillermo, 6; compared with Bogosian, 45
Goodman, Nelson, autographic versus allographic art, 107–08
Gray, Spalding: vii, 4, 5, 18, 22, 25, 26, 31, 36, 37, 41, 44, 48–79, 81, 95, 110, 113, 116, 119, 120, 144, 174, 178, 179, 193, 195, 196; acting career, 53; AIDS, 75, 128–29; aura of authorship, 13; as author, 19, 54, 145–46; as autographic, 107; avant-garde, 77; Bogosian's satire of, 200; Christian Science, 73; colonialism, 57, 76, 108, 152–53; commercialism, 70; compared to Tim Miller, 126; compared to Kornbluth, 126–27; compared to Shawn, 156–57; compared to Bogosian, 80, 199; compared to Clay, 201; compared with Hal Holbrook, 71; compared to Wooster Group, 77; confessional style, 56; critics' difficulties in categorizing, 50; as event, 79; as epitomizing first person monologue, 14; defended by Shank, 77; defended by Demastes, 77–78; deviance, 130–31, 145; doubled consciousness, 54; event, 62, 71–72; expanding frame, 68–69, 78–79; as famous performance artist, 49; heterosexuality, 123, 126–27; historical importance, 52; homophobia, 200; homosexuality, 200; in popular culture, 49; introspection, 175–76; irony, 79; Jewish performers, frequently compared to, 50; marketing, 70; objectivity, 54; parenthood, 62; performance as present event, 55; as "platform performance," 25; postmodernism, 79; presence, 54–55, 64, 78; production process, 54; race, 154–55; racism, 74; the real, 69, 146; as theatrical, 49–50; therapy, 61; Shafransky, repeated mention of, 129; Shafransky as director, 71; setting, 173; as "sit-down comic," 35; television adaptation, 56; transgression, 182–83; universality, 56, 76–77; unmediated address to audience, 17; virtuosity, 67; whiteness, 75, 150, 152–55; women, 140–41; performances with Wooster Group, 53
Works:
—*Booze, Cars, and College Girls*, 55–56, 145, 182–83
—*47 Beds*, 200
—*Gray's Anatomy*, 72–76
—*Impossible Vacation* (novel), 24, 70, 200
—*Interviewing the Audience*, 60–65, 197; compared to Brechtian Lehrstuck, 62–63; compared to David Letterman, 63; compared to dwarf tossing, 64–65; as monologue, 65
—*Monster in a Box*, 24, 70–72; celebrity in, 71; compared to *Swimming*, 70; liveness in, 71–72
—*A Personal History of the American Theatre*, 65–70, 126–27; audience in, 67–68; celebrity in, 69; presence in, 69; random structure in, 66
—*Sex and Death to the Age 14*, 55–56, 145, 182
—*Straight Talk* (film), 123
—*Swimming to Cambodia*, 56, 57–60, 131, 141, 152–53, 197
—*Terrors of Pleasure: The House*, 56–57, 58

Hall, Donald, on poetry readings, 29
Heterosexism, and assumption of heterosexuality, 8
Heterosexuality, 123–32; assumed, 7, 130, 132, 140; and the body, 124–25; compared with whiteness and maleness, 150; and form, 124–28; functional heterosexuality of performers, 127–28; heterosexual versus "straight," 8; importance of term, ix, 7–9; "in-ing" as opposed to "outing," 8; as insecure, 129–30; as performative, 123; "queer" as term compared with "straight," 8; "straight" (term), 192; in Bogosian, 123, 125; in Gray, 76, 123, 126–27; in Kornbluth, 126–28; in Leary, 148
High art: and real objects, 17–18; compared with Gray, *Personal History*, 66
High culture, poetry as exemplifying, 26
Hoch, Danny, viii, 50, 118, 160, 194, 202; AIDS, 167; audience, 164; audience identification with, 27–28; author, 169–70; autobiography, 168–69; compared to Bogosian, 165; female characters, 203; identity politics, 172; Jewishness, 162, 168, 170–71; laughter, 167; marketing, 166; presence, 170; racism, 172; real, 169–70; setting, 202; *Some People*, 161–72; universality, 165, 171; virtuosity, 165; whiteness, 168–69, 170–71; women, 165
Holbrook, Hal, 24, 25; compared with Gray, 71; not perceived as author, 26
Homelessness, in Bogosian, 91, 97–98, 100, 104, 106
Homophobia, 150; in Bogosian, 87–88, 129; in Clay, 143; in Gray, 200; in Leary, 148
Homosexuality: "invention" of, 9; in Bogosian, 129; in Gray, 200; in Hoch, 165
Homosociality: in Clay, 137; in Kornbluth, 121

Hope, Bob, 34
Houston-Jones, Ishmail, 6, 44
Hughes, Holly, 6, 175; compared with Gray, 45

Identity, viii; and postmodernism, 6; as performative, 11; of performer as marginal, 15; produced through performance, vii; social construction of, 9
Inoculation (Barthes), 124
Intention: in poetry performance, 29; and "successful" reading of dramatic monologue, 27; in Bogosian, 91, 112, 117; in Clay, 91
Irony, 176, 194; definitions of, 27; and dramatic monologue poetry, 27–28; undermined by performance, 28; in Bogosian, 89–92, 96, 112, 115–16, 177; in Gray, 54, 79; in Shawn, 160

Jewishness: and whiteness, 170–71; in Bogosian, 153; Gray's whiteness established in contrast to, 50; in Clay, 171; in Hoch, 162, 168, 170–71; in Kornbluth, 120, 171

Kaprow, Allen, 66
Killing Fields, The (film), 57–58
Kirby, Michael, definition of performance art, 41
Kornbluth, Josh, viii, 50, 119, 120–23, 137, 144, 153, 176, 183; compared to Bogosian, 127; compared to Clay, 143; compared to Gray, 126–27; deviance, 131, 145; heterosexism, seeming critique of, 132; heterosexuality, 125, 127–28; homosociality in, 121; Jewishness, 120, 171; laughter, 128; male community, 121–22; nostalgia, 121; *Red Diaper Baby*, 120–23; relationship of comedy and performance art, 15; sexuality and politics, 120; women, 140; women, absent, 121

Laughter: in stand-up comedy, 36; in Becker, 134; in Bogosian, 99–100,

128; in Clay, 128; in Hoch, 167; in Kornbluth, 128
Leary, Denis, viii, 119, 181; audience, 147; compared to Clay, 137, 147; disability, 147; heterosexuality, 148; homophobia, 148; masculinity, 148; *No Cure for Cancer*, 147–50; racism, 149–50; transgression, 148; whiteness, 148–50
LeCompte, Elizabeth, 41, 53
Leguizamo, John, 171, 201; setting, 174; *Spic-o-rama*, 144
Letterman, David, compared with Gray, *Interviewing*, 63
Lighting, as part of monologic apparatus, 4
Liveness, in Gray, *Monster*, 71–72
Lunch, Lydia, 174

McCauley, Robbie, 6
McCowen, Alec, 25
Magic, in performance art, 101
Maleness: and essentialism, 178–80; and monologue, 6; and universality, 178; compared with whiteness and heterosexuality, 150; importance of term, ix
Marginality, of performance art, 15–16
Marketing: as allographic, 108; as constructing performance art, 37, 39; as constructing stand-up comedy, 37; of Gray, 70; of Hoch, 166
Masculinity, 139–47; and assumption of heterosexuality, 140; and sexuality, in Clay, 143; in Bogosian, 176–77; in Bogosian, *Men Inside*, 88; in Clay, 201; in Leary, 148
Men's movement, 115, 142, 187, 188; political potential, 201; as reactionary culture, 10; and Becker, 134–35; and Leary, 148
Miller, Tim, 44, 186; compared to Gray, 126
Modernism: return to, in performance art monologues, 47; and identity, 10
Monologic apparatus, 4–5; and identity privilege, 6; genius, 5; in Shawn, 156–57
Monologue: as cultural impulse, 46; defined, 193; as novelty, 4; as traditional mode of drama, 3; and "writing," 46–47; Gray, *Interviewing* as, 65
Monopolylogue, defined as subgenre of performance art monologue, 14
Montano, Linda, 40

Nostalgia: in Clay, 139; in Kornbluth, 121
Novelty, 4, 24, 25

Objectification, in Clay, 139
Objectivity: in Bogosian, 100; in Gray, 54; of dramatic monologue poetry, 28
Originality: and the avant-garde, 203; and voice, 203
Outing, versus "in-ing," 192

Performance art: and actuality of signs, 17; autobiography in, 48; as autographic, 108; and the body, 12, 18, 40, 43; Bogosian's work as, 100–03; as challenge to art gallery conventions, 40; as challenge to theatrical conventions, 43; and collectivism, 47; and commercialism, 42; compared to entertainment theatre, 26; compared to popular culture, 91; compared to sculpture, 39; as contested term, 21–22; contradiction of presence and authorship, 20; and dada, 39; definitions, 38–42; indefinable by formal means, 38; development through galleries, clubs, theatres, 41–42; discursive construction of, 13–14; documentation, 106; event in, 47; and feminism, 39; formal criteria, 12–13; and futurism, 39; and magic, 101; as marginal form, 16; and modernism, 47; multiple-character, compared to poetry reading, 32; novelty, 24; and postmodernism, 47; and presence, 47;

and the real, 12–13, 43, 47; straight white male, impossibility of, 189; "theatrical" versus "art world," 42–43
Performance art monologues: defined, 14, 45–46; as genre, vii, 13, 40–41; sub-genres, 14; importance of, viii; similarities to other forms, 22; and white men, 6
Performance group, 53, 67, 196; and theatrical performance art, 43
Performance space, as part of monologic apparatus, 4–5
Performativity, and identity, 11
Performer-specatator relationship, 4–5
Phallus, microphone in stand-up comedy as, 34
Phelan, Peggy, 76; autobiography in performance art, 48; critique of *Swimming to Cambodia* (film), 59–60
Photography, and the aura of art objects, 18–19
Plath, Sylvia, 195
Poetry in performance, 28–31; and community, 194–95
"Political correctness," 10, 148, 200
Politics, viii, 15; and straight white male performance, 187; in Hoch, 172
Pomo Afro Homos, 44
Popular Culture: compared with high art, 18; compared with performance art, 91; and Gray, 49
Postmodernism, 180; and crisis of identity, 6, 11; and performance art, 47; in Bogosian, 111–12; in Gray, 79
Presence: anti-presence, in Becker, 133–34; defined, 16–17; and modernist performance art, 47; in performance art, 20; in poetry reading, 32; referential versus theatrical, 64; undermined by writing, 18, 195–96; in Bogosian, 84–85, 96; in Gray, 54–55, 64, 69, 78; in Hoch, 170
Privilege, 11, 15; and monologic apparatus, 6

Race: and the avant-garde, 154; ignoring of, 151; and universality, 108; in Gray, 154–55
Racism: in Becker, 152; in Bogosian, 87–88, 153–54; in Clay, 138, 143; in Gray, 74; in Hoch, 172; in Leary, 149–50
Real: in performance art, 12–13, 43–45, 47; real objects and high art, 17–18; in Bogosian, 102–03, 109; in Gray, 69, 146; in Hoch, 169–70
Realism: compared to Bogosian, 100; in dramatic monologue poetry, 31
Representation, described by Barthes as effect, 48
Responsibility of performer to audience, 30
Rich, Frank: favorable review of Bogosian, *Sex, Drugs, Rock & Roll*, 98, 100; favorable review of Bogosian, *Funhouse*, 93
Rosenthal, Rachel, 6
Rosmarin, Adena, 22
Royko, Mike, defense of dwarf tossing, 65

Sayre, Henry, 20; photography as threat to presence, 18–19
Schechner, Richard, 53, 67, 196, 198, 200; mentioned in Bogosian, *Pounding Nails*, 114–15
Schneeman, Carolee, 175–76
Sculpture, compared with performance art and theatre, 39
Setting: and stand-up comedy, 174; and universality, 173–74; in Becker, 174; in Bogosian, 173–74; in Gray, 173; in Hoch, 202; in Leguizamo, 174
Sexuality and politics, in Kornbluth, 120
Shafransky, Renée, 57, 70, 75, 128; as director of Gray, 71; repeated mention of, in Gray, 129
Shamanism: and performance art, 198; and stand-up comedy, 34; in Bogosian, 100–03, 108, 111

Shank, Theodore, defense of Gray, 77
Shawn, Wallace, viii, 5, 119; audience, 159–60; autobiography, 157; celebrity, 156; compared to Gray, 156–57; as event, 157; irony, 160; *The Fever*, 155–60; transgression, 183; universality, 159; whiteness, 158–59
Smith, Anna Deveare, 6; compared with Bogosian, 95
Snyder, Gary, 29, 30
Solo drama, 22–26; as personally meaningful to performers, 25; novelty, 24; "impersonated legend performances," 24; "platform performances," 24
Solo performance art, as genre, 44–46
Speech: as excremental, 35, 195; as phallic, 35, 195
Sprinkle, Annie, 175
Stand-up comedy, 5, 32–38; and "assholes," 135; autobiography in, 33; comedian as "shaman," 34; compared to performance art, vii, 33, 35–37; concept comedy, 14; defined, 33; and microphone as phallic, 34; and neutral setting, 174; high/low distinction in, 36; hostility to audience, 181–82; social function, 33–34, 35; in Becker, 132–35; in Clay, 135–39; compared to Gray, 57
Star Wars (film), 18
Stellarc, 101
Stereotypes (Barthes), 6–7
Storytelling, 3, 191

Television adaptation: of Bogosian, 109–11; of Gray, 56–57; of Hoch, 202
Theatrical apparatus, 111
Thespis, 3
Tomlin, Lily, 26
Transgression: and the avant-garde, 181; and the body, 183; in Bogosian, 182; in Gray, 182–83; in Leary, 148; in Shawn, 183

Universalism/Universality, 174; and the avant-garde, 181; and maleness, 178; and neutral setting, 173–74; and race, 108; and whiteness, 150; in Bogosian, 88, 113, 125–26, 154, 155; in Gray, 56, 76–77; in Hoch, 165, 171; in Shawn, 159

Vawter, Ron, 60
Virtuosity: in Bogosian, viii, 85, 89, 98, 108; in Gray, *Personal History*, 67; in Hoch, 165
Vulnerability of performer, 29–30

"White male paranoia," as context for study, 10–11
Whiteness, 150–55; and audience, 171–72; compared with heterosexuality and maleness, 150; importance of term, ix; and Jewishness, 50, 170–71; and monologue, 6; and universality, 150; white culture inseparable from others, 151; white performance influenced by non-white traditions, 202; white supremacism, 186; in Becker, 202; in Bogosian, 150, 153–55; in Gray, 75, 150, 152–53, 154–55; in Hoch, 162, 168–69, 170–71; in Leary, 148–50; in Shawn, 158–59
Williams, Emlyn, 24
Wilson, Robert, 39, 43
Women: and autobiographical performance, 178; as performance artists, 174–75; in Becker, 140, 142; in Bogosian, 141–42; in Clay, 137, 142–43, 144; in Gray, 140–41; in Hoch, 165; in Kornbluth, 140; in Leguizamo, 144
Wooster Group, 41, 54, 60, 196, 197; compared to Gray, 77; and theatrical performance art, 43; as doing "performance," 42; performances with Gray, 53

Young, Iris Marion, 185–86